MODERN AIR-LAUNCHED WEAPONS

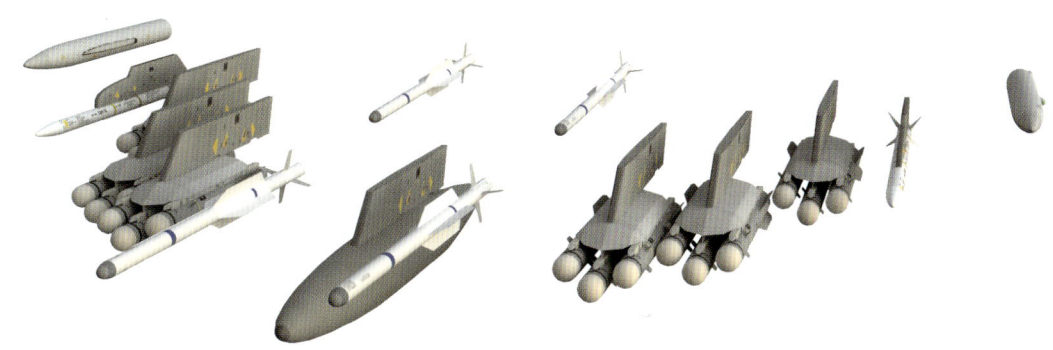

MODERN AIR-LAUNCHED WEAPONS

MARTIN J. DOUGHERTY

amber
BOOKS

First published in 2010 by
Amber Books Ltd
Bradley's Close
74–77 White Lion Street
London N1 9PF
United Kingdom
www.amberbooks.co.uk

Copyright © 2010 Amber Books Ltd.

All rights reserved. With the exception of quoting brief passages for the purpose of review no part of this publication may be reproduced without prior written permission from the publisher. The information in this book is true and complete to the best of our knowledge. All recommendations are made without any guarantee on the part of the author or publisher, who also disclaim any liability incurred in connection with the use of this data or specific details.

ISBN: 978-1-907446-30-6

Project Editor: James Bennett
Picture Research: Terry Forshaw
Design: Joe Conneally

Printed in China

PICTURE CREDITS

All digital illustrations courtesy of Military Visualizations, Inc.

All photographs courtesy of U.S. Department of Defense except for the following:

Air Team Images: 159, 166, 174, 177, 182, 184, 186
Art-Tech/Aerospace: 8/9, 10
BAE Systems: 103
Oleg Belyakov: 155, 160, 179
Cody Images: 12
Corbis: 171 (Alain Nogues), 185 (EPA)
Dassault: 2, 134, 135, 136, 138
Eurofighter: 126, 127, 129, 131
Gripen: 142, 143, 144, 146/147
Andrei Nesvetaev: 170, 175

Contents

Introduction	6
A-10 Thunderbolt II	20
F-15A-D Eagle	28
F-15E Strike Eagle	36
F-16 Fighting Falcon	44
F/A-18 Hornet & Super Hornet	52
F-22 Raptor	60
B-52 Superfortress	68
F-111	76
B-1B Lancer	84
B-2 Spirit	92
F-35A/B/C Lightning II	100
AV-8B Harrier II	108
Tornado	116
EF2000 Typhoon	124
Rafale	132
Gripen	140
Su-27/30/35 & Chinese Variants	148
MiG-29/35	156
MiG-31	164
Su-25	172
Post-Soviet Bombers: Tu-22M, Tu-160 and Tu-95	180
Directory of Modern Air-Launched Weapons	188
Index	223

MODERN AIR-LAUNCHED WEAPONS

INTRODUCTION

A combat aircraft is, above all else, a delivery platform for its weapons. However impressive the aircraft's performance might be, it is only as good as its weaponry, and it can only perform the tasks it is configured for. That configuration is termed a 'loadout', and choosing the correct loadout is vital to mission success.

This book does not attempt to show every possible configuration of weapons and other equipment a given aircraft can carry, but it does demonstrate the loadouts likely to be chosen for a given mission. Notes on each aircraft featured are complemented by a discussion of the missions and the weapons used to complete them, creating a comprehensive picture of what it takes to fight a modern air campaign.

History of Air-Launched Weapons

The use of air power in warfare dates back to the battle of Fleurus in present-day Belgium in 1794, when an observation balloon was used for the first time. Balloons made useful reconnaissance platforms and were even occasionally used to

Left: An F-15E Strike Eagle over Afghanistan, carrying a range of external stores for both ground attack and air-to-air combat. The bulges outboard of the engine intakes are conformal fuel and stores (FAST) packs. Originally an add-on for the F-15 A–D models, they are incorporated as standard on the F-15E.

MODERN AIR-LAUNCHED WEAPONS

direct artillery fire. However, it was not until the invention of the fixed-wing aircraft that air power became capable of directly intervening in ground combat.

Initial attempts to attack ground targets were rather crude, involving hand-dropped grenades and explosives. There are accounts of early pilots throwing heavy metal darts or even bricks out of the cockpit. None of these measures justified the expense of sending an aircraft over enemy positions, but it was not long before specialist air-dropped weapons were developed. The first of these were small bombs carried on a rack under the wings or fuselage of the aircraft and released by a lever in the cockpit.

In the meantime, the fledgling air forces of the world began seeking a means to deny the use of the air to the enemy. Rude gestures between pilots gave way to amateurish potshots with shotguns and revolvers, and finally to machine-guns either in fixed mounts or operated by a second member of the crew. Machine-guns were useful against ground targets in addition to other aircraft, enabling ground-strafing runs at very low level.

The smaller aircraft, originally known as 'scouts', became 'fighters' with air-to-air combat as their primary mission, though reconnaissance and artillery spotting were also of considerable importance. Larger aircraft, designated 'bombers', were dedicated to the ground-attack role, with multi-role 'fighter-bombers' falling somewhere in between. These distinctions mapped out the basic roles of the combat aircraft and are still relevant today, though the range of missions has increased greatly.

Early Ground-Attack Missions

The first bombing of ground targets in wartime was carried out by the Italian air force, attacking Turkish positions in 1911. From this rather humble beginning the ground-attack mission quickly expanded. New technology followed, with aircraft becoming capable of delivering explosive and incendiary bombs, rockets and torpedoes.

World War I (1914–18) saw aircraft attacking an ever-increasing range of ground targets. As well as strikes and bombing attacks on hostile troops, aircraft attacked artillery positions, supply convoys, railways and other rear-area targets that had previously been unreachable. 'Strategic' bombing against cities and industrial centres proved ineffectual, but this did not stop various governments from concluding that 'the bomber will always get through' and investing in a large fleet of bombers to strike at the enemy heartland. Other experiments, such as the launch of aircraft from ships or even submarines, were carried out with varying degrees of success.

Right: World War II Royal Air Force pilots scramble in response to an air attack. By 1939, air forces had matured from a useful novelty into a fully fledged combat arm capable of significantly affecting the outcome of a campaign.

INTRODUCTION

Improvements in technology between the wars enabled aircraft to carry out an even wider range of missions in the World War II. Early in the conflict the German military demonstrated what could be achieved by close cooperation between strike aircraft and mobile ground forces, with fighter-bombers acting as 'flying artillery' to support the armoured advance. 'Tankbusting' aircraft soon arrived on the scene, armed with powerful cannon and rockets to destroy enemy armour. Similar weapons proved effective against lightly armoured ships.

By the end of World War II, virtually all the aircraft missions recognized today had been attempted, including

MODERN AIR-LAUNCHED WEAPONS

Above: World War I bombers like the German Gotha had very limited capabilities and tended towards 'operational losses' not connected with enemy action. But they demonstrated the concept of the heavy bomber and paved the way for more advanced aircraft.

strategic bombing using nuclear weapons. Crude guided missiles had been successfully launched from aircraft, and it was here that the great revolution in air-launched weapons began.

In order to achieve an accurate strike with unguided ('dumb') weapons, it was necessary to fly close to the target, often straight and level, while the weapon was aimed and launched. This made the aircraft an easy target for hostile fighters and ground-based weapons. The development of guided weapons allowed an accurate strike from a much greater distance, increasing aircraft survivability. Very small targets could also now be attacked with a greater chance of success.

Since the first appearance of observation balloons, countermeasures had been attempted in the form of hopeful cannon shots and later rifle fire directed at aerial targets. However, once the aircraft developed into a credible threat to ground forces or ships, air defence became an important area of military capability. Machine-guns mounted on high-angle carriages led to light automatic cannon and heavier guns, assisted first by searchlights and later by radar. More esoteric defences included cables, either held aloft by tethered balloons or sometimes launched into the path of an oncoming aircraft by rocket. Eventually, ground-launched guided weapons were developed, offering defenders a far greater chance of a hit on hostile aircraft.

However, the greatest threat to the attacking bomber or strike aircraft has always been the fighter. Initially equipped with machine-guns, fighters gained rapid-fire cannon and guided weapons of their own, greatly increasing their deadliness. To defeat the defending fighters, a range of countermeasures was invented. These included defensive guns on the bomber, fighter escorts, improvements in operational ceiling or the speed of attack aircraft, decoys and electronic countermeasures to defeat missiles, and lately the invention of 'stealth' technologies to make the bomber harder to detect and intercept.

Thus the history of air-launched weapons is one of ever-developing technologies as the bomber strives to get through and the defender seeks to prevent it with air- and ground-launched weapons. The advantage has at times lain with the attacker and at others with the defender. However, technology must also be effectively used. Tactical considerations play an important part in getting the weapon to the launch point, but equally it is vital to configure the aircraft correctly to suit its mission.

A combat aircraft must set out on its mission with weapons capable of successfully attacking the target. It must also be able to reach the target, taking into account

INTRODUCTION

defences and the distance that must be flown, and it must be able to get its crew safely back to base. There is a limit to what can be carried on any given airframe, so selecting the correct balance of equipment – the right loadout – is vital to the success of a mission.

Combat Aircraft Missions

Most air missions fall into three broad categories: air combat; ground attack (which in this context also includes attacks on maritime targets); and support missions. The latter incorporates the very first of all wartime air missions, reconnaissance of enemy forces and capabilities. It also covers other activities that help defeat the enemy by making the missions of other aircraft safer or easier, or putting assets in place to carry out those missions.

The first group of missions is aimed at ensuring control of airspace, either to deny it to the enemy or to enable friendly aircraft to reach their targets. This requires aircraft that can engage and destroy their hostile counterparts, usually by means of guns and missiles. The general anti-aircraft mission is termed Air Superiority, and is obviously the task of fighters or multi-role aircraft that can effectively undertake air combat.

Air-superiority fighters must combine agility, acceleration, and speed and have good sensor equipment in addition to their weapons. Modern radar can track many targets at once, assisting a pilot in keeping track of where the enemy is and what threats exist. A second member of crew is carried by some fighters to assist with visual observation, radar handling and some weapons use. There are advantages and disadvantages to carrying another crew member, notably the extra space and cockpit systems required.

Fighter pilots are often assisted by Fighter Control Officers, who are sometimes unkindly referred to as 'Scopedopes'. FCOs may be ground-based or aboard a support aircraft with powerful radar. In some air forces FCOs provide information and advice to pilots and warn them of threats. In other countries the FCOs instruct pilots on exactly what manoeuvres to perform.

Once the air-superiority fighter has located a target, combat ensues. The traditional 'dogfight', with two fighters turning hard to try to get a shot at each other, is generally

Below: The dropping of the first atomic bombs from the B-29 Superfortresses 'Enola Gay' and 'Bockscar' represented a rare occasion where air power achieved a decisive result.

MODERN AIR-LAUNCHED WEAPONS

not favoured in air combat doctrine. Indeed, it is axiomatic that the longer a pilot spends in dogfighting the more likely he is to be shot down by an opponent he has lost track of. Dogfights also waste fuel, which can be problematic on a long mission.

Ideally, enemy aircraft are downed by missiles fired from a safe distance, or by a 'slashing' gun attack. In the latter case the fighter makes a fast pass, ideally diving from above to gain the benefits of additional speed, then vanishes into the distance before any surviving hostiles can engage. This tactic of 'one pass and haul ass' is less dramatic than a turning fight but it is more efficient and survivable than dogfighting.

However, it is not always possible to engage in combat under ideal conditions, so air-superiority fighters are designed to be highly manoeuvrable, with a tight turning circle and the ability to quickly regain speed and altitude. In a dogfight, acceleration is more important than top speed; turning hard slows an aircraft down, and moving slowly makes it an easy target. Fighter pilots assert that 'speed is life' so not only does good acceleration enable fighters to pursue targets more effectively, it also increases life expectancy.

So long as it has sufficient range, a good air-superiority fighter is also capable of effectively escorting strike aircraft or bombers. Specialist long-range escort fighters have also been designed and manufactured at times. In either case, the escort's job is to keep enemy fighters away from the ground-attack planes. It is not so important whether or not the hostiles are shot down; what matters is that the strike force is protected. If an enemy can be drawn into dogfighting with the escorts instead of engaging the bombers, then the escorts' mission is considered a success.

Below: Although conceived as a nuclear bomber, the Avro Vulcan reverted to a conventional role during the 1982 Falklands Conflict. Flying out of Ascension Island, RAF Vulcans attacked Argentine targets 14,800km (8000 nautical miles) away.

INTRODUCTION

Interceptors are more specialized than air superiority fighters, and are often less effective in the standard fighter role. Their task is to intercept enemy strike or reconnaissance aircraft as far from the target as possible and either shoot them down or force them to abort the mission. For this reason interceptors often have a very high top speed and rate of climb, enabling them to reach a firing position before a high-flying bomber gets out of range. Turning characteristics are usually inferior as this is far less important when intercepting bombers. Most interceptors carry long-range missiles, increasing their effective combat radius.

The ground-attack mission is somewhat more varied than the air-to-air role, with several possible subdivisions. As a general rule missions can be classified according to how close to the combat area the target lies.

Close Air Support missions are flown against enemy forces in close proximity to friendly troops, often upon request by commanders on the ground. CAS missions require a high degree of precision to avoid hitting friendly targets. Ideally, guided weapons are used or the aircraft flies very low and relatively slowly to allow targets to be carefully identified and weapons to be delivered with a high probability of an accurate hit.

One variation on the Close Air Support theme was developed during the 1991 Gulf War. The term 'Tank Plinking' came to be associated with the use of such guided weapons as laser-guided bombs to attack armoured vehicles, or sometimes with using any excessively powerful weapon for this purpose.

Strike operations can be directed against troop and vehicle concentrations that are not in close proximity to friendly forces, or against the logistics chain that supports them. By attacking supply convoys directly, or the bridges that they must pass over, it is possible to reduce the effectiveness of enemy combat forces. Attacks on command posts and communications centres can disrupt

Above: A B-52 Stratofortress drops a stick of retarded bombs. Note the drogue parachutes deploying to slow the bombs almost immediately they leave the bomb bay. At low level this gives the aircraft time to clear the blast area.

the enemy chain of command even if critical personnel do not come to any harm.

For 'hard' targets, such as command bunkers, or when attacking targets in close proximity to civilian areas, precision is vitally important and guided weapons are normally used. This is generally referred to as the Precision Strike mission. Precision strikes are also used against targets such as bridges and air defence installations, though the latter mission has a specific title of its own.

These attacks on the enemy's support structure, and also on troops advancing towards the combat area, are collectively known as Interdiction. The intent is to effectively cut off the enemy forces in contact with friendlies from reinforcements and supports, making their defeat more likely.

Attacks can also be launched against a nation's war-fighting capability. For example, bombers might deliver bombs or missiles against factories, oil refineries, power stations and the like in the enemy rear. While this will not impact the combat troops at the front immediately, it will reduce the enemy's ability to prosecute a war and can force the government to open negotiations in the hope of avoiding serious economic damage. Attacks of this sort normally fall under the heading of Strategic Bombing or Strategic Strike. Attacks on population centres, possibly with nuclear weapons, are also considered to be strategic bombing missions.

All strike and bombing missions are subject to interception by enemy fighters and surface-to-air missiles. The survivability of strike aircraft is greatly increased by being able to fly fast and either very high or very low. Some bombers are designed to cruise to the target area at an economical speed and high altitude, then sprint through the enemy defences at high speed and close to the ground.

A low-flying aircraft is hard to detect with radar, while one at high altitude may be out of range of many interceptors and missiles. Combined with speed, this makes interception problematical for the defender. A successful intercept can be made even more unlikely by using low-observable ('stealth') technology. Stealth does not make an aircraft invisible but it does reduce the range at which it can be detected. By picking a suitable route between radar positions it is possible for a stealth aircraft to slip thorough enemy defences undetected.

If a bomber or strike aircraft is detected, it can defend itself against fighters with cannon or missiles if suitably equipped, though few bombers are a match for a pure combat aircraft. Missiles can be countered with electronic countermeasures (ECM) or decoy launchers. Alternatively, enemy defences can be attacked before the mission begins or even during it. This is the SEAD (Suppression of Enemy Air Defences) mission.

SEAD can be accomplished in a variety of ways. Anti-radiation missiles are designed to home in on the emissions of air defence radars, forcing them to remain shut down or risk destruction. It is also possible to attack radar and missile sites with other weapons, notably precision-guided missiles and bombs.

Similarly, enemy air assets can be rendered ineffective by a range of measures falling under the general title of counter-air operations. These range from sending escort fighters to attack enemy interceptors to strikes against enemy airfields. Whether or not the actual aircraft are destroyed, enemy air operations become less effective if fuel and munitions stocks are attacked, or if ground crews cannot work due to bombing attacks on the airfield.

Runway-denial is another standard tactic, cratering the runway to prevent its use until repairs are made.

Attacks against shipping can be considered to be quite similar to strikes on ground targets. Against warships, it is possible that a SEAD strike to weaken air defences might made before the main strike, which might use anti-ship missiles or precision-guided weapons. Transport vessels are vulnerable to direct attack but, being mobile and relatively small compared to the surrounding ocean, still require precision weapons to make a hit likely.

Support missions are intended to make other air operations more successful. This includes 'ferry' missions, where aircraft transfer between bases, and mundane but vital logistics flights to bring supplies and personnel to the base. Tanker aircraft provide in-flight refuelling, greatly extending the range of a combat mission, while electronic warfare planes might accompany a strike force to protect it against enemy radar detection and weapons guidance.

Airborne Early Warning aircraft also contribute to the air combat package by providing information on the location, speed and heading of enemy forces, and sometimes carry fighter control officers to advise the combat pilots. AEW is really just an advanced and specialized form of the original air mission – reconnaissance of enemy forces.

The Air Campaign

It is not really possible to defeat an enemy through air power alone, except perhaps in extreme circumstances where nuclear weapons are used. However, a successful air campaign can change the course of a ground war. Such a campaign comprises several interrelated elements, each aimed at either weakening the enemy or making other operations more successful and safer for friendly forces.

Ground troops in contact with friendly forces are damaged by Close Air Support missions, while being starved of reinforcements, supplies and fuel by interdiction strikes. Enemy forces not in yet contact with friendlies are harassed by air strikes, possibly including carpet bombing by heavy bombers. Their movements are made difficult by strikes against bridges and railways. Meanwhile, command and control of these forces is disrupted by the destruction of command bunkers and communications sites.

Morale is eroded by psychological operations such as the dropping of leaflets offering good treatment as prisoners and outlining the hopelessness of the situation. Further back, smashed factories, sunken supply ships and

INTRODUCTION

Above: An F-16C Fighting Falcon takes off on a SEAD mission. It carries the AGM-88 Homing Anti-Radiation Missile (HARM) as its mission payload, supported by external fuel tanks to increase range and AIM-9 Sidewinder missiles for self-defence.

disrupted ports make manufacturing additional munitions difficult, while the destruction of power stations adds to confusion in the rear echelon as well as causing political and economic damage.

Electronic warfare aircraft accompany the bombers and strike planes, reducing the effectiveness of the enemy's response, while opposition to the ground attack missions is reduced by SEAD strikes and attacks on airfields destroy enemy fighters or keep them grounded. Those that do venture up to fight are attacked by escort fighters who receive tanker support in order to stay with the bombers. Airborne Early Warning aircraft advise the escorting fighters to expect a threat, greatly increasing the odds against the enemy.

Against this backdrop, a constant round of reconnaissance takes place, informing the commanders of ground and air forces of the effectiveness of their strikes and the locations of new targets. Enemy reconnaissance is countered by air-superiority and interception missions as, of course, are attempts to take the initiative in the air campaign.

No campaign ever goes this well, of course, but the ideal pattern is one of mutually supporting air operations that crumble away the enemy's resistance by strikes at the tactical and strategic level, making the task for ground (or perhaps, naval) forces easier.

Aircraft Weapons and Support Systems

Setting up an aircraft for a mission is an exercise in compromise. The more stores that are carried on external mounts, the greater the drag the plane experiences, reducing its speed and range. Fuel tanks and pods, if in use, must be mounted instead of weapons because there is only so much space available for them. This reduces the payload that can be carried on a long mission. If air-to-air and air-to-ground weapons are both to be carried, a suitable combination must be decided upon.

Most combat aircraft have an internal weapons bay and/or mounting points (pylons) on the wings and fuselage. Some of these are 'plumbed', allowing fuel tanks to be carried instead of weapons. Pods containing electronic warfare equipment, targeting devices, decoy

MODERN AIR-LAUNCHED WEAPONS

launchers and cameras for reconnaissance are also often carried. Some loadouts restrict an aircraft's ability to manoeuvre in the air, while certain stores are sufficiently big or heavy as to make it impossible to carry other items on some stations. Choosing the correct loadout for a mission is of vital importance if success is to be achieved.

Guns

Small-calibre machine-guns were the first practical air-to-air weapon but, because they lack range and hitting power, are no longer effective against modern aircraft. The last fighter to be downed by a bomber-mounted machine-gun was in 1972; cannon superseded the machine-gun as a fighter weapon long before this time.

Modern aircraft guns are usually automatic cannon in the 20–30mm range. Rotary, or 'Vulcan' cannon are often used to increase rate of fire and therefore the chance of a hit. Even with modern sighting aids, hitting a fast-moving target with a cannon is difficult at best, and at one point it was believed that the guided missile had made cannon obsolete. Experiences in the Vietnam War proved otherwise; cannon remain an important weapon for close-range engagements and allow combat to continue after an aircraft's limited supply of missiles has been used up.

Cannon are often mounted internally, but some aircraft are able to carry one or more gun pods; self-contained mounts holding the weapon (or weapons) and ammunition. Shells are not ejected from the aircraft after firing, but are held in a container to be unloaded after landing.

Cannon can be used, like their predecessor the machine-gun, for short-range ground attack. This is not an ideal role for such weapons, but some strike aircraft can carry multiple gun pods for attacks on 'soft' targets in an environment where the threat to the aircraft is relatively low. The cannon of the A-10 Thunderbolt is an exception to this rule. It is the aircraft's main weapon and is designed specifically for low-level ground attack. Capable of destroying tanks, the cannon can also be used to attack most other kinds of target.

Air-to-Air Missiles

Missiles offer two main advantages to a combat pilot. They can strike from greater range than cannon, and can guide themselves to attack an evading target. Chances of a successful attack are increased by the use of proximity fuses, which detonate the missile's warhead when

Left: A modified F-15A launches an ASM-135 anti-satellite (ASAT) missile. The test was successful and the target, a derelict satellite, was destroyed. The ASM-135 missile is no longer in service.

it is close to the target. The resulting shower of fragments can riddle the target with holes, cutting fuel lines and control circuits in addition to causing structural damage or harm to the aircraft's crew.

Missiles are normally guided either by radar or by seeking the target's infrared (heat) signature. As a general rule, longer-range missiles use radar homing while short-range 'dogfight' missiles home in on infra-red radiation, i.e. heat. Early infrared missiles were not very reliable, requiring a clear view of the target's jet exhausts (the hottest part of an aircraft) in order to obtain a lock. This necessitated a rear attack, but more modern missiles can attack from any angle.

Similarly, these early missiles were easy to distract with decoys such as magnesium flares, which burned hotter than the target aircraft and thus presented a more attractive target. Some missiles would even lock onto the sun if it was within the seeker head's field of view. More advanced missiles have better defined targeting parameters and are harder to distract with decoys.

Some specialist air-to-air missiles exist or have been experimented with. Extremely long-range missiles, such the U.S. Phoenix missile, are primarily useful for attacking relatively large targets, such as bombers. They extend the engagement range of the carrying aircraft and thus allow hostiles to be attacked farther from their target. Missiles designed specifically to attack enemy airborne early warning planes effectively perform the SEAD mission against airborne radar platforms.

The U.S. AIM-135 ASAT anti-satellite missile also falls into the category of air-to-air missiles, more or less. Launched from an F-15 fighter at the top of a high-speed climb, this missile was designed to be capable of intercepting a satellite in orbit at a height of up to about 560km (350 miles). It was successfully tested but is no longer in service.

Bombs and other Dropped Weapons

The most basic bomb is simply a container filled with explosives, with a vaguely aerodynamic shape and fins to ensure a predictable flight path. Unguided bombs are sometimes termed 'dumb' or 'gravity' bombs, because they simply fall under the effects of gravity with no control input. In theory the point of impact is predictable, but the vagaries of wind can carry dumb bombs far off of the target. Inaccuracy becomes more of a problem as delivery height increases, to the point where a fairly small inaccuracy in the drop point calculation can result in a large margin of error by the time the bomb actually hits the ground.

Inaccuracy can in some ways be useful; an area can be 'carpet bombed' by delivering large numbers of bombs so that they spread out, creating a pattern of destruction rather than a single impact point. This is useful primarily against 'soft' targets, such as personnel, but can result in unacceptable levels of collateral damage, for example, the destruction of civilian areas close to the target.

The accuracy of a 'dumb' bomb can be increased by delivering it from a very low level, but not only does this expose the delivering aircraft to ground fire, but may result in damage from the bomb itself. Retarded bombs were developed to counteract this. By deploying air brakes after launch, the weapon loses much of its forward velocity, allowing the strike aircraft to leave the area before impact. Precision is also greatly improved by the use of guidance devices, which are discussed below.

Originally, bombs contained only explosives, but more sophisticated munitions were developed for special purposes. A bomb can carry almost any payload, including incendiary, chemical or even nuclear warheads, and can be configured to penetrate deep into earth or concrete before detonating. This is useful when attacking bunkers and other hard targets, including caves and tunnels, which would otherwise protect the personnel inside from attack.

Various other munitions can be dropped in the same manner as a bomb, often from the same pylons or mounts. These include submunition delivery containers, the commonest of which are cluster bombs. These scatter many small 'bomblets' over a considerable area, making them highly effective against personnel but much less so against hard targets such as armoured vehicles. Dispensers similar to those used in cluster bombs can deliver mines or other items, such as propaganda leaflets. Napalm tanks are dropped in the same manner as bombs, though in many services they have been superseded by cluster bombs.

Rockets and Missiles

The only real difference between rockets and missiles is guidance. Rocket weapons are unguided, and are often launched in salvoes from a pod containing several munitions. They are not very accurate weapons, so are usually employed by low-flying aircraft carrying out close air-support or strike missions. The usual warhead is explosive but smoke is sometimes used for target marking.

MODERN AIR-LAUNCHED WEAPONS

Above: Munitions are brought up on deck of a US Navy aircraft carrier deployed to the Persian Gulf. The bombs in the foreground are GPS-guided 453kg (1000lb) GBU-31 Joint Direct Attack Munitions.

Air-to-ground missiles range from fairly short-ranged weapons, such as the AGM-65 Maverick, to cruise missiles, such as the Storm Shadow missile used by several European air forces. Missiles are fairly precise weapons, allowing attacks on small and/or mobile targets, such as armoured vehicles and command bunkers. Missiles can also be used to launch 'standoff' strikes at a considerable distance from the target. This allows the launching aircraft to remain outside the close air defence region around the target, improving survivability. This was the thinking behind the development of the Air Launched Cruise Missile (ALCM). Rather than flying to the target and bombing it, ALCM allowed a bomber to launch its weapons hundreds of kilometres from the target area, possibly beyond the range of enemy air defences.

Missile payloads vary considerably. Explosive warheads can be employed, or the weapon can be used to deliver submunitions, such as air-scattered mines or cluster bombs. Nuclear and chemical warheads might also be employed by some users, though the consequences of utilizing such weapons are an effective deterrent in most cases.

Anti-ship missiles are not very different from those used to attack land targets. Indeed, the Harpoon naval missile, originally designed to be launched against maritime targets by ships and aircraft, evolved into a land-attack missile. However, specialist maritime strike missiles do exist. These are often designed to fly very low ('sea-skimming') to make detection and defence a problem, though some attack from above the target ('high-diving'). Very long-range maritime strike missiles are essentially specialized cruise missiles.

Weapon Guidance Systems

Weapons can be guided by a variety of means. Guidance not only allows small targets to be attacked, or hard targets to be cracked by hitting at just the right point, but it also offers other benefits. Ordinarily it might require several strikes and a great deal of ordnance to hit a given target, exposing many aircraft to enemy defences and making them unavailable for other operations. Guided weapons allow a target to be reliably neutralized, often by a single aircraft.

An air force can only generate so many sorties per unit time, meaning that it can only put so many aircraft out on missions in a given day, week, or campaign. Each sortie risks an aircraft and requires maintenance time as well as using up disposables like fuel and munitions. Thus the ability to strike with precision enables resources to be more effectively distributed. True, guided weapons are more expensive than 'dumb' ones, but this is offset by the savings possible and the ability to spread the number of available sorties out among several or even many targets.

Some munitions use the Global Positioning System (GPS) to guide themselves to a preset aim point. While not as precise as some other systems, GPS guidance is relatively cheap. In fact, kits are available that can be fixed to a standard 'dumb' bomb to convert it to GPS guidance. The U.S. Joint Direct Attack Munition (JDAM) works this way, converting standard Mk 82, 83 and 84 gravity bombs to GPS-guided precision munitions. GPS guidance is automated; once the weapon is launched it finds its own way to the target.

Laser guidance systems home in on the reflection of a laser designator from the target. So long as the laser is kept on target, the weapon will strike very close to the designated point. It is possible to launch a stream of laser-guided weapons and move the designator aim point to the next target as each is destroyed, though this is a tricky business. Laser designation, or 'lasing' can be carried out by the launching aircraft in some cases, or

INTRODUCTION

by another aircraft. Designation by ground personnel is also possible.

Some weapons are command-guided, i.e. they are 'flown' to the target using an electro-optical system (essentially a TV camera, which may be infrared or conventional) mounted in the nose of the weapon. Others use electro-optical systems but 'lock' the target image into the guidance system, allowing the missile to seek the target on its own. This 'fire-and-forget' system has the obvious advantage of allowing the aircraft crew to move on to other tasks.

Other systems home in on emissions from the target. These might be infra-red (or thermal) or emissions such as radar systems. Such weapons are also fire-and-forget systems. Some will retain the target location even if it ceases emitting, allowing a radar system that shuts down to be accurately targeted by a seeking missile.

Reconnaissance and Support Systems

Support systems are designed to make the aircraft's mission easier or more survivable. They also include fuel tanks, which can sometimes be dropped once or empty, or may be brought back to base. External fuel tanks slow down an aircraft and, ironically, increase fuel consumption, but they are often necessary in order to reach a distant target.

Other systems that might be carried include decoy launchers to distract enemy heat-seeking or radar-guided missiles, and electronic warfare pods with jammers that counter enemy radar systems. Reconnaissance pods contain cameras and other instruments positioned to look forwards, downward or sideways. Visual images captured by cameras are added to infra-red data and detection of enemy signals and radar emissions. Combining a variety of systems builds up a picture of enemy capabilities and weaknesses that can be exploited by air and ground forces.

Below: This F-15E Strike Eagle carries fuel tanks and medium and short-range air-to-air missiles in addition to 227kg (500lb) and 453kg (1000lb) GPS-guided bombs. Note the addtional pylons on the conformal fuel tanks, located outboard of the engine intakes.

MODERN AIR-LAUNCHED WEAPONS

A-10 Thunderbolt II

Experience in the Vietnam War showed the U.S. that they still needed a dedicated Close Air Support and Strike aircraft. At the time, fast jets were becoming prevalent. However, a slower aircraft capable of attacking from a very low level increased accuracy, which was crucial when supporting troops in close contact with the enemy. Of course, low speed and altitude also exposed the aircraft to ground fire, so any future CAS plane would have to be highly survivable.

GAU-8 Avenger cannon
The A-10's primary armament is the 30mm GAU-8 Avenger cannon. The cannon is mounted slightly offset so that the firing barrel is directly on the aircraft's centreline. This reduces the effect of recoil on the Thunderbolt's flight path.

Heavy protection
The cockpit and gun are heavily armoured against hits from underneath, to prevent a single hit from disabling the aircraft by killing the pilot or detonating cannon ammunition. The A-10 can survive hits in most other areas with only slightly impaired performance.

External hardpoints
The Thunderbolt has eight wing pylons and three fuselage stations. These are capable of carrying guided and unguided bombs, air-to-ground missiles, cluster munitions, rocket pods and Sidewinder missiles. The A-10 generally uses unguided ordnance, but it flies slowly enough that it can deploy rockets and iron bombs accurately.

A-10 THUNDERBOLT II

LOAD 1

Close Air Support

1 2x AIM–9 Sidewinder
2 4x LAU–131 rocket pod
3 1x ALQ-131 ECM pod
4 2x AGM–65 Maverick
5 1x AN/AAS–35(V) Pave Penny targeting pod

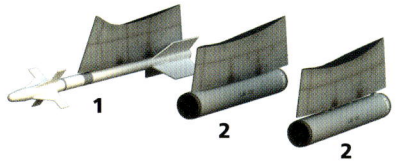

LOAD 2

Ground Attack

1 2x AIM–9 Sidewinder
2 1x ALQ-131 ECM pod
3 1x AN/AAS–35(V) Pave Penny targeting pod
4 2x AGM–65 Maverick
5 6x Mk82 unguided bomb

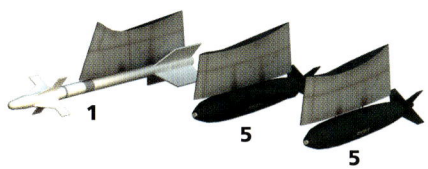

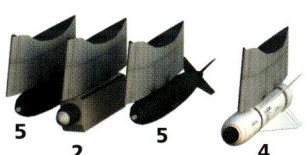

LOAD 3

General Support

1 2x AIM–9 Sidewinder
2 1x ALQ-131 ECM pod
3 1x AN/AAS–35(V) Pave Penny targeting pod
4 2x AGM–65 Maverick
5 4x CBU–87 cluster munition

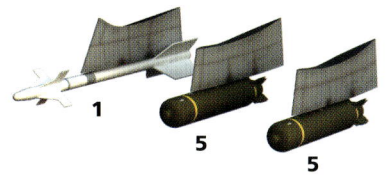
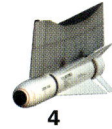

MODERN AIR-LAUNCHED WEAPONS

The U.S. Air Force 81st Training Wing operated A-10s from 1978–93.

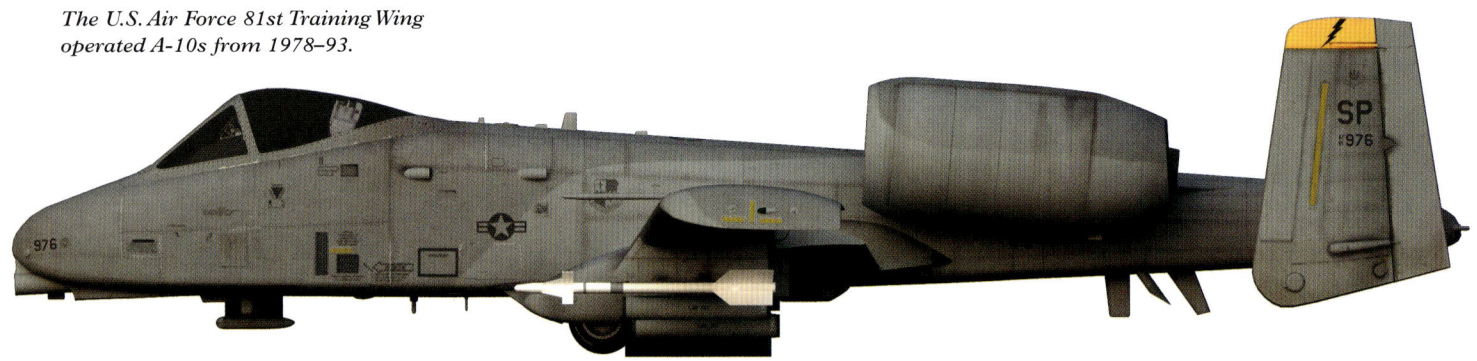

 LOAD 4 Forward Air Control

1 2x AIM–9 Sidewinder
2 1x ALQ–131 ECM pod
3 4x LAU–68 rocket pod (smoke rockets)
4 1x AN/AAS–35(V) Pave Penny targeting pod
5 4x LAU-131 Hydra rocket pod (smoke rockets)

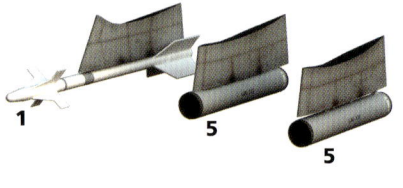

First flown 1972, the A-10 Thunderbolt delivered a range of ordnance, yet was highly resistant to the potential damage that could be caused by an attack. Redundant control systems and the ability to remain airborne even with parts of the wings and tailplane shot off give it improved get-home capability. Critical systems (the engines, pilot and main armament ammunition) are extremely well protected.

The pilot is shielded by a titanium 'bathtub' that withstands shells of up to 23mm and, in some cases, even 57mm, fired from the most likely angles beneath the aircraft. Cannon ammunition, which could destroy the aircraft if detonated by a direct hit, is also located behind thick armour.

The curious position of the A-10's engines also improves survivability. They are protected from ground fire by the wings and tailplane, while their location places the tail section between the hot exhaust and any heat-seeking missiles used by enemy ground forces. This makes the A-10 a more difficult target for such weapons. At the same time, the low altitude at which it flies limits engagement times and makes it unlikely that most missile gunners will even acquire the aircraft as a target before it passes behind a terrain obstruction. The engine position also reduces the chance of it being damaged by debris thrown up from the surface of a hastily prepared forward airstrip.

The A-10 is not an attractive aircraft, hence its unofficial nickname of 'Warthog' or just 'Hog'. It is, however, justifiably well respected. Even flying 'clean', i.e. without any external stores, the A-10 is a formidable ground-attack platform. This is due to the power of its GAU-8 seven-barrel 30mm cannon.

There is nothing new about the concept of putting a powerful gun on an aircraft for the ground-attack role. Guns of up to 75mm were carried by various World War II aircraft for 'tankbusting' missions. However, the GAU-8 is the most powerful gun ever carried by an aircraft, and is easily capable of destroying armoured vehicles with just a few rounds.

A-10 THUNDERBOLT II

Above: The A-10 is a formidably versatile aircraft, capable of carrying a wide range of ordnance on its many hardpoints. A loadout need not be symmetrical, further increasing the range of weapons that can be carried.

For combat, the GAU-8 cannon is normally loaded with 1150 rounds, but it can carry as many as 1174. Most rounds are armour-piercing incendiary (API), with a depleted uranium penetrator to punch through armour and a secondary incendiary effect. Every fifth round in the feed system is High Explosive Incendiary (HEI) ammunition, which produces even better results against 'softer' targets.

The gun is set up to fire 3900 rounds per minute, though it can handle a higher rate. In practice, pilots are expected to fire one- or two-second bursts to prevent the barrel from heating up excessively and wasting ammunition, but the gun can theoretically fire continuously. Its recoil is so powerful, though, that the weapon must be mounted so that the firing barrel is directly on the centreline. This stops the weapon's extreme accuracy being wasted or compromised by recoil forces.

Although the GAU-8 cannon is the Thunderbolt's main weapon, it is by no means its only one. Up to 7260kg

MODERN AIR-LAUNCHED WEAPONS

LOAD 5 — Tank Hunting

1 2x AIM–9 Sidewinder
2 1x ALQ–131 ECM pod
3 1x AN/AAS–35(V) Pave Penny targeting pod
4 6x AGM–65 Maverick

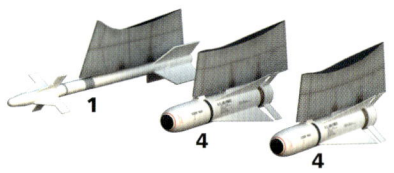

LOAD 6 — Hard-Target Strike

1 2x AIM–9 Sidewinder
2 1x ALQ-131 ECM pod
3 2x AGM–65 Maverick
4 1x AN/AAS–35(V) Pave Penny targeting pod
5 1x SNIPER targeting pod
6 5x GBU–12 laser-guided bomb

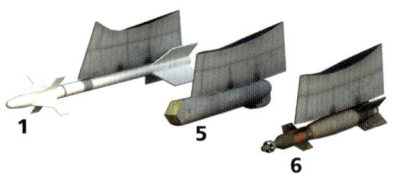
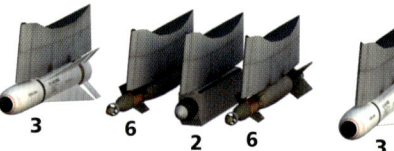

LOAD 7 — SCUD Interdiction

1 2x AIM–9 Sidewinder
2 1x ALQ-131 ECM pod
3 2x AGM–65 Maverick
4 1x AN/AAS–35(V) Pave Penny targeting pod
5 2x LAU–131 rocket pod
6 4x CBU–89B munitions dispenser with GATOR mines

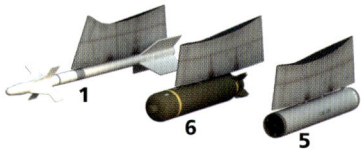
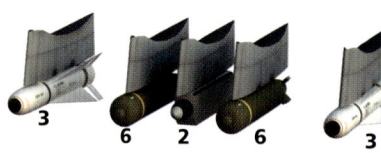

(16,000lb) of stores can be carried on 11 pylons. These include unguided rockets and bombs as well as more advanced weapons. The A-10 is commonly associated with the AGM-65 Maverick missile, a short-range weapon guided by an infra-red system that can also be used by the pilot in the absence of a dedicated Forward-Looking Infra-Red (FLIR) system.

Some A-10s, redesignated OA-10, have served in the Forward Air Controller (FAC) role. These planes retain their capabilities but are armed with rocket pods loaded with smoke warheads, which are used to mark targets for other aircraft. The slow speed of the A-10 makes it an excellent platform for observation and target marking, leaving it to the faster jets to attack accurately. Low speed also makes the A-10 suitable for escorting and supporting helicopters used for Search and Rescue missions or for carrying Special Forces personnel.

Most A-10s fly with an ALQ-131 electronic countermeasures (ECM) pod for defence against enemy radar-guided weapons, and a pair of AIM–9 Sidewinders for air-to-air combat. The A–10 was never intended to function as a fighter, though its excellent manoeuvrability does give it advantages in a turning fight. This capability is defensive; the A-10 is a ground-attack aircraft and is wasted in any other role.

For the ground-attack mission, laser-guided weapons can be used, but this is uncommon. The Thunderbolt can deliver iron bombs and other unguided

Low-Level Gun Attack

Guns, no matter how powerful, have a limited range and are thus only useful against ground targets if they are fired from low altitudes. Aiming can be problematical when travelling at high speed close to the ground, as there is very little time for the pilot to identify a target and line up a shot. Even with the most advanced targeting systems, accurate shooting requires great skill.

A rapid-fire cannon is a good choice for this role, as the volume of fire increases the chances of a hit. It is much more useful to fire 100 rounds just as the aim point is about to cross the target than to fire three times as many over a few seconds and hose the burst onto the target. Most of the ammunition used in this way is wasted, and the actual target area receives relatively few rounds, which may be ineffective.

Lining up a cannon shot requires the aircraft to enter a dive and pull up once the target has been 'serviced'. Raising the nose of the aircraft during firing spreads out the burst just at the moment when it needs to be concentrated. The aircraft may or may not be turning as the shot is aimed, but afterwards it is desirable to execute a hard turn to make aiming more difficult for any ground-based personnel firing back at the plane.

There is obviously a danger of flying into the ground, so the pilot must think ahead, set up a good pass and be willing to recognize if a given target is too close to permit an attack. It is also necessary to pull up and abort a pass that has begun to go awry; no target is worth crashing into the ground for.

Ground-attack training teaches pilots these skills and gives them the confidence to select a fleeting target and attack it, or to make the decision not to launch a low-percentage run that risks aircraft loss or damage for no real chance of a result. Despite this, ground strafing remains a remains a real challenge; in its own way it is every bit as difficult as dogfighting.

An A-10 firing its 30mm Avenger cannon during a low-level pass. The cannon has an effective range of more than 1200m (4000ft), but accurate shooting is difficult from a moving aircraft.

MODERN AIR-LAUNCHED WEAPONS

ordnance with considerable accuracy; other aircraft are better suited to launching precision strikes of this sort.

The Thunderbolt arrived too late to see service in the Vietnam War, but became a mainstay of U.S. tactical air capability. Had the Cold War 'gone hot', Thunderbolts would have been a critical component of the NATO response to massed Soviet tank advances across Europe. The 'tankbusting' role would have absorbed most of the A-10 squadrons' attention, along with close air support and interdiction missions.

However, nothing ever happens the way it was predicted or planned for. In the late 1980s the A-10 was mainly operating in an observation/FAC role, and was scheduled for replacement by faster jets. The 1991 Gulf War allowed the Thunderbolt to show its strengths in an environment not entirely unlike the one it was designed for; the Iraqi army used Soviet-supplied tanks and possessed them in vast numbers.

The A-10 proved to be everything its designers could have hoped for, accounting for nearly a thousand enemy tanks and twice as many other military vehicles. Strikes against artillery positions were equally successful. Thunderbolts even downed two enemy helicopters with their main guns. In return they suffered just four aircraft shot down in 8100 sorties.

A-10s flew support, observation and strike missions during the Balkans conflicts of the late 1990s, and against the Taliban in Afghanistan from 2002 onwards. They also participated in combat operations in Iraq during Operation Iraqi Freedom, with one aircraft shot down and another returning to base despite very serious damage.

Among the many targets for A-10 strikes in Iraq were mobile SCUD missile launchers, which proved difficult to find in the desert terrain. SCUD erector-launchers are not especially 'hard' targets and do not require extremely powerful weapons to destroy them. Among the options open to the A-10 strike pilots was a direct attack with guns, the use of rockets or Maverick missiles, or the seeding of air-dropped anti-vehicle mines to limit the lauchers' movements even if they could not be destroyed.

Thunderbolts flew a range of missions in Iraq, including close support and strikes against the enemy's logistics chain. Psychological Operations (PsyOps) were also conducted by A-10s, using air-dropped leaflets to undermine the morale of hostile forces. Such measures are unlikely to be effective without a credible threat, but the presence of A-10s in the combat area was almost certainly sufficient to provide one.

It was expected that the A-10 would be phased out in favour of such fast aircraft as the F-16, but experience in the Gulf War and the Balkans showed that a dedicated close air support platform was still a sound investment. Instead of being retired, the Thunderbolt has instead been given a Service Life Extension Programme, demonstrating the value military planners now placed on it.

Upgrades to the A-10 include greatly improved instrumentation for the pilot, along with targeting equipment that allows the use of GPS and laser guided weapons. This enhances the Thunderbolt's precision-strike capability and will eventually be incorporated into all A-10s. At present it is planned that the A-10 will remain in service until at least 2028. Its intended replacement is another fast mover, the F-35, so perhaps the venerable Warthog might soldier on even after that date.

Below: Unguided 'iron bombs', such as these 226kg (500lb) Mk82 devices, can be delivered with impressive accuracy from an A-10. In many cases laser guidance does not significantly increase weapon accuracy.

A-10 THUNDERBOLT II

LOAD 8

Infrastructure Strike

1. 2x AIM–9 Sidewinder
2. 1x ALQ–131 ECM pod
3. 6x Mk84 JDAM

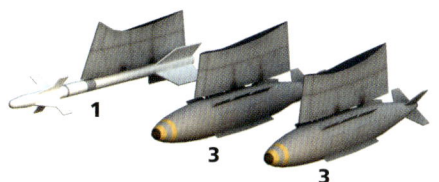

LOAD 9

Precision Strike

1. 2x AIM–9 Sidewinder
2. 1x ALQ–131 ECM pod
3. 1x AN/AAS–35(V) Pave Penny targeting pod
4. 4x GBU–12 laser-guided bomb

LOAD 10

Extended-Range Strike

1. 2x AIM–9 Sidewinder
2. 1x ALQ–131 ECM pod
3. 1x AN/AAS–35(V) Pave Penny targeting pod
4. 2x 2271l (600gal) fuel tank
5. 3x Mk 84 JDAM

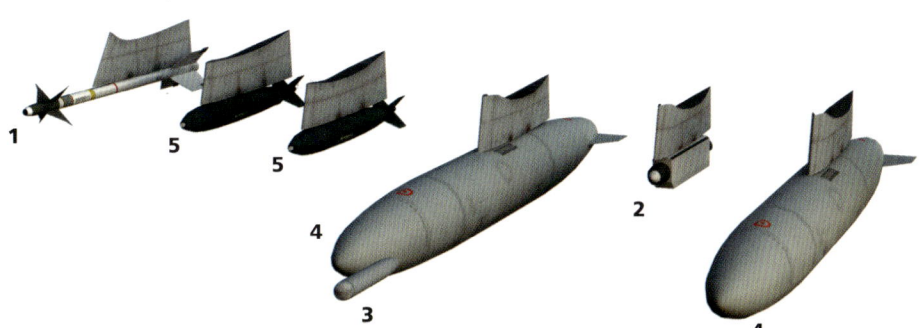

MODERN AIR-LAUNCHED WEAPONS

F-15A–D Eagle

The U.S. Air Force emerged from the era of the Vietnam War with the excellent F-4 Phantom serving in a variety of roles. This versatile aircraft started out as a fighter but proved its value as a multi-role air-combat and ground-attack platform, as well as in such specialist roles as reconnaissance and SEAD (Suppression of Enemy Air Defences). However, the Americans recognized that the Phantom would need replacing at some point, and that they were in need of a counter to the new generation of Soviet fighters then starting to appear.

Radar assistance
The F-15's radar system is mounted in the nose and accessed through a side panel. Look-down, shoot-down capability allows the F-15 to engage low-flying targets that might otherwise be able to hide in the 'ground clutter'.

Fuselage mounts
The F-15 carries up to four medium-range air-to-air missiles in semi-recessed fuselage troughs. This reduces drag produced by the weapon, which can be significant when undertaking high-level interception. A six-barrel Vulcan 20mm cannon is also carried in a fuselage mount.

Wing pylons
Additional air-to-air missiles can be carried on wing pylons, or on the 'shoulders' of fuel tanks carried on the wing stations. A fuel tank can be carried on the centreline station, but this station cannot accommodate shoulder-mounted missiles on the tank.

F-15A–D EAGLE

LOAD 1
Interception

1 2x AIM–9 Sidewinder
2 2x AIM–7 Sparrow
3 3x 2271l (600gal) fuel tank

Any new fighter would need to be able to intercept high-flying bombers as well as engage in air-superiority combat at all altitudes. This required both a high rate of climb and excellent turning characteristics, coupled with the ability to maintain a high speed for long periods in order to make an early interception. To enable the new fighter to defeat its likely opponents, it would also need advanced electronic systems, notably radar.

The aircraft that emerged to meet these specifications was the F-15, whose extremely powerful engines enabled it to outperform most rivals without engaging the afterburners. A power-to-weight ratio of greater than one enabled it to accelerate even in a

Below: The ability to carry missiles on the 'shoulders' of fuel tanks enables aircraft to make best use of a limited number of pylons. More recent aircraft generally have more hardpoints than the F-15.

MODERN AIR-LAUNCHED WEAPONS

Above: The F-15's gun uses a linkless feed system, which recycles the cases of fired rounds back into the storage system. It is not practical to eject spent rounds from an aircraft moving at speed.

vertical climb and to reach very high altitudes quickly, as well as regaining speed lost in a turning fight.

The F-15 entered service with the U.S. Air Force in 1976, and was subsequently exported to Japan, Israel and Saudi Arabia. The original aircraft was designated F-15A, with a two-seat trainer version designated F-15B. An upgraded C variant (and associated two-seat D version) was constructed starting in 1979 and onwards. The main enhancements were in terms of improved avionics and electronics, it was also given the capability to use conformal fuel/systems packs. The F-15 also formed the basis for experimental aircraft, such as the proposed F-15N, which was to be carrier-capable, and licensed versions, such as the F-15J. The latter version was built in Japan.

The F-15 A-D carries a 20mm M61A1 rotary cannon, normally loaded with 960 rounds for combat. It has four semi-recessed fuselage hardpoints for external stores, a centreline pylon and two wing pylons. Up to four AIM–9 Sidewinder missiles can be carried for short-range combat, with up to four AIM–120 AMRAAM or AIM–7 Sparrow missiles for longer-range engagements. The centreline pylon can carry a fuel tank or other stores including reconnaissance pods.

The range of a C or D model F-15 can be extended by using conformal FAST (Fuel and Sensor, Tactical) packs on the wing roots. These allow the aircraft to carry extra fuel and/or other stores without using up pylons as drop tanks do. Conformal tanks of this sort can only be removed while the

F-15A–D EAGLE

LOAD 2 Ferry

1 2x AIM–9 Sidewinders
2 3x 2271l (600gal) fuel tanks

LOAD 3 Standoff Interception

1 7x AIM–120 AMRAAM
2 1x AIM–9 Sidewinder

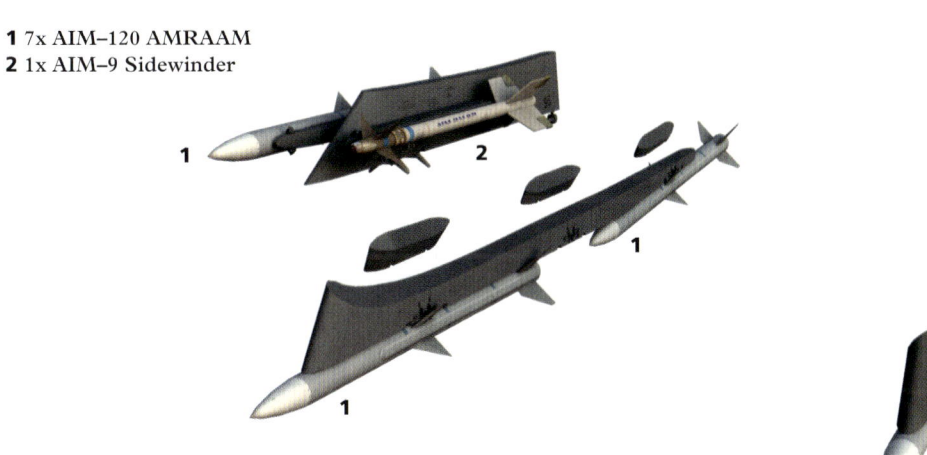

aircraft is on the ground, so they cannot be discarded when empty. However, they cause little drag and do not greatly increase radar cross-section.

Using FAST packs proved successful enough that the F-15E (Strike Eagle) now carries them as standard and would need modification to fly without them. Essentially, this makes the F-15E a slightly different aircraft to the A–D version – conformal tanks are an optional extra on the C and D models but are part of the aircraft on the Strike Eagle.

The F-15A-D is an air-superiority fighter and would not normally engage ground targets. Its gun is not well suited to this role and it does not carry air-to-ground weapons. It is, however, an excellent air superiority fighter, andas such is capable of engaging a wide range of targets.

As the F-15 closes for an interception, it can engage from far beyond visual range. Originally this capability was provided by AIM–7 Sparrow missiles. Early model Sparrows relied on radar guidance by the launching aircraft, which meant that the F-15 had to continue flying towards the target. This was acceptable when intercepting a bomber (one of the F-15's original roles) but when engaged in combat it proved to be unacceptably hazardous. Against fighters that could evade violently, such early missiles were ineffective.

Later model Sparrow missiles extended the Eagle's reach out to 50km (30 miles) but suffered from the same guidance problems. An attempt to mount the long-range fire-and-

MODERN AIR-LAUNCHED WEAPONS

F-15A–D EAGLE

An F-15C Eagle of the 44th Fighter Squadron, 18th Fighter Wing, based at Kadena Air Force Base in Japan.

LOAD 4

Air Superiority

1 4x AIM–9 Sidewinder
2 4x AIM–120 AMRAAM

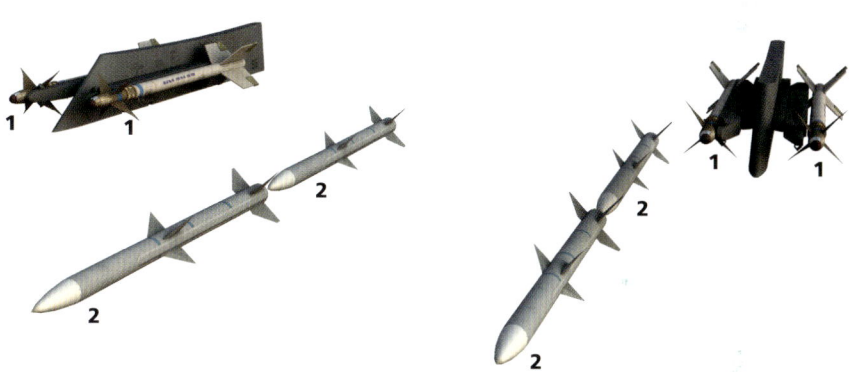

forget AIM-54 Phoenix missile on a modified Eagle was abandoned in favour of the new AIM–120 AMRAAM missile, which offered the capability for intercepts beyond visual range out to about 50km (30 miles).

While not as impressive as the range of the Phoenix missile, which exceeded 160km (100 miles), AMRAAM offered good intercept capability and, more importantly, active homing. After being guided to the general target vicinity by data from the launching aircraft, the missile

Left: This F-15 is carrying a classic air-to-air loadout, comprising a centreline fuel tank and four AIM–120 AMRAAM missiles on the fuselage, as well as four AIM–9 Sidewinders on the wing pylons.

activates its own radar and begins its attack manoeuvres. At closer ranges the AIM–120 can engage its own radar almost immediately, and can also home in on an enemy aircraft's radar jammers, rendering electronic countermeasures far less effective.

The AIM–120 AMRAAM allows an F-15 to engage up to four targets with radar-guided missiles, and to engage in defensive or offensive manoeuvres before the weapons have reached their targets. At closer ranges, the AIM–9 Sidewinder infra-red guided missile offers an all-aspect attack capability. Earlier Sidewinder models required a launch position behind the target aircraft for their seeker heads to acquire the target, but

modern weapons can acquire a fast-moving jet fighter from any angle.

The Sidewinder is also a fire-and-forget weapon, so it can be launched at an enemy aircraft from a range of up to 18km (11 miles) and requires no further input from the pilot. This is essential in a dogfight situation or where there are more than one targets available. Once these missiles are expended, or where a target is closer than the Sidewinder's arming distance of about 2.5km (1.5 miles), the cannon can be used.

The Eagle's high speed and agility enable it to make a rapid approach to the target, launch missiles or make a gun pass, and escape before a response can be mounted. If a dogfight does

MODERN AIR-LAUNCHED WEAPONS

Engagement Ranges

The ranges of engagement for air combat can be subdivided into four categories. Long- and medium-range attacks occur beyond visual range (BVR), while short and 'gun' range attacks are made at a distance where the target can be seen from the launching aircraft.

A long- or medium-range weapon must be fast enough to cover the distance to the target before it moves out of range or manoeuvres in such a way that tracking is lost. This calls for a powerful engine and enough fuel to reach the target. Once within range, the missile needs to be able to manoeuvre violently enough to hit an evading target. For this reason, longer-range missiles are large and heavy.

Missile attacks from BVR rely on radar data gathered by the launching aircraft or another radar platform. Target identification can be difficult, and rules of engagement may prohibit the use of long-range weapons to protect neutral and civilian aircraft. This would not be much of a problem in an all-out war, but most modern conflicts are limited in scope to the point where civilian air traffic may be present in a contested air zone.

Because of this, such extremely long-range weapons as the Phoenix missile may not be able to exploit their full capabilities, and even medium-range weapons, such as AMRAAM, have to be used with care. Visual-range attacks with short-range missiles such as Sidewinder allow the pilot to 'eyeball' the target and positively identify it before firing. A short-range weapon can be lighter and thus easier to carry, enabling it to be positioned on wingtip pylons that could not support heavier weapons. However, engaging at close range does involve more danger to the aircraft.

As a result of these factors, weapons of a very long range are of relatively limited use, while guns are primarily a fallback system for use when other weapons are not appropriate or available. Thus most air-superiority fighters tend to fly with a combination of medium- and short-range weapons, enabling them to fire effectively at the most likely engagement ranges.

An F-15 fires an AIM–120 AMRAAM missile as part of a combat evaluation programme.

ensue the Eagle is extremely agile and can maintain high speed even in a turning fight; if this goes against it then the ability to accelerate away, even in a climb, allows the Eagle to get itself out of trouble and return to the combat on its own terms. Even if the aircraft is heavily damaged it can often survive – one F-15 lost a wing about 60cm (2ft) from the fuselage due to a mid-air collision and still managed to return to base under sufficiently good control to make a landing.

No F-15A–D has ever been shot down by enemy aircraft. Eagles have scored 104 air-to-air victories, the majority of which are credited to Israeli pilots. During the 1991 Gulf War, F-15s downed almost all the Iraqi aircraft destroyed by U.S. pilots, including some 34 aircraft ranging from fighters and strike planes to transport aircraft and helicopters. Most used missiles and not guns. The F-15 was also successful in air-to-air combat operations over the Balkans.

Since the cessation of the Cold War, the need for a top-end air-superiority fighter might perhaps have diminished somewhat. Ground attack, especially against insurgent bases, is proving to be increasingly important at present. Most of these forces cannot deploy a credible air-combat or ground-attack force, and most potential enemies lack the capability to field modern fighters. Despite this, air superiority remains a precious commodity, and its full value

F-15A–D EAGLE

LOAD 5   **Maritime Long-Range Interception**

1 1x 2271l (600gal) fuel tank
2 4x AIM–7F/M Sparrow
3 4x AIM–9 Sidewinder

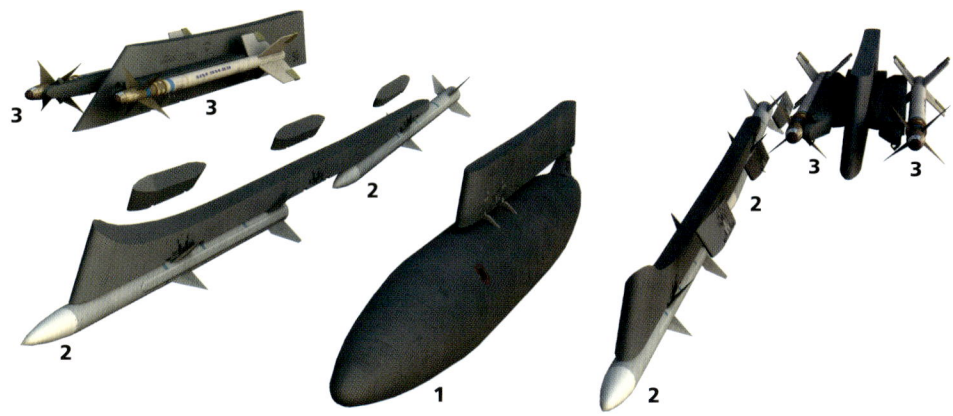

may not even be appreciated until it is in danger of being lost. For this reason, the high-capability air-superiority fighter remains a vital component of the arsenal of the major powers today and will remain so for the foreseeable future.

However, the Eagle is now beginning to show its age. All A and B models have been withdrawn from U.S. Air Force service, with the C and D models being gradually replaced by the F-22 Raptor. There are plans to keep some updated F-15Cs in USAF service even after the introduction of the F-35, and certain foreign air forces may still continue to use the Eagle for many years in the future. In common with the Phantom before it, this excellent air-combat machine has developed into a versatile multi-role aircraft which will continue to give many more years of service.

Below: The F-15 still remains one of the world's best fighter aircraft, and it may continue to receive upgrades extending its service life into the 2030s and beyond.

MODERN AIR-LAUNCHED WEAPONS

Above: An F-15E in Iraq, configured for a multi-mission profile. Some aircraft in a flight provide fighter defence, while others make ground attacks, then descend from top cover position to drop their own bombs.

The Strike Eagle was intended to replace the F-111 as a tactical strike aircraft. It was conceptualized at a time when precision weaponry had already demonstrated how valuable it could be, so the capability to deploy advanced weapons was built in at the design stage. This included the ability to programme weapons, such as the Joint Direct Attack Munition (JDAM) and Joint Standoff Weapon (JSOW), in flight. Improved electronics systems were also incorporated, including night vision equipment and an advanced cockpit interface.

The F-15E is still being developed, refined and upgraded. For example, the F-15E was the first U.S. fighter ever powered by a blend of traditional and synthetic aviation fuels in flight. An upgraded version (designated F-15K) was built for export to the Republic of Korea, and a low-observable (stealth) variant designated F-15S, also known as the 'Silent Eagle' was demonstrated in 2009.

The Strike Eagle retains the air-to-air capabilities of its predecessor, including the M61 20mm Vulcan cannon and the ability to carry Sidewinder and/or AMRAAM missiles. This gives the Strike Eagle a measure of 'self-escort' capability and enables it to fight its way into or out of enemy airspace as needed. Its primary role is as a strike platform, and for this it can carry a wide range of stores.

The F-15E can deliver a single B61 nuclear bomb or a range of conventional ordnance including cruise missiles and shorter-range missiles, such as the AGM-65 Maverick or AGM-84 Harpoon. It can drop laser-guided bombs of the Paveway family and GPS-guided or 'dumb' bombs, along with cluster bombs and air-dropped mines. The Strike Eagle is also capable of carrying specialist ordnance, such as the CBU-107 Passive Attack Weapon. This weapon is non-explosive and allows targets in close proximity to non-combatants or civilian structures to be attacked with a minimal chance of collateral damage.

F-15E STRIKE EAGLE

LOAD 4 Standoff Anti–Armour

1 2x AGM–154B JSOW each carrying 6x BLU–108B submunitions
2 1x 2271l (600gal) fuel tank
3 3x AIM–120 AMRAAM
4 1x AIM–9 Sidewinder
5 1x AN/AAQ–13 LANTIRN navigation pod
6 1x SNIPER targeting pod

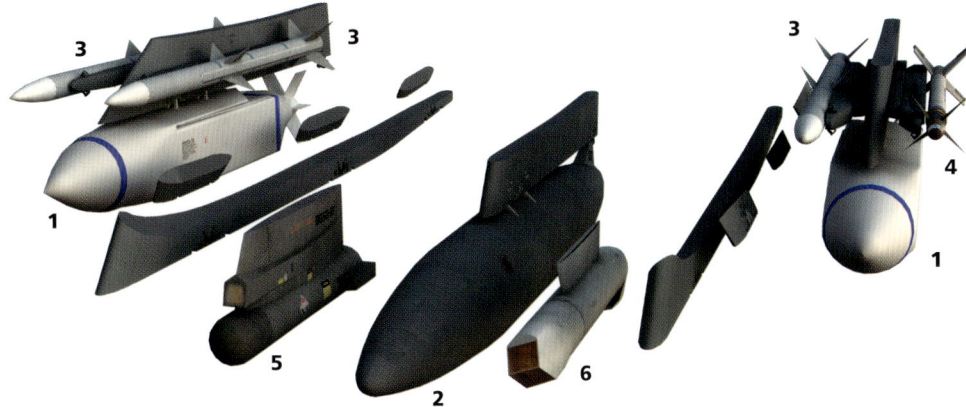

LOAD 5 Offensive Counter-Air

1 3x AIM–120 AMRAAM
2 3x CBU–87 cluster bomb
3 2x GBU–12
4 1x AIM–9 Sidewinder
5 1x 2271l (600gal) fuel tank
6 1x AN/AAQ–13 LANTIRN navigation pod
7 1x SNIPER targeting pod

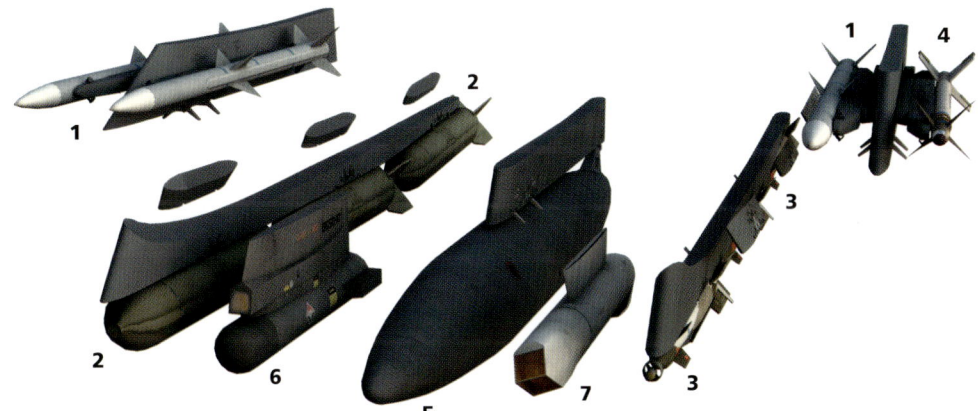

Most weapons handling is tasked to the Weapons Systems Officer (WSO), seated behind the pilot. Both pilot and WSO use advanced radar systems and a LANTIRN navigation and targeting system. This includes Forward-Looking Infrared (FLIR) sensors that can automatically guide the aircraft in terrain-following mode. This allows safe flight at very low levels, down to about 60-70m (200–230ft), which helps hide the Strike Eagle from hostile weapons and radars.

The Strike Eagle first saw action in the initial Gulf War, flying close support missions in addition to deeper strikes. These included strikes against enemy armoured forces and several 'decapitation strike' missions intended to kill enemy high commanders by bombing their possible locations.

The Iraqi air force was suppressed by strikes against its bases, with many fighters destroyed on the ground. Occasional brushes with enemy fighters did not lead to any kills, but the Strike Eagle did score a very unusual air-to-air kill when a laser guided bomb hit the ground beneath an Iraqi helicopter and destroyed it.

After the 1991 Gulf War, Strike Eagles were utilized to help police the no-fly zones set up around Iraq, flying with a combination of stores to allow immediate-response attacks on whatever units broke the ceasefire conditions. This flexibility greatly shortened reaction times in comparison with a sortie that must

MODERN AIR-LAUNCHED WEAPONS

The F-15E can be easily distinguished from the air-superiority C version because it carries a second crew member and has conformal fuel and weapon packs alongside the engine intakes as standard. The presence of ground-attack weapons is another obvious indicator.

LOAD 6 — Interdiction Strike

1. 8x GBU–39 Small Diameter Bomb
2. 3x CBU–87 cluster bomb
3. 3x AIM–120 AMRAAM
4. 1x AIM–9 Sidewinder
5. 2x 2271l (600gal) fuel tank
6. 1x AN/AAQ–13 LANTIRN navigation pod
7. 1x SNIPER targeting pod

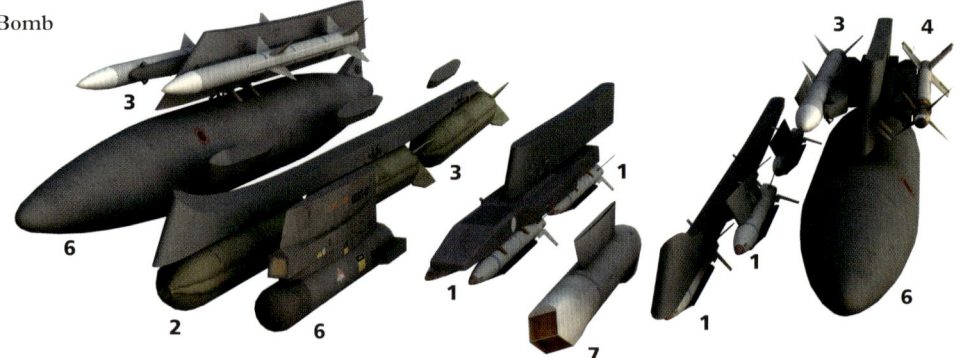

be authorized, planned, and loaded before the aircraft can even take off.

Limited operations against Iraqi targets were carried out in the late 1998s because of its non-compliance with UN resolutions. At this time, Strike Eagles were forced to operate in a 'war-like situation'. The rules of engagement were very strict – avoiding collateral damage was a primary concern. In the event, laser-guided bombs proved to be highly effective against Iraqi surface-to-air missile sites, munitions stores, command posts and communications facilities.

The Strike Eagle was also highly active over Iraq in 2003, striking key command and control sites, such as the headquarters of the ruling Ba'ath party and Republican Guard. At the beginning of the 2003 war, Strike Eagles suppressed enemy air defences and communications equipment. They also flew in support of Special Forces teams operating deep in Iraq, attacking targets pinpointed by ground personnel and assisting teams in contact with the enemy.

During the 2003 war in Iraq, Strike Eagles severely mauled the Iraqi air force, catching many fighters on the ground and eliminating them, in addition to making air bases unusable. Strikes against Republican Guard armoured units debilitated them, greatly assisting the ground campaign. F-15Es also located targets for other aircraft, including heavy bombers.

The F-15E also operated over the Balkans, destroying anti-aircraft weapons that had fired on UN forces operating in the area. Again, laser-guided bombs proved very effective. The first incidences of Strike Eagles flying Close Air Support missions soon followed, with some missions launched from bases in Britain. This required flight time of several hours to and from the combat area, necessitating mid-air refuelling. The aircraft carried a mixed armament of air-to-air and air-to-ground weapons, allowing them to cover one another's attacks in case of interference by enemy fighters.

The AGM-130 missile was used from Strike Eagles against various targets that merited its considerable

Above: An F-15E banks hard over Afghanistan. The current primary mission for the Strike Eagle is close air support and interdiction of enemy logistics using precision-guided weapons.

expense. These included grounded enemy aircraft and bridges located in terrain that made an attack problematic. Terrorist training camps in Afghanistan and tunnels suspected of housing munitions stores or Taliban forces were also attacked with these weapons, as well as laser-guided penetrator bombs designed to explode after they had punched deep into the ground. Precision delivery of these weapons is vital to effectiveness.

MODERN AIR-LAUNCHED WEAPONS

LOAD 7

Standoff 'Bridge Busting' against heavily defended target

1. 1x ALQ–131 ECM pod
2. 2x GBU–15
3. 4x AIM–120 AMRAAM

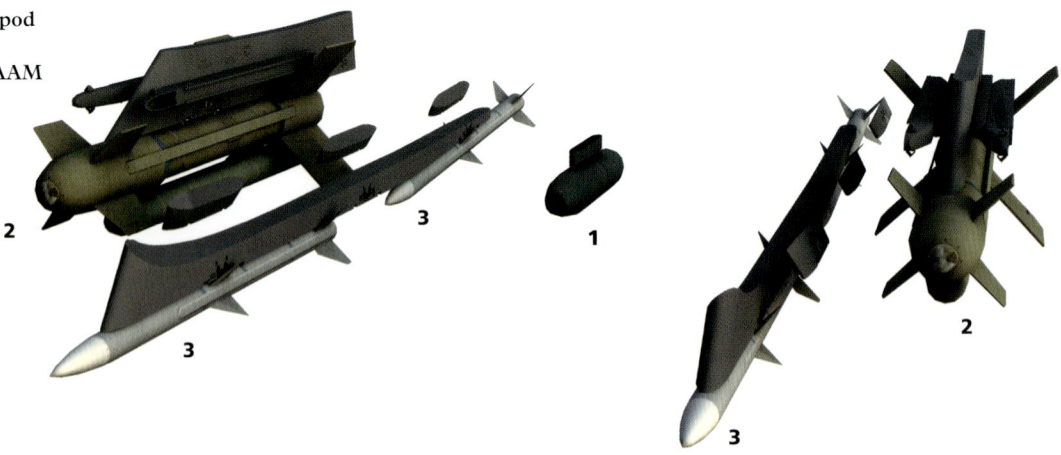

LOAD 8

Standoff 'Bunker Busting'

1. 2x AGM–130 missile with BLU–109 penetrator
2. 3x AIM–120 AMRAAM
3. 1x AIM–9 Sidewinder
4. 1x 2271l (600gal) fuel tank
5. 1x AN/AAQ–13 LANTIRN navigation pod
6. 1x AN/AAQ–14 LANTIRN targeting pod

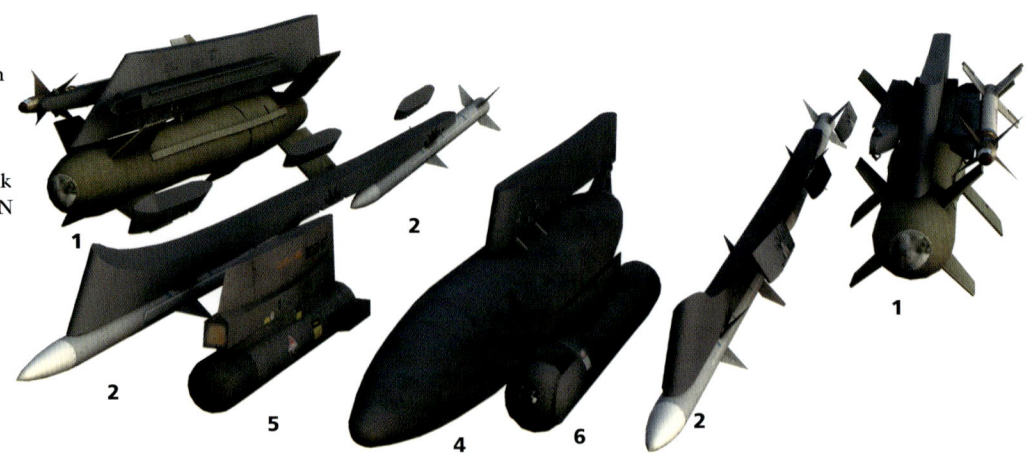

LOAD 9

Anti-Electrical

1. 3x AIM–120 AMRAAM
2. 2x AGM–154 JSOW carrying CLU–94 or BLU–114B munitions
3. 1x 2271l (600gal) fuel tank
4. 1x AIM–9 Sidewinder
5. 1x AN/AAQ–13 LANTIRN navigation pod
6. 1x SNIPER targeting pod

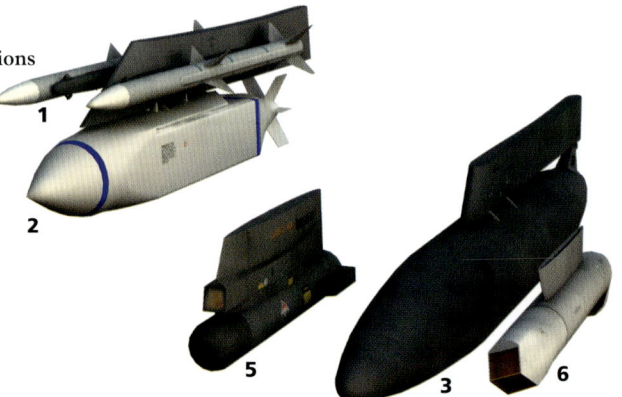

F-15E STRIKE EAGLE

During operations against the Taliban in Afghanistan, a force of Strike Eagles carried out the longest-duration mission ever undertaken by fighters, spending almost 16 hours in the air and refuelling from airborne tankers no fewer than 12 times. Precision-guided bombs were the usual weapon for Strike Eagle missions over Afghanistan, but on some occasions ground attacks were made with 20mm cannon.

Industry Standard

In addition to U.S. forces, the F-15E and its variants are in service with Israel, Saudi Arabia, Singapore and South Korea. Because it is capable of delivering such a wide range of weapon systems, this aircraft can be considered the 'industry standard' when a new system is developed. A planned replacement in some roles by the F-35 Lightning does not guarantee that the F-15E will be retired when the Lightning enters service. It likely that the Strike Eagle will be flying into the 2030s and possibly beyond.

Bridge-Busting (infrastructure strike)

It is not possible to destroy every single supply vehicle or reinforcement unit that attempts to move into the combat zone, although a proportion can be targeted. The remainder can be delayed and the reinforcement or resupply process badly disrupted by attacks on the routes leading from rear-area bases to the battle zone.

Rivers, ravines and other terrain obstacles create 'choke points' through which enemy forces and logistics convoys must pass. The destruction of a bridge at a key point can force enemy units to undertake a lengthy detour to find an alternate route. This not only causes delay but also increases the logistics burden of the move in terms of fuel use and the inavailability of vehicles elsewhere. The longer a convoy or unit is on the move, the more time is available for additional air units to locate it and launch direct attacks.

Ever since air units became capable of the tactic, 'bridge-busting' has been an important strategy. However, a blowing up a bridge is not an easy objective. A bridge is relatively small, and strongly constructed. Scoring a hit requires the accurate delivery of a powerful weapon capable of shattering reinforced concrete.

The weapon of choice for bridge-busting is a laser-guided bomb, such as the GBU-24 Paveway III. This weapon is designed to be launched from low level and is highly manoeuvrable to allow it to make a very precise strike. Its 910kg (2000lb) warhead is powerful enough to drop a span of most bridges.

Before such bombs were available, several aircraft were needed to attack a bridge, and there were often heavy casualties from enemy anti-aircraft fire. Today, a single aircraft can reliably deny the enemy the use of a key route, significantly affecting the outcome of the ground campaign and totally justifying the considerable expense of the weapon used.

An F-15E drops four laser guided Mk84 bombs. Immediately after launch the bombs' guidance fins deploy and they begin seeking the targeting laser. If laser targeting is lost the weapons will revert to a 'dumb' ballistic path, which may still put them somewhere near the target.

MODERN AIR-LAUNCHED WEAPONS

F-16 Fighting Falcon

The F-16 is a single-seat multi-role fighter aircraft that was first designed to fulfil the 'lightweight fighter' niche. Lightweight fighters are designed to offer excellent value for money rather than cutting-edge performance in return for an astronomical investment. The F-16 clearly satisfies this expectation, as it is the world's most widely exported fighter aircraft.

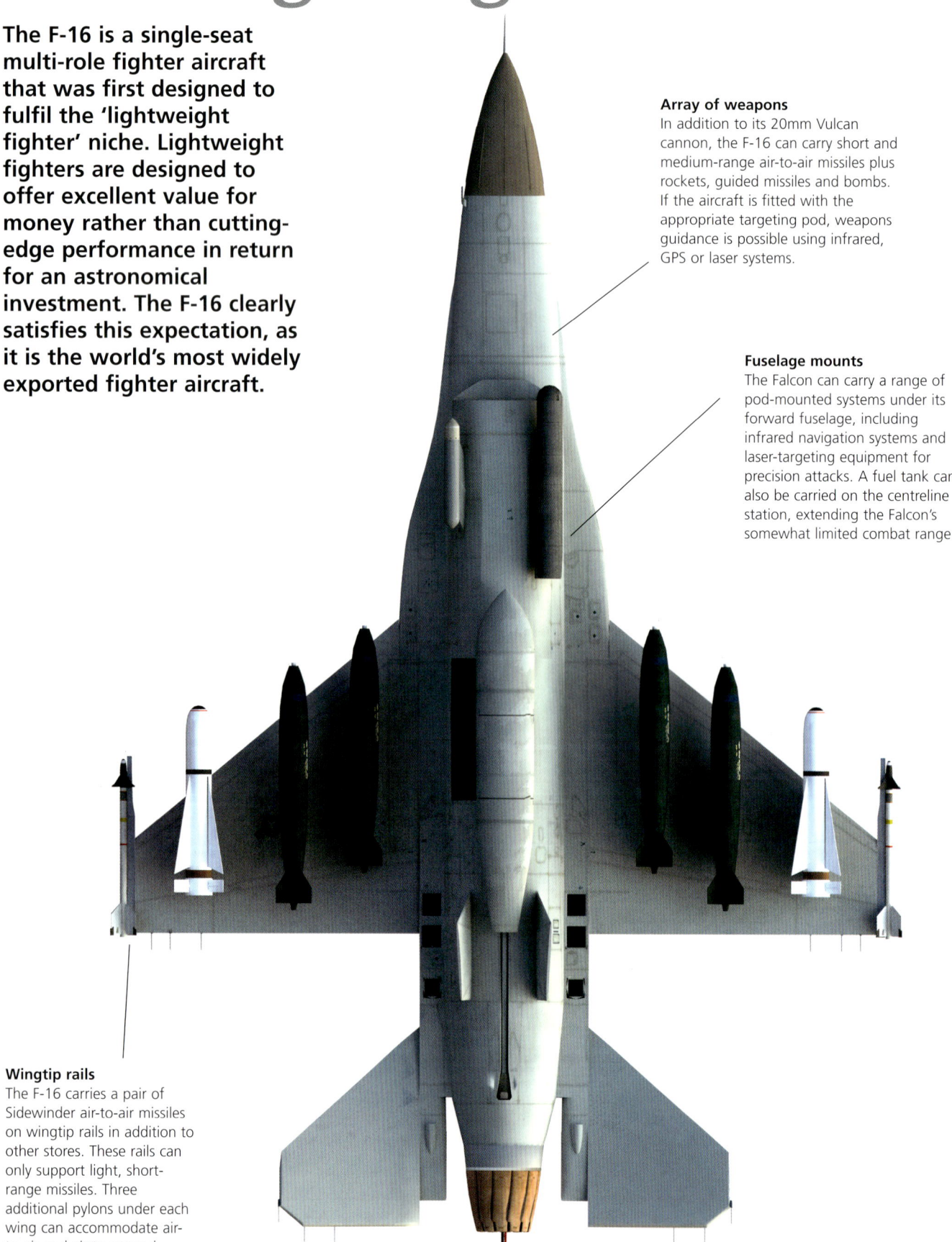

Array of weapons
In addition to its 20mm Vulcan cannon, the F-16 can carry short and medium-range air-to-air missiles plus rockets, guided missiles and bombs. If the aircraft is fitted with the appropriate targeting pod, weapons guidance is possible using infrared, GPS or laser systems.

Fuselage mounts
The Falcon can carry a range of pod-mounted systems under its forward fuselage, including infrared navigation systems and laser-targeting equipment for precision attacks. A fuel tank can also be carried on the centreline station, extending the Falcon's somewhat limited combat range.

Wingtip rails
The F-16 carries a pair of Sidewinder air-to-air missiles on wingtip rails in addition to other stores. These rails can only support light, short-range missiles. Three additional pylons under each wing can accommodate air-to-air and air-to-ground weapons.

F-16 FIGHTING FALCON

LOAD 1

Combined Air to Air/Air to Ground

1. 2x AIM-9 Sidewinder
2. 2x AGM-65 Maverick
3. 4x Mk84 unguided bomb
4. 1x 1552l (410gal) fuel tank

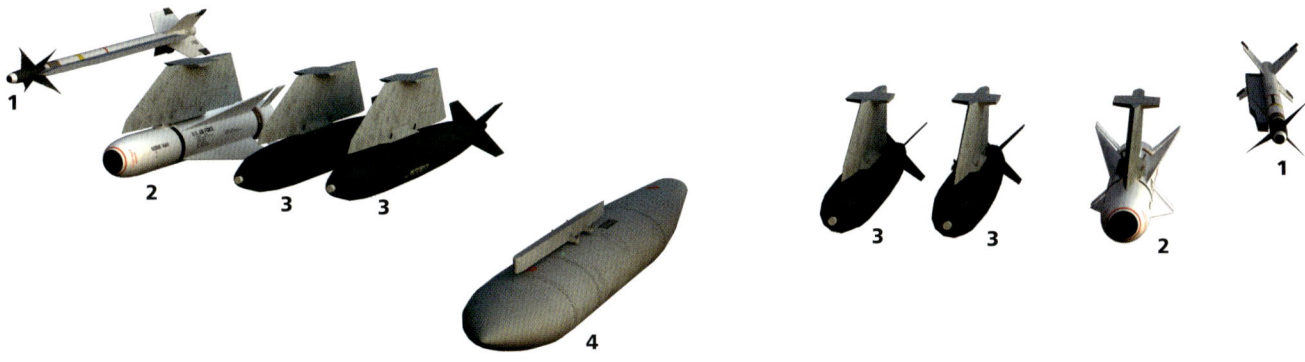

LOAD 2

Air to Air

1. 4x AIM-9 Sidewinder
2. 2x AIM-120 AMRAAM

LOAD 3

Iron Bomb

1. 2x AIM-9 Sidewinder
2. 2x AIM-120 AMRAAM
3. 6x Mk82 unguided bomb
4. 2x 2309l (610gal) fuel tank

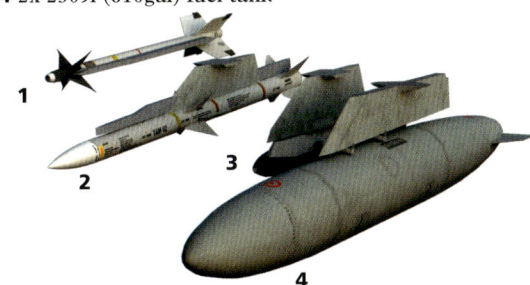

MODERN AIR-LAUNCHED WEAPONS

Above: High-g manoeuvres stress the airframe when conducted with heavy stores on the wings. This can be offset by placing the heaviest stores, in this case large fuel tanks, close to the wing roots.

Unofficially nicknamed the 'Viper', the F-16 entered service in 1979 and has been gradually updated ever since. Among the enhancements it has received are improved radar and ECM equipment, bolt-on targeting pods and the capability to employ an ever-increasing array of weaponry. This is carried on six underwing and one centreline pylon. Two wingtip mounts can accommodate short-range air-to-air missiles. The F-16 also carries a M61A1 Vulcan 20mm cannon internally.

The F-16 was designed from the outset to be extremely manoeuvrable. Indeed, it was the world's first fighter built with the intent of exceeding 9gs in a turn, though this capability is limited by the amount of stores being carried. Its single engine provides a high power-to-weight ratio, enabling the aircraft to maintain or regain high speeds in a turning fight.

To enhance manoeuvrability, the F-16 was designed to be essentially unstable. Most aircraft are designed with a built-in tendency to return to straight and level flight in the event that control is lost. This is important for safety reasons but it makes the aircraft less responsive to the pilot's instructions. The F-16 was designed with a tendency to depart from straight, level flight, making it virtually uncontrollable without computer assistance, but the pay-off is greatly improved manoeuvrability.

The pilot can exploit this almost frightening level of manoeuvrability by using a multiply-redundant fly-by-wire control system. This automatically corrects the aircraft's instability when it is not making use of it. The pilot's seat is deeply reclined to reduce the effects of high-g turns, and the 'bubble' canopy allows excellent all-round visibility.

Versatility Justifies Cost

These factors clearly mark the F-16 as a high-capability air-superiority fighter, and in this role it can use short-range missiles such as the AIM-9 Sidewinder as well as Beyond-Visual-Range (BVR) weapons such as

F-16 FIGHTING FALCON

The F-16's small size and high manoeuvrability are assets in a dogfight, and it can carry a very respectable warload despite its limited dimensions. These factors contribute to the Falcon's popularity as a multi-role export fighter.

LOAD 4 — Infrastructure Strike ('Bridge-Busting')

1 2x AIM–9 Sidewinder
2 2x AIM–120 AMRAAM
3 2x GBU–12
4 2x 2309l (610gal) fuel tank
5 1x AN/AAQ–13 LANTIRN navigation pod
6 1x AN/AAQ–14 LANTIRN targeting pod

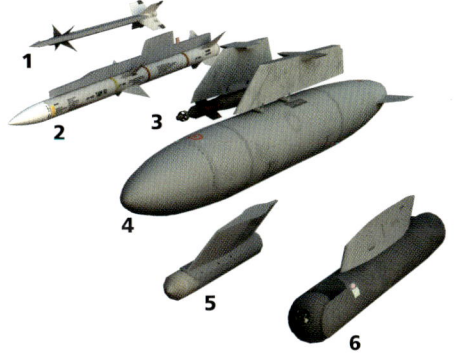

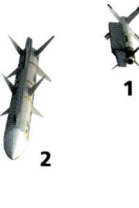

AIM-7 Sparrow and AIM-120 AMRAAM. However, the Falcon is also capable of undertaking ground-attack and strike missions.

This is a factor in its very considerable export success, and is also important in today's military environment, where a purchasing government needs to justify the cost of every aircraft. A large-scale war against enemies possessing advanced weapon systems are unlikely, but the capability to fight one must be retained. At the same time, conflict with an opponent of lesser capability is far more likely.

A cheap, light ground-attack aircraft might seem like an attractive alternative to a more expensive high-capability fighter-bomber, and such an aircraft could be very effective in relatively low-threat environments or against a low-capability enemy. However, small numbers of advanced weapon systems can be purchased by almost any combatant, posing a risk of heavy casualties among cheap attack aircraft or even making some missions impossible. In addition, such an aircraft would be almost useless against a major opponent.

This means a government without unlimited funds to spend must try to provide for all eventualities as best it can. An advanced lightweight fighter with the capability to deliver a wide range of weapons represents a good all-round investment. It may not be as effective as a cutting-edge air-superiority fighter, nor as potent as a dedicated strike plane, nor as cheap as a low-end counter-insurgency aircraft, but it can be switched from each of these tasks to another as the need arises. It is this capability to handle almost any task competently, and some tasks very well indeed, that has recommended the F-16 to some 25 air forces in addition to its home service.

F-16s can employ a range of missiles including AGM-84 Harpoon and AGM-119 Penguin for anti-shipping strike, and AGM-88 HARM for SEAD operations. The AGM-65 Maverick can be carried for a variety

MODERN AIR-LAUNCHED WEAPONS

Hard Target Strike ('bunker-busting')

Hard targets, such as deeply buried bunkers, require special munitions for a successful attack. A concrete bunker might be shattered by a large explosion, and craters can be blasted in earth, but when the two are combined their defensive effects are multiplied.

Most weapons will detonate on contact with the ground, causing considerable surface damage. However, earth absorbs a blast extremely well, deadening the shock wave. A concrete bunker is likely to withstand this attenuated blast without undue damage, protecting personnel or equipment inside. Thick rock covering a cave or tunnel will function the same way.

In order to defeat this level of protection, penetrator warheads are used. These are very robust, allowing the weapon to break through earth or even rock if it strikes hard enough, and still remain in a condition to function. A delay fuse detonates the warhead once it has buried itself, concentrating the effect of the blast against the target rather than dissipating it into the surroundings.

Penetrator weapons are only useful if they are delivered precisely; an underground burst has a very limited radius of effect. They must also impact with great force to enable them to penetrate deeply, which can make delivery problematical. One solution is precision guidance, which enables a fast-moving aircraft to deliver the weapon with a high probability of success. Laser-guidance is ideal for this purpose, allowing a precise impact point to be chosen.

The standard 'bunker-busting' weapon in U.S. service is the BLU-109, a modified 910kg (2000lb) bomb capable of punching through 1.8m (6ft) of reinforced concrete before detonating. It is available as an unguided gravity bomb but is most effective as part of the GBU-24 laser-guided penetrator bomb.

Variations on this concept include the Massive Ordnance Penetrator, designed to pierce through a tunnel complex and destroy it despite internal blast doors and other defensive measures, and capable of penetrating several times as far as the standard GBU-24. The use of penetrators, perhaps delivered by cruise missile, to deliver Agent Defeat Warheads against bunkers thought to contain chemical or biological weapons, is also being investigated.

Traditionally, messages have been written on bombs for as long as they have been dropped from the air. This GPS-guided Joint Direct Attack Munition is to be loaded into B1-B Lancer, but the sentiment would be familiar to previous generations of aircrew.

F-16 FIGHTING FALCON

LOAD 5

Low-Altitude Ground Attack

1. 2x GBU–24
2. 2x AIM–120 AMRAAM
3. 2x AIM–9 Sidewinder
4. 1x AN/AAQ–14 LANTIRN targeting pod
5. 1x ALQ–131 ECM pod
6. 2x 2309l (610gal) fuel tank

LOAD 6

SEAD

1. 2x AGM–88 HARM
2. 3x AIM–120 AMRAAM
3. 1x AIM–9 Sidewinder
4. 2x 2309l (610gal) fuel tank
5. 1x AN/AAQ–13 LANTIRN navigation pod
6. 1x ALQ–131 ECM pod

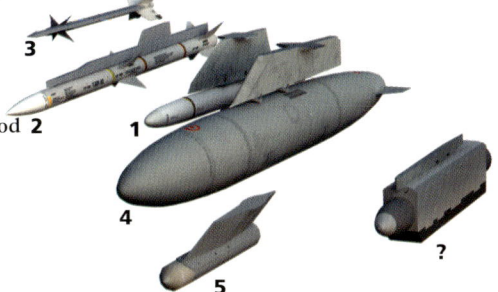

LOAD 7

Anti-Shipping

1. 2x AGM–65 Maverick
2. 3x AIM–120 AMRAAM
3. 1x AIM–9 Sidewinder
4. 2x 2309l (610gal) fuel tank
5. 1x AN/AAQ–13 LANTIRN navigation pod
6. 1x AN/AAQ–14 LANTIRN targeting pod
7. 1x ALQ–131 ECM pod

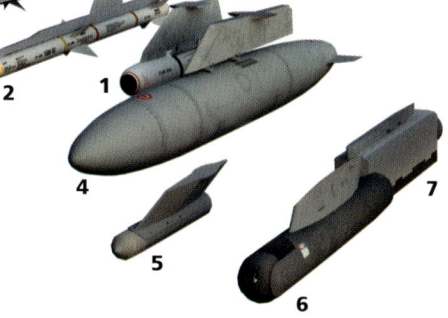

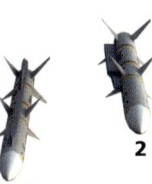

MODERN AIR-LAUNCHED WEAPONS

of missions, and the AGM-154 JSOW to allow standoff strikes. Guided bombs, including GPS and laser-guided weapons, are put to use against precision targets.

The F-16 can also carry and deliver unguided weapons including conventional 'iron bombs', i.e. unguided explosive bombs, and strafing rocket pods as well as cluster bomb and air-dropped mine dispensers. Other capabilities include the nuclear strike role with a single B61 nuclear bomb and a variety of special missions. These include PsyOps, dropping leaflets from a converted cluster bomb dispenser. A range of targeting and defensive pods are available if required.

The F-16 has been built in a range of variants, including planes designed to demonstrate an experimental 'cranked arrow' wing configuration. Many export customers have requested specific modifications to the basic aircraft, and those in USAF service have been updated during their lives in an attempt to keep pace with advancing technology.

The largest force of F-16s deployed outside the USA is with the Israeli Air force, which, in 1981, undertook the first air-to-air combat missions flown by the Falcon. Later that year eight F-16s took part in the historic Osirak reactor attack, aimed at preventing Iraqi development of nuclear weapons. Israeli F-16s have seen combat on several occasions since, being highly successful in air-to-air combat against MiG-21 and Mig-23 aircraft and unmanned air vehicles, as well as against ground targets.

Right: The F-16 has served in several conflicts. This F-16 flies over Afghanistan, supporting Operation Enduring Freedom. It has Sidewinders on its wingtips but there is no real air-to-air threat in this environment.

Other foreign air forces have had good service out of the F-16; Pakistan's Falcons intercepted aircraft during the Soviet-Afghan war while Venezuelan F-16s operated against rebel air and ground forces during the 1992 coup attempt. F-16s from Greece and Turkey clashed in 2006 as part of an ongoing dispute. A dogfight ensued, resulting in a loss of one Greek and one Turkish F-16 due to mid-air collision although no shots were fired by either side.

In U.S. service, the F-16 was the mainstay of strike missions in the 1991 Gulf War, flying more sorties than any other Coalition aircraft. F-16s also formed the core of the largest single strike package of the war, a 72-ship attack on targets in Baghdad. After the war, F-16s patrolled the no-fly zones, downing two Mig-25s with AMRAAM missiles. Resumption of hostilities in 1998 saw F-16s striking various targets as part of Operation Desert Fox.

Very few F-16s were lost in Iraq during any of the various operations there. One loss, in 2003, however, highlighted the dangers of ground-attack missions when a Falcon hit the ground while strafing enemy vehicles with its cannon. Among the successes scored by the F-16 during the most recent round of conflict in Iraq was the destruction of an Al-Qaeda safehouse by precision-guided bombs (one laser-guided and one using GPS), resulting in the death of the head of Al-Qaeda in Iraq.

In the Balkans, F-16s engaged in air-to-air combat and attacked ground targets in support of UN operations. Although hampered by rules of engagement, the F-16 force was successful against J-21 Jastreb and J-22 Orao and Mig-29 fighters. Although Falcons were lost to ground fire, no air-to-air losses occurred. In Afghanistan, where there is no real air-to-air threat, F-16s have flown ground-attack missions against Taliban targets. Modified aircraft using high-resolution infrared cameras have also proven effective in the reconnaissance role.

The F-16 may continue to serve with the Air National Guard for some years to come, but there are plans to replace it with the F-35 Lightning in the U.S. Air Force service in 2025. Foreign sales continue to be strong, however, suggesting that the F-16 may remain in service overseas even after it has finally been phased out in its country of origin.

F-16 FIGHTING FALCON

The F-16 has a relatively short range compared to a dedicated strike platform, but this can be extended by the use of external fuel tanks and standoff weapons, such as the AGM-154 JSOW, which also improves survivability.

LOAD 8

Standoff Anti-Armour

1 2x AGM–154 JSOW each carrying 6x BLU–108/B SFM
2 2x AIM–120 AMRAAM
3 4x AIM–9 Sidewinder
4 1x 1552l (410gal) fuel tank

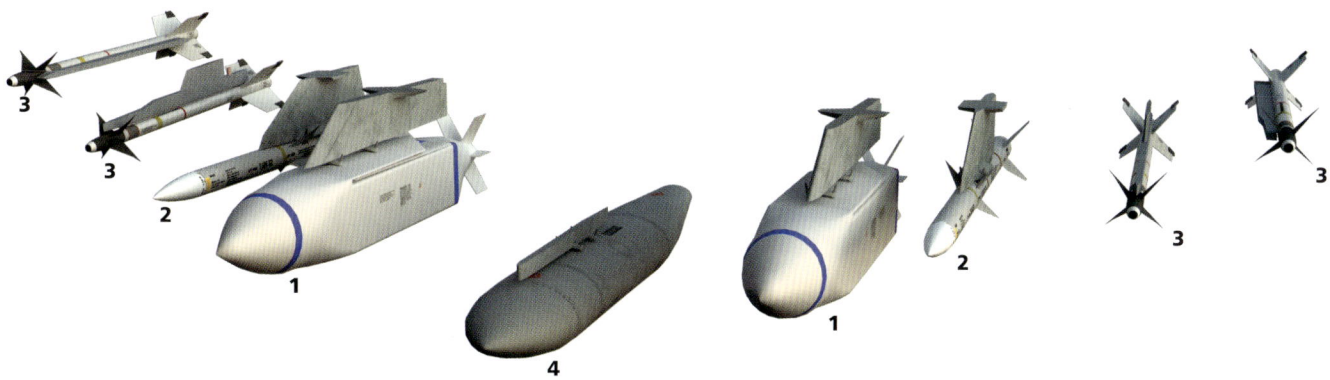

LOAD 9

Logistics Interdiction

1 2x AIM–9 Sidewinder
2 4x Mk83 JDAM
3 2x CBU–87 cluster bomb

MODERN AIR-LAUNCHED WEAPONS

F/A-18 Hornet & Super Hornet

First flying in 1978, the F/A-18 Hornet was developed for use aboard U.S. aircraft carriers, offering both fighter and attack capabilities in a relatively inexpensive airframe. Evolutionary development through models A–D eventually led to the introduction of the redesigned and larger E and F model 'Super Hornet'. This airframe is also used as the basis for the EA-18G Growler electronic warfare aircraft.

Wing stations
The F/A-18 can carry light air-to-air missiles on its wingtip rails. There are also four underwing pylons capable of handling a range of air-to-air and air-to-ground weapons. The Hornet can launch anti-ship, anti-radar and general-purpose missiles in addition to bombs and cluster munitions.

Fuselage stations
The Hornet mounts a six-barrel Vulcan 20mm cannon in the fuselage, and can carry a fuel tank on the centreline to extend its rather limited combat radius. Two missiles can be carried in semi-recessed fuselage stations.

Twin engines
The Navy, whose aircraft operate extensively over water, required a twin-engine design.

F/A-18 HORNET & SUPER HORNET

LOAD 1 — Carrier Defence

1 2x AIM–9 Sidewinder
2 6x AIM–7 Sparrow
3 1x 1249l (330gal) fuel tank

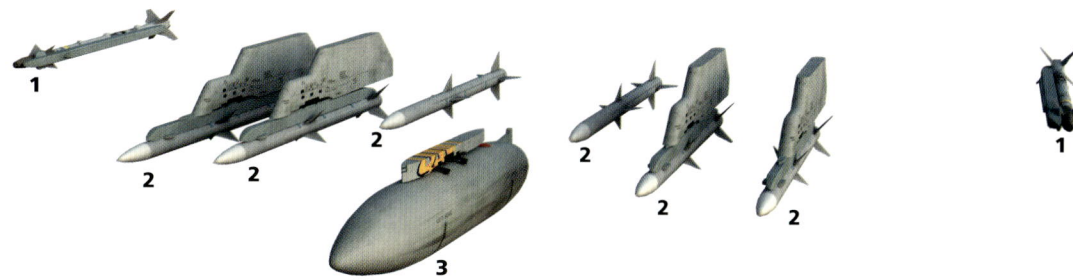

LOAD 2 — Anti-Ship Strike

1 2x AIM–9 Sidewinder
2 4x Harpoon
3 1x 1249l (330gal) fuel tank

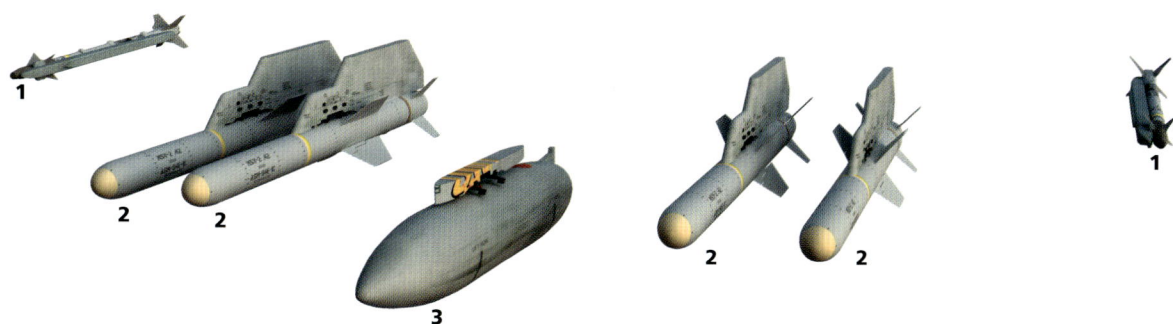

The Hornet is a fast, agile aircraft. It lacks range using its internal fuel only, so external fuel tanks are carried on most missions. The design of the Super Hornet somewhat corrected this deficiency, enhancing range by means of an increased fuel fraction (the proportion of takeoff weight contributed by onboard fuel as opposed to airframe, engines and systems) but external tanks are still necessary for longer missions.

Replacing the F-14 Tomcat with the Hornet as the U.S. Navy's carrier-based fighter raised a number of questions. The F-14 had a much greater range and could carry the long-range Phoenix missile, extending its engagement range still further. However, the Hornet's greater versatility outweighs this loss by allowing a carrier force to undertake a greater range of missions with the same number of aircraft.

The Hornet is also extremely robust and survivable. Aircraft have returned to base with significant damage, including one F/A-18 hit in both engines over Iraq, and yet have been quickly returned to service. In addition to the obvious benefits of power and acceleration, the possession of two engines provides superior get-home capability in the case of damage. This is considered essential in carrier-based aircraft, which are expected to

MODERN AIR-LAUNCHED WEAPONS

Above: A Hornet with a very large external fuel load launches from USS Dwight D. Eisenhower. *With no external weapons, this aircraft is clearly transferring to another base, rather than expecting combat.*

operate over water most of the time. The F/A-18's engines are reliable and far less prone to such problems as flameouts and compression stalls than those of the F-14.

Ease of maintenance is also crucial in naval aircraft. Carriers operate far from their bases and cannot carry unlimited supplies of spares and components. Nor can a carrier air group afford to have a high proportion of its planes down for maintenance or repair. Space and facilities are limited, so in this environment an aircraft that is easy to keep flying is a major asset.

And while it is not too challenging to start an air campaign with an air group that is in good shape to carry out high-tempo operations, keeping it in action throughout a long campaign is a difficult business. This is made somewhat easier by having aircraft that are simple and easy to maintain, and the Hornet has met with favourable comment in this regard.

In addition to its Vulcan 20mm cannon, the F/A-18 can carry 8500kg (17,750lb) of stores on six underwing pylons, a centreline pylon, two wingtip missile rails and two semi-recessed under-fuselage troughs. The latter can carry AIM-7 Sparrow or AIM-120 AMRAAM missiles, while the wingtip rails carry such smaller missiles as the AIM-9 Sidewinder or AIM-132 ASRAAM. This means that engagement is possible beyond visual range in addition to dogfighting.

As a carrier-based attack aircraft, the F/A-18 is expected to be able to strike at land or maritime targets. For the latter role it carries the AGM-84 Harpoon missile, and the Harpoon-based SLAM-ER (Standoff Land Attack Missile, Extended Range) can be used against distant targets, as can AGM-154 JSOW standoff weapons. Anti-radiation missiles are available for the SEAD mission.

For guided attacks at shorter ranges the Hornet can deploy AGM-65 Maverick missiles as well as a combination of AGM-65 Maverick missiles and laser- and GPS-guided bombs. A range of unguided weapons

F/A-18 HORNET & SUPER HORNET

LOAD 3 — Air Superiority

1 8x AIM–120 AMRAAM
2 2x 2309l (610gal) fuel tank
3 2x AIM–9 Sidewinder
4 1x 1816l (480gal) fuel tank

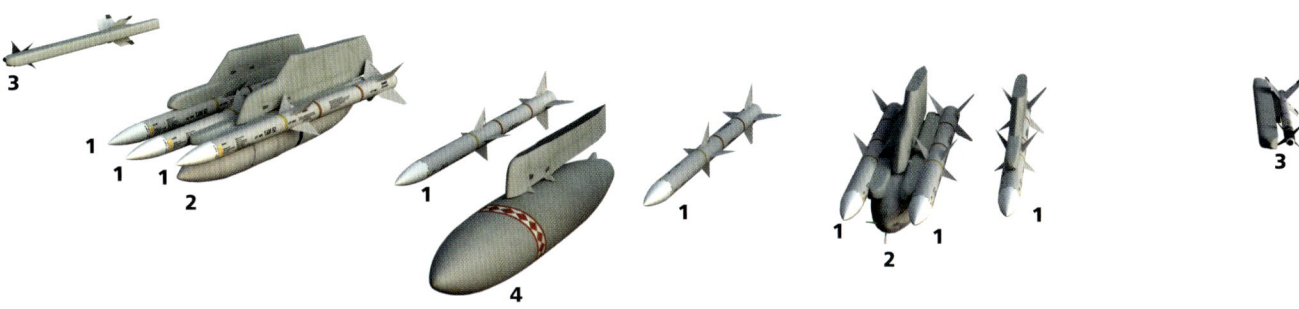

LOAD 4 — Standoff Land Attack

1 2x AIM–9 Sidewinder
2 4x AGM–154 JSOW
3 1x 1816l (480gal) fuel tank
4 1x AN/AAQ–14 LANTIRN targeting pod

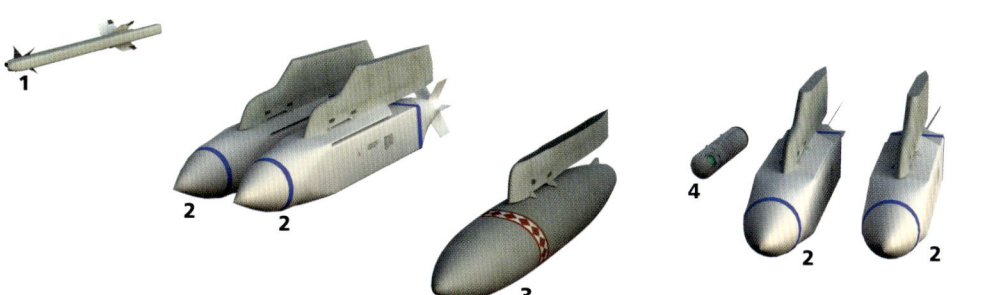

LOAD 5 — SEAD

1 2x AIM–9 Sidewinder
2 4x AGM–88 HARM
3 1x 1816l (480gal) fuel tank

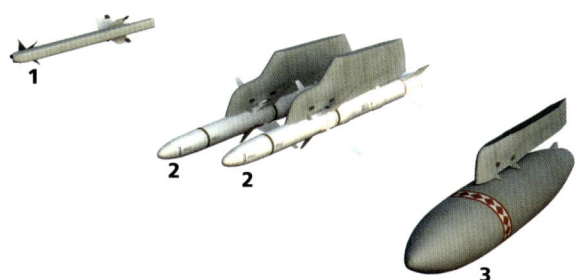
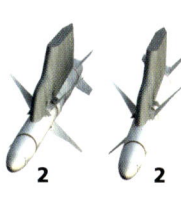

SEAD (Suppression of Enemy Air Defences)

SEAD (Suppression of Enemy Air Defences) is one of the most hazardous missions a combat aircraft can be tasked with. If it can be successfully achieved, a SEAD campaign reduces losses among friendly aircraft and makes otherwise suicidal missions possible. However, it does require sending out aircraft against weapons specifically designed to shoot them down, and deliberately going 'in harm's way' in order to make an attack.

The primary asset of air defence forces is radar. This can be mobile or fixed, and may be associated with a weapon system or deployed elsewhere. There are two ways to render enemy radar ineffective; either destroy it or force it to shut down by the threat of destruction. It does not greatly matter whether a given radar is out of commission or merely hiding; either way it is not gathering data for the air defence system, and is therefore of little use to the enemy. Obviously, destroying an enemy radar set is of more lasting benefit than merely forcing it to shut down, but to aircrew flying a strike mission both options are of immense value.

Radar systems can be located by detecting their emissions. A clever enemy commander may keep some of his radars off the air, hopefully allowing them to evade detection until a major strike force is in the area and thus increasing their effectiveness. However, at some point these radars will have to begin emitting. SEAD missions sometimes involve a certain amount of 'coat-trailing' as aircraft try to tempt enemy air defence radars to lock onto them. Of course, this is usually followed by the launch of anti-aircraft weapons, so these airborne matadors require good defensive ECM and decoy systems.

Once enemy radars have been detected, or if the weapons themselves can be located, they can be attacked. Anti-radiation missiles (ARMs) will home in on the emissions of a radar set. Early ARMs could be defeated by switching off the radar, but many modern systems are able to guide themselves to the target area and make an attack even if the radar ceases emitting.

Radar units are relatively 'soft' targets which can be successfully attacked with cluster bombs that will destroy equipment as well as killing personnel. Cluster munitions offer good area coverage and can be used against targets whose location is known only in general, or which are dispersed. Guided bombs are also highly effective; the effects of a large explosion on sensitive radar or missile technology can be considerable even if the target is not directly hit.

The AGM-88 Homing Anti-Radiation Missile (HARM) can locate and attack an enemy radar emitter from 50km (30 miles) away. Its supersonic speed gives the target little warning time to react to an attack.

F/A-18 HORNET & SUPER HORNET

LOAD 6
Ground Attack

1 2x AIM–9 Sidewinder
2 4x Mk84 JDAM
3 1x 1816l (480gal) fuel tank
4 1x AN/AAQ–14 LANTIRN targeting pod

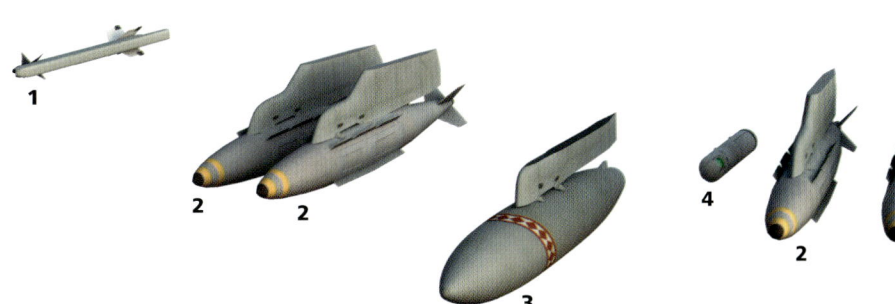

LOAD 7
Anti-Armour

1 2x AIM–9 Sidewinder
2 2x GBU–12
3 2x AGM–65 Maverick
4 2x 1816l (480gal) fuel tank
5 1x GBU–24

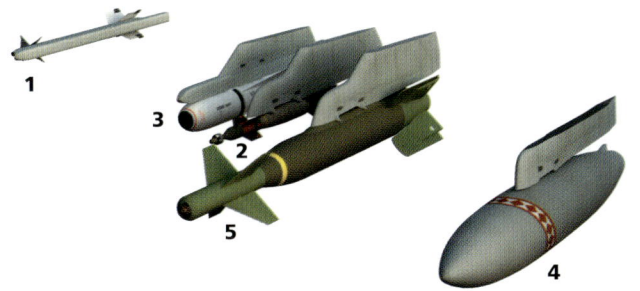
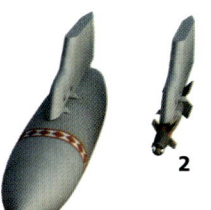

LOAD 8
Extended-Range Carrier-Based Land Attack

1 2x Harpoon SLAM–ER
2 3x 1816l (480gal) fuel tank

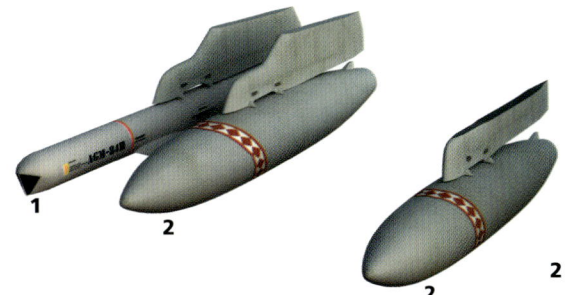
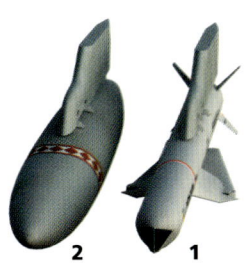

MODERN AIR-LAUNCHED WEAPONS

ranging from rockets to cluster bombs and air-scattered mines can be used along with unguided 'iron bombs'. Hornets can also carry the B61 nuclear bomb.

These weapons are augmented by a forward-looking infrared sensor that also houses a laser designator with which the F/A-18 can self-designate its own laser-guided weapons or 'buddy lase' for a companion aircraft. Other sensors include an advanced radar system that can simultaneously track air and ground targets, providing

Below: An F/A 18C Hornet armed with Paveway laser-guided bombs drops a thermal decoy flare. Such decoys offer an attractive target for the missile's seeker head to lock on to, instead of the aircraft.

targeting data on both to the advanced cockpit computer. The pilot's interface uses touch-sensitive controls and a helmet-mounted cueing system. This permits the pilot to lock a missile onto a target by simply looking at it as well as providing information without the pilot having to look down at the instruments and possibly losing visual contact with a target.

In addition to speed, agility and relatively small size, the Hornet is also protected by a countermeasures system that advises the pilot about threats and can conduct jamming operations as well as launching decoy flares and chaff to distract enemy missiles. Hornets engaged in reconnaissance missions can carry a multi-sensor pod capable of simultaneously monitoring the air and surface (sea or land) environments.

Carrier-based F/A-18s flew SEAD missions against Libyan targets in 1986 and later served in the 1991 Gulf War. There, Hornet pilots made history by being the first engage and destroy enemy fighters with air-to-air weapons and then go on to complete their original mission, which was a strike against ground targets at an Iraqi airfield. Subsequent service included operations over the Balkans and a return to Iraq.

The Hornet is theoretically a competitor to the F-16 Fighting Falcon for export sales, but for a variety of reasons it has never enjoyed

F/A-18 HORNET & SUPER HORNET

The F/A 18 suffers from a lack of range. This can be offset by the use of external fuel tanks, but only at the cost of reducing weapons payload. However, it is a very capable and versatile combat aircraft even with this limitation.

LOAD 9 — Precision Strike

1 2x AIM–9 Sidewinder
2 2x AGM–65 Maverick
3 2x GBU–24
4 1x 1816l (480gal) fuel tank
5 1x AN/AAQ–14 LANTIRN targeting pod

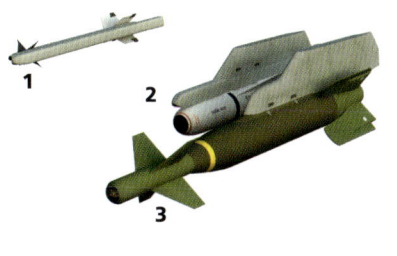   

the same success. Several nations have evaluated the Hornet and, despite viewing it favourably, have eventually selected a different machine – often the F-16. It is possible that the F/A-18's designation as a carrier-based aircraft counts against it when competing for selection by land-based air forces. Still, modest numbers have been purchased by air forces as diverse as those of Canada, Switzerland, Finland, Spain, Kuwait and Malaysia.

It is likely that the Hornet will be replaced in service by the F-35 Lighting at some point in the future, but as has been the case with several successful airframes in the past, it may continue to serve in deployment as a reconnaissance or electronic warfare platform long after it has been displaced from the fighter and attack roles.

Right: *The two-seat Super Hornet devotes more of its internal volume to fuel than the original, increasing range. A second crew member handles navigation and many attack tasks, easing the pilot's workload.*

59

MODERN AIR-LAUNCHED WEAPONS

F-22 Raptor

The F-22 Raptor entered service with the U.S. Air Force in 2005 after a protracted development period. Its first flight was in 1990, and in the intervening years a number of design changes had to be made. The end result was an enormously expensive single-seat fighter, but one with extremely high capabilities and incorporating a number of new technologies.

Side weapons bay
The F-22 can carry two small air-to-air missiles in side-mounted bays. At present only the AIM–9 Sidewinder can be carried in this position. A six-barrel 20mm Vulcan cannon is carried in a bay of its own. Normally the gun bay door is kept closed to reduce radar cross-section.

Main weapons bay
Weapons are carried in internal bays to reduce radar signature. When ordnance is launched the bay doors open for about a second, during which the weapon is ejected downwards. The amount of stores that can be carried this way is limited, however, resulting in a small warload when operating stealthily.

Wing pylons
Two pylons under each wing can carry fuel tanks or air-to-air missiles, albeit at the cost of reduced stealth. If fuel tanks are carried on the wings, additional missiles can be accommodated on the 'shoulders' of the tanks.

F-22 RAPTOR

LOAD 1
Air to Air (Stealthy)

1 2x AIM–9 Sidewinder
2 6x AIM–120 AMRAAM

LOAD 2
Ground Attack (Stealthy)

1 2x AIM–9 Sidewinder
2 2x AIM–120 AMRAAM
3 2x Mk83 JDAM

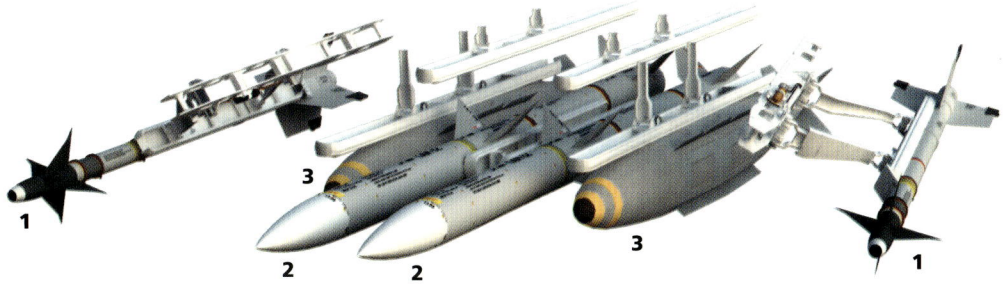

LOAD 3
Alternate Ground Attack (Stealthy)

1 2x AIM–9 Sidewinder
2 2x AIM–120 AMRAAM
3 8x GBU–39 Small Diameter Bomb

MODERN AIR-LAUNCHED WEAPONS

Above: The F-22 Raptor is less susceptible to bad weather than early stealth aircraft. A storm like this one would have damaged the stealth coatings of a B-2 bomber.

The Raptor was first developed in response to the U.S. Advanced Tactical Fighter Programme, which was established to find a replacement for the F-15. The latter was initially developed as a pure air-to-air combat machine, with the designers pursuing the ideal of 'not a pound for air-to-ground', but developed into a multi-role strike platform. The Raptor, too, had to show it could perform more than one role to avoid cancellation. For this reason the project was redesignated F/A-22 for a time before reverting to a pure fighter designation.

During the development process, doubts were voiced about the need for this aircraft. No opponent existed or, at that time, was even nearing entry into service that could justify the cost of a fleet of Raptors. It was suggested that Raptor money would be better spent on the F-35, which could handle more tasks less expensively. However, the desire to retain cutting-edge air-superiority capability won out and the Raptor was finally ordered, though in smaller numbers than planned.

One reason for the Raptor's great expense and long development time was the incorporation of several new technologies. These give the Raptor significant advantages in terms of agility, speed and the ability to avoid detection. While not a pure 'stealth' aircraft designed solely around this concept, the Raptor makes use of low-observable technologies for both attack and defence.

Offensively, the F-22's small radar signature can enable it to close with an opponent and launch a surprise attack, or to slip through enemy air defences to strike a ground or air target. Defensively, low thermal and radar signature makes the task of enemy missiles more difficult and improves

F-22 RAPTOR

Low-Observable (Stealth) Technology

There are essentially four ways to cope with a high-threat environment where the enemy has plentiful and powerful radar equipment. Three rely on what amounts to brute force one way or another: enemy radars and the weapons they guide can be attacked and destroyed; or the aircraft can try to fly too high and fast to be engaged; or a combination of ECM and decoys can be used to defend the aircraft.

The fourth method is more subtle. If an aircraft is not detected then it cannot be attacked. Tactics such as staying low and using 'ground clutter' to confuse enemy radars, or simply staying as far away as possible from enemy radar, can be reasonably effective, but modern technology offers other alternatives.

Low-observable (commonly referred to as 'stealth') technology refers to a range of measures designed to make an aircraft harder to detect. Concepts as simple as camouflage have been in use for decades, and can be effective against visual detection, but against technical systems such as radar, a more sophisticated approach is needed.

Radar detection works by reflecting energy from the target. Sharp corners and perpendicular surfaces reflect radar best, so by building aircraft that scatter radar energy rather than reflecting it straight back, the radar 'cross-section' can be reduced. This cannot make a plane invisible to radar but it does reduce the range at which a given radar set can detect the aircraft. Radar cross-section can be further decreased by using materials that absorb energy rather than reflecting it, and by ensuring that such weapons as bombs and missiles are carried internally rather than on pylons where their sharp edges will reflect radar energy.

Thermal signature must also be reduced as much as possible, to avoid detection by infra-red systems. The siting of engines such that their hot surfaces and exhaust gases are screened by parts of the airframe helps reduce this signature, though it is not possible to entirely eliminate it.

The F-15 Eagle (banking) was designed to outfly any other fighter, but can now be outmanoeuvred by the Raptor, even if the F-22 is not able to sneak up undetected and attack it.

MODERN AIR-LAUNCHED WEAPONS

This side view of the F-22 shows the main and one of the secondary weapons bays open. The latter reveals an AIM–9 Sidewinder missile. If possible, external stores are expended first, enabling the Raptor to become more stealthy.

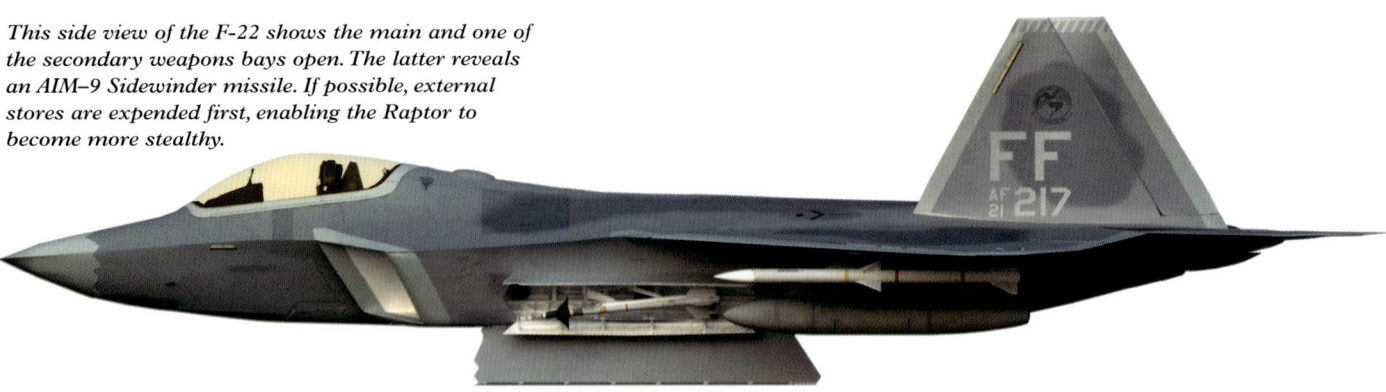

LOAD

4 Air to Air (Non-Stealthy)

1 2x AIM–9 Sidewinder
2 10x AIM–120 AMRAAM
3 2x 2271l (600gal) fuel tank

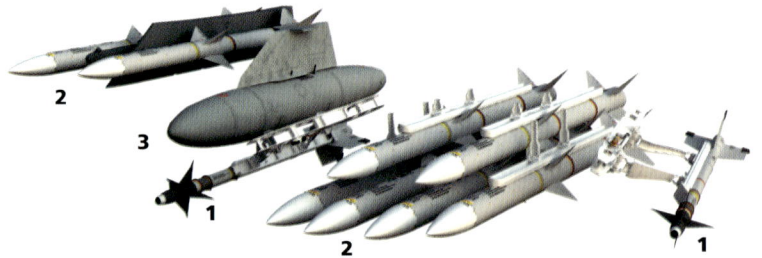
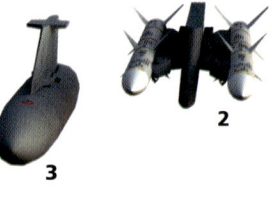

the Raptor's chances of breaking off combat and escaping.

The shape of the Raptor is a key component of its low signature. Blended and non-perpendicular surfaces eliminate the sharp corners that increase radar return, while weapons are carried in an internal bay wherever it is possible. Additional ordnance can be carried externally, but this reduces the Raptor's level of stealth. Heat signature is reduced by hiding the hot exhaust with the tail

Left: This head-on view of an F-22 on the ground shows its lack of perpendicular surfaces. As well, the wings blend into the fuselage and the fins are angled. Such construction helps reduce radar return.

F-22 RAPTOR

Above: The Raptor was conceived as a pure air-to-air fighter but had to justify its enormous cost with additional capabilities. A range of air-to-ground weapons can be launched from the wing pylons or, as here, from the internal weapons bay.

section, and by using advanced engines that produce enormous thrust even without using afterburners.

The Raptor's engines enable it to 'supercruise', i.e. to travel faster than sound without afterburning. This reduces fuel use as well as thermal signature. Although the F-22 has a slightly lower power-to-weight ratio than the F-15 (roughly 1.1:1 rather than 1.2:1), its rate of climb is higher. The Raptor can also make use of vectored thrust, creating a tighter turning circle and increasing agility.

The F-22 mounts an M61A2 20mm Vulcan cannon, with 480 rounds normally carried. The main internal weapons bay can hold two AIM–120 AMRAAM missiles plus either two 450kg (1000lb) GPS guided bombs or eight 115kg (250lb) small-diameter bombs. The bay can alternatively hold six AMRAAM, while each of the smaller side bays can hold an AIM–9 Sidewinder or similar small air-to-air missile. Weapons are ejected vertically from the bays by a pneumatic ordnance management system. Opening a weapon bay increases radar signature, but launch can be completed and the bay doors closed again in under a second.

At the price of a higher radar signature, the Raptor is capable of carrying additional stores on its four wing hardpoints. Each wing position is rated for 2,270kg (5000lb) of stores, which can include fuel tanks (on the inner pylon) or additional air-to-air missiles. Pylons can be jettisoned after ordnance is expended, reducing radar signature.

Although the Raptor uses a fairly traditional hands-on-throttle-and-stick (HOTAS) control system, its instrumentation and electronics are extremely sophisticated. There are no traditional dials or indicators; the entire cockpit display is electronic.

MODERN AIR-LAUNCHED WEAPONS

LOAD 5
Long Range Air to Air (Non-Stealthy)

1 8x AIM–120 AMRAAM
2 4x 2271l (600gal) fuel tank

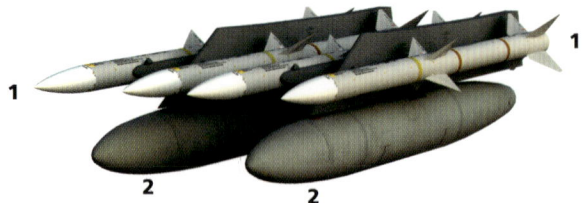

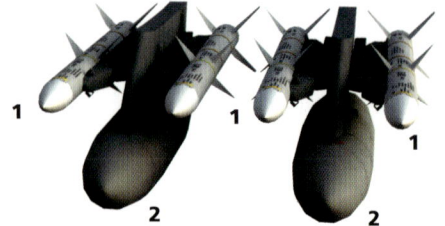

The communications and sensor fit is also extremely sophisticated. The Raptor's radar uses low-probability-of-intercept (LPI) technology to reduce the chance that hostile forces will pick up its emissions. Raptors can share information gathered by their radar with one another, and designate targets for other aircraft such as F-15s and F-16s, essentially functioning as an Airborne Early Warning aircraft.

Having entered service recently, the F-22 has not yet faced a credible challenge in air-to-air combat. Nor has it seen service in the attack role. There are several aircraft in the U.S. inventory that can perform ground-attack missions more effectively and at lower cost; it would not be possible to justify deploying F-22s for strike missions just to allow them to win their spurs in combat.

However, performance in exercises has been very promising. Among the advantages enjoyed by the F-22 is the ability to cruise at high altitude, increasing radar range and granting an advantage at the start of a combat. A small force of Raptors was thus able to annihilate a much greater number of F-15s and F-16s during exercises held in 2006. While this is not conclusive – only actual combat is a true test of a warplane's abilities – it seems that the Raptor is indeed vastly superior to the previous generation of fighters.

The Raptor is sufficiently advanced that export outside the USA is banned. An export variant, with some of the most sensitive technologies downgraded, may become available at some point but many potential customers are more interested in the F-35 as this is seen as better value for money. Another possible future variant is a fighter-bomber version with larger wings, capable of carrying a larger payload, or a naval version. Both have been proposed and rejected, but future need may result in a resurrection of these concepts, or a wholly new application of the Raptor's formidable capabilities.

Future in Peril

The Raptor is in the early stages of its career, but its future is already in jeopardy. A planned large purchase was reduced, and there is doubt as to whether a mid-life upgrade programme will justify the expense. The main problem is that the F-22 lacks a suitable opponent. The current combat environment calls for cost-effectiveness and flexibility, while the Raptor is a specialized aircraft with massive capabilities but a high price.

If and when a suitably high-performance fighter begins to appear in foreign hands, it is likely that the Raptor will become once again a highly desirable part of the U.S. arsenal. 'Air sovereignty' is extremely precious; indeed, the ability to remove enemy high-end fighters from the equation is one of the factors that allows other aircraft to carry out their missions. The Raptor cannot rival the Strike Eagle or the Thunderbolt in their intended role, but it may turn out to be indispensable to their missions all the same.

Right: An F-22 banks over California with its side weapons bays open. Each bay can carry a single AIM–9 Sidewinder missile for air-to-air combat.

MODERN AIR-LAUNCHED WEAPONS

B-52 Stratofortress

The B-52 has already completed more than half a century in service. Originally conceived as a long-range deep-penetration nuclear bomber, it has matured into a highly capable conventional strike platform. It has the capacity to deliver a range of conventional munitions including bombs, cluster munitions, mines and missiles.

Targeting pods
The B-52 carries two steerable turrets under its nose for an electro-optical system. This incorporates Forward-Looking Infrared (FLIR) in the starboard turret and a low-light television camera in the port turret.

Wing pylons
Although early B-52 models carried only internal stores, the current B-52H can also deploy weapons from its wing pylons. Such weapons were originally intended to have been nuclear cruise missiles, but a range of conventional weapons can now be carried. The internal bay can carry bombs or missiles.

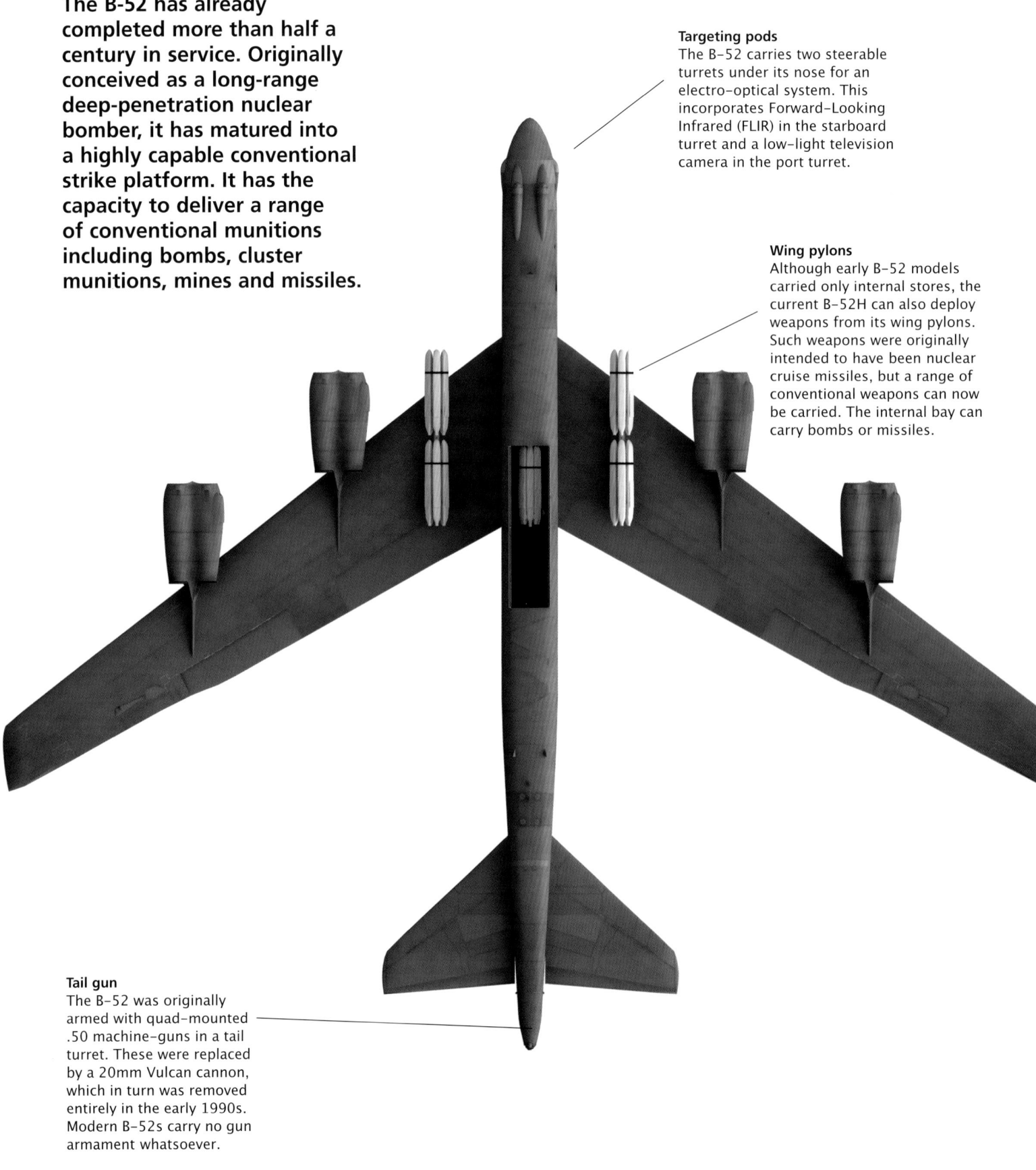

Tail gun
The B-52 was originally armed with quad-mounted .50 machine-guns in a tail turret. These were replaced by a 20mm Vulcan cannon, which in turn was removed entirely in the early 1990s. Modern B-52s carry no gun armament whatsoever.

B-52 STRATOFORTRESS

LOAD 1 Cruise-Missile Strike

1 12x AGM–86C on wing pylons
2 8x AGM–86C in rotary bomb bay

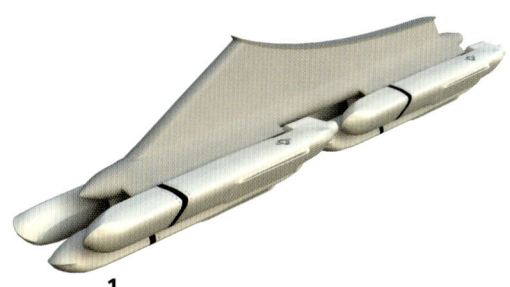

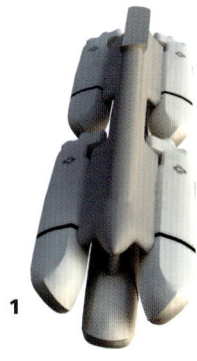

The idea of an intercontinental bomber was conceived during World War II, when it was feared that bases in Britain would be overrun. Seeking a means to carry on the war across the width of the Atlantic Ocean, defence planners in the U.S. came up with the idea of producing a bomber with a range of almost 13,000km (8000 miles). However, by the time it was delivered not only was the likely threat now the Soviet Union, and no longer Nazi Germany, but the environment in which the intercontinental bomber must operate had also changed significantly.

Below: The idea of a strategic bomber flying close-support missions might once have seemed risible, but this B-52's arsenal of guided weapons enables it to engage targets in close proximity to friendly troops.

MODERN AIR-LAUNCHED WEAPONS

Above: A B-52 fires a JDAM GPS-guided bomb as part of a weapons evaluation mission. A wide range of weapons has been integrated with the Stratofortress, some requiring hardware or software upgrades.

The mainstay of U.S. long-range bombing capability in the late 1940s and early 1950s was the B-50, which was an aircraft that had been derived from the B-29 Superfortress. The original design of its replacement, which became the B-52 Stratofortress, was clearly derivative, with straight wings and turboprop propulsion. Jet bombers were then coming into service, but the fuel economy benefits of turboprops made them a natural choice for aircraft with a long range.

The development of improved jet engines, and new airborne refuelling technology, allowed a redesign that incorporated pairs of turbojet engines in pods suspended from the wings, and an altered wing design. Swept rather than straight wings offered a good lift-to-drag ratio, and their thickness allowed fuel tanks to be installed in later models. Other deviations from the original design included side-by-side flight-crew seating in the manner of an airliner, whereas the original design called for tandem seating.

It was in this form that the prototype A model first flew in 1952. The B-52A was built in very small numbers and never saw service, instead being used for development. An almost identical B model entered service in 1955, replacing the B-50 with operational squadrons. Further models quickly followed, usually incorporating new advances in electronics or flight systems, though the B-52B remained in service alongside them. The B-52C carried additional fuel in wing tanks as well as upgraded avionics and improved bombing and navigation systems, but was supplanted by the D model after only 35 aircraft had been built.

The B-52D, which formed the backbone of U.S. heavy bomber capability during the Vietnam War, was little different to the B-52C but for slight modifications to improve the strength of the airframe. A 'Big Belly'

B-52 STRATOFORTRESS

LOAD 2 Carpet Bombing

1 18x Mk84 unguided bomb

modification was made to some D models to allow more ordnance to be carried. Advances in anti-aircraft technology then forced a move away from high-level penetration. The B-52E was given enhanced flight electronics, allowing low-altitude flight and bombing, and was followed by the F model with improved engines.

The B-52F was the last of the 'first generation' B-52s. The G model, which first flew in 1958, was in many ways a new aircraft that used the same airframe and general design but incorporated a number of advanced features. Most notably, the B-52G was designed to launch missiles as well as drop bombs and used a 'wet wing' fuel structure to carry more fuel than previous versions.

Redesigned and Improved

A number of other modifications were made, including new and improved flight and fuel management controls, as well as improvements designed to reduce crew fatigue. The tail-gun arrangement was redesigned, moving the gunner from the turret itself to a remote-control station in the main crew area. The H model followed on with these changes, adding better engines and electronics plus a 20mm Vulcan cannon in the tail turret rather than the quad machine-guns previously mounted.

The B-52H is the only model still in service, and has been gradually updated over the years with improved sensors and the ability to deploy a wide range of conventional weapons. These include freefall 'dumb' bombs and dispensed munitions (cluster bombs and mines) as well as GPS-guided bombs, AGM-84 Harpoon anti-shipping missiles and standoff weapons including cruise missiles.

B-52s equipped with nuclear weapons served in the deterrent role for several decades, including airborne deterrent flights, until 1968. In this role, fully armed nuclear bombers remained aloft in loitering areas for up to 26 hours at a time. This ensured that at least part of the bomber force would survive a first strike to retaliate. Airborne alert flights ceased in 1968, by which time the B-52 had demonstrated its capability as a conventional bomber.

Right: The tail turret assembly is clearly visible on this B-52. The B-52 is the largest aircraft ever to score an air-to-air kill, but today the Stratofortress relies on electronic defences rather than guns.

MODERN AIR-LAUNCHED WEAPONS

B-52 STRATOFORTRESS

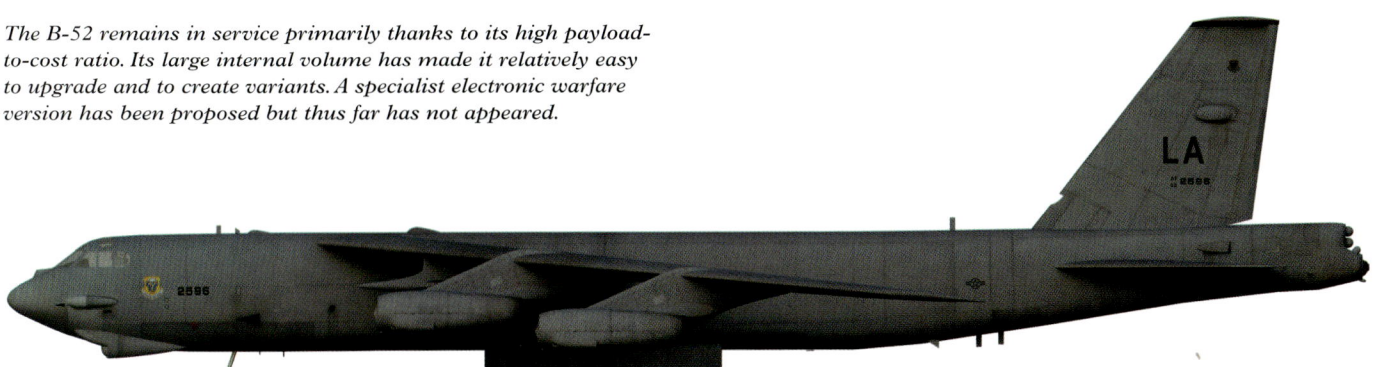

The B-52 remains in service primarily thanks to its high payload-to-cost ratio. Its large internal volume has made it relatively easy to upgrade and to create variants. A specialist electronic warfare version has been proposed but thus far has not appeared.

LOAD 3

Close Air Support

1 92x GBU–39 Small Diameter Bomb

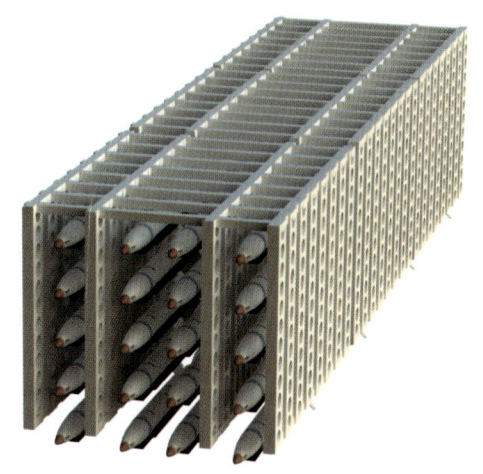

From 1965–73, B-52s flew more than 125,000 sorties against targets in North and South Vietnam. The usual tactic was carpet bombing by six aircraft in two groups of three all releasing their bombs simultaneously. While not precise, such attacks were effective against dispersed personnel or base areas and, according to survivors, severely affected enemy morale in the areas under attack.

During the 1991 Gulf War B-52s exploited their great range and large payload, flying from bases in the UK,

Left: The B-52 can deliver such naval weapons as this Mk56 mine. Its immense operating radius makes it possible to lay mines at strategic 'choke points' or outside harbours almost anywhere in the world.

Spain, Saudi Arabia and the Indian Ocean. After an initial round of cruise missile strikes against Iraqi command and control centres, the bombers engaged a range of targets. These included SCUD missile launching sites as well as enemy combat formations. To create gaps in Iraqi minefields, carpet-bombing techniques were used. The resumption of attacks against Iraqi targets in 1996 saw the combat debut of the B-52H, launching standoff attacks against Iraqi air defence sites.

A similar pattern of operations was used in the Balkans, with missile attacks at the start of the campaign giving way to bombing missions against hostile ground forces, and again in Afghanistan against Taliban targets. There, GPS-guided weapons were used to give close support to friendly ground troops in addition to more conventional bomber missions.

In 2003, the B-52 returned to the skies over Iraq, using a combination of unguided bombs and GPS-guided JDAM weapons. The Stratofortress achieved another first during this period, launching laser-guided weapons for the first time. Propaganda leaflets were also dropped – a rather older bomber mission but one that remains a useful part of the package when fighting wars.

The B-52 has been tagged for replacement more than once. The B-70 project and later the B-1B derived

MODERN AIR-LAUNCHED WEAPONS

Making Dumb Bombs Smart

This 910kg (2000lb) bomb is little different from the iron bombs of previous generations apart from the addition of a JDAM tailkit. This transforms it into a precision weapon and enormously increases its accuracy.

It is possible to increase the likelihood of a hit with conventional 'dumb' gravity bombs by dropping a great many of them, or by delivering them from a low altitude. Both measures have their drawbacks, and do not entirely eliminate the inherent inaccuracy of an unguided weapon dropped from a height.

The Joint Direct Attack Munition (JDAM) unit makes use of the existing Global Positioning System (GPS) system to provide guidance. It takes the form of a kit that can be attached to the tail of a conventional bomb, converting an existing weapon into one that is much more precise.

Although less accurate than a laser-guided weapon, GPS-guided bombs are reliably capable of striking within 10–11m (33–36ft) of the target point, which is sufficient for most uses. They also have the advantage of a fairly passive guidance system. The GPS satellites are always broadcasting, so there is nothing to indicate that an attack is imminent. Nor is it necessary for an aircraft to remain in the target vicinity to designate the target; GPS-guided weapons can be dropped and then forgotten about.

The JDAM unit was originally used with Mk83 450kg (1000lb) and Mk84 910kg (2000lb) bombs, though it has also been applied to other weapons such as the BLU-109 penetrator warhead and Mk80 115kg (250lb) bombs. Smaller bombs such as the Mk80 were for some time considered too light to be effective under most circumstances, but improvements in accuracy thanks to GPS guidance have greatly improved their effectiveness, allowing an aircraft to carry more individual bombs for the same weight and thus increasing mission flexibility.

Continued upgrades to the JDAM system may in future include a terminal guidance unit that improves accuracy to within 3m (10ft), the same degree of precision possible with laser guidance. This would potentially replace laser designation as the precision strike method of choice.

B-52 STRATOFORTRESS

Above: A B-52 makes its final landing approach. The enormous range of this aircraft enables it to strike distant targets from bases located within the USA.

from it were both intended to supplant the ageing B-52 fleet. However, the relatively low cost of operating the Stratofortress and its utility in a wide variety of roles make it difficult to find a more cost-effective alternative.

The size of the aircraft makes modification possible without undue loss of capability and continuing upgrades add new capabilities, enabling B-52s to carry out missions that the original designers cannot possibly have imagined. The addition of a LITENING targeting pod to the B-52H fleet added the capacity for laser guidance and high-resolution infrared imaging. This not only made it possible to deploy additional weapon systems, but also allowed B-52s to gather reconnaissance data and transmit it to other friendly forces in the area.

The same capacity for modification and upgrade makes the B-52 a useful testbed for such research projects as the implementation of synthetic aviation fuel. The first flight of a U.S. military jet using a 50/50 combination of synthetic and more traditional fuel was conducted aboard a B-52. A later flight marked the first time a military aircraft had been entirely fuelled by such a blend. It is this capacity to receive upgrades, along with the ability to deliver large and varied payloads over long distances, at a relatively low cost per flight hour in terms of both maintenance time and actual dollars, that keeps the B-52 flying. It is currently envisaged that the B-52 fleet will remain in service until 2040.

MODERN AIR-LAUNCHED WEAPONS

F-111

First flying in 1964, the F-111 Aardvark was for many years the main interdiction and strike platform for the U.S. Air Force. Despite its 'F' designation, the F-111 was deployed as a bomber, and never undertook air-to-air combat missions. The last F-111s in service, with the Royal Australian Air Force, retired in 2010, making the F-111 one of the longest-serving combat aircraft ever.

Precision weapons
The F-111 has achieved considerable combat success in the precision strike role using laser-guided bombs. Targets as diverse as command bunkers, bridges and individual tanks have been successfully attacked by F-111s using the PAVEWAY family of laser-guided bombs.

Weapons bay
The internal weapons bay can carry a range of ordnance, including nuclear weapons on some models. A 20mm cannon was originally carried internally as well, but was eventually deleted as unnecessary.

Pivoting pylons
Variable-geometry wings can be positioned forward at low speeds, and swept back to reduce drag. The four wing pylons can pivot to keep the weapons correctly oriented.

F-111

LOAD 1 'Tank Plinking'

1 4xGBU–12

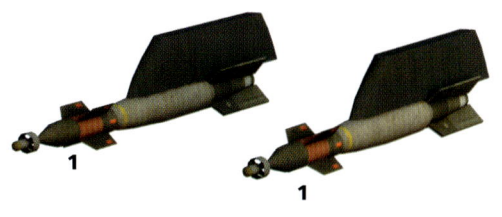

LOAD 2 Air to Air

1 4x AIM–9 Sidewinder
2 2x AIM–120 AMRAAM

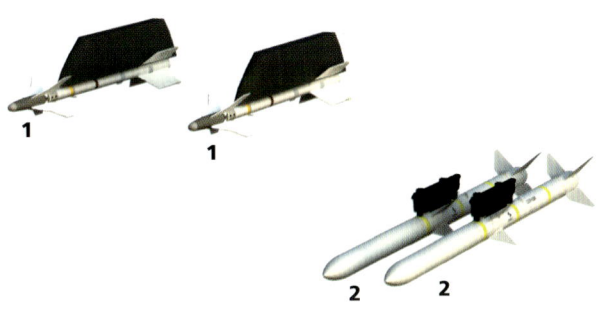

The definitive Aardvark is the F-111F, which served in the Gulf War. This model, like all others, did not mount a gun as standard but could carry an M61 20mm Vulcan cannon. This capability was rarely used, however. In addition to the internal bay the Aardvark could carry a range of weaponry on eight underwing pylons. Most commonly, this would be 500 450 and 910kg (1000 and 2000lb) laser-guided or 'dumb' bombs but cluster munitions and runway-denial weapons could also be carried.

The F-111 could also fly with AIM–9 Sidewinder missiles aboard for air-to-air self-defence but, despite the designer's original intentions, it was never agile enough to even pretend to be an air-superiority fighter. Speed and low altitude were more important to aircraft survivability than the possibility of defeating an interceptor in a missile fight.

The F-111, with its curious 'fighter' designation, arose from a design concept that called for a single aircraft to meet the needs of the Navy for fleet defence and the air force for a multi-role fighter-bomber. At the time, the development of effective guided missiles had opened up new opportunities for airspace defence. Instead of specialist fighters capable of high speed and possessing great agility, an airborne missile platform equipped with long-range radar could perhaps undertake this role.

This line of thinking led to the Douglas Missileer, a project that was eventually scrapped but which led, indirectly, to the F-14 Tomcat. The

77

MODERN AIR-LAUNCHED WEAPONS

'Tank Plinking'

There is nothing new about the concept of aircraft attacking hostile armoured vehicles. Guns, bombs and rockets were used in World War II, with large guns fitted to often entirely inappropriate aircraft in an effort to thin out enemy armoured forces. However, with the advent of guided weapons the anti-tank mission has taken on an entirely new dimension.

The term 'tank plinking' was unofficially applied during the 1991 Gulf War and afterward to the practice of making attacks on armoured vehicles with powerful guided weapons. A laser-guided bomb will change course to pursue a fleeing or evading tank so long as the designator is kept focussed on the vehicle, making attacks on mobile forces far easier. However, not all 'tank plinking' missions were against forces on the move.

Reconnaissance using thermal imaging equipment allows armoured vehicles to be spotted even at night, especially if they have been running recently and are therefore still significantly warmer than their surroundings. A bomb can be delivered by an aircraft flying high enough and sufficiently distant that it may not be heard by forces on the ground, and even if it is, there is nothing to indicate a specific threat.

Thus the phenomenon of tanks that mysteriously exploded during the night was terrifying and demoralizing to Iraqi armoured vehicle crews during the Gulf War. They quickly learnt that sleeping inside the tank for warmth was unsafe, and that it was better to be some distance from the nearest vehicle, just in case.

Various aircraft carried out 'tank plinking' missions during the Gulf War, inflicting losses on the enemy and seriously affecting morale among vehicle crews. The foremost tank-plinkers were found to be F-111s armed with laser-guided bombs. With air defences largely suppressed, an exchange rate of one tank to one bomb, with little risk to the air forces involved, represented a good return in investment.

With air defences almost entirely suppressed, there was little the Iraqis could do to prevent the F-111s from roaming the skies in search of armoured vehicles to destroy. No tank could survive even a near miss from a large warhead.

F-111

Above: An F-111 closes with a tanker for refuelling over the North Sea. Note the asymmetric loadout – as long as weight is reasonably balanced there is no need to carry exactly the same stores on each wing.

naval version of the Aardvark, designated F-111B, also fell by the wayside because of technical problems, but this intention – to use the aircraft in what had traditionally been a fighter role – was one factor in its designation as a fighter rather than a strike aircraft or bomber.

The F-111 incorporated a number of what were, at the time, new concepts. The most obvious was the use of variable-geometry or 'swing' wings, which could change position at need. When positioned well forward, they generated additional lift for takeoff, landing and low-speed operations, but could be swept back to reduce drag when operating at high speeds. Despite the aircraft's considerable weight, its afterburning engines could drive it at speeds of 2225km/h (1450mph) but at the cost of high fuel consumption.

SEAD Missions

Terrain-following radar was also incorporated to allow high-speed low-level penetration of enemy airspace. This feature enabled the F-111 to fly SEAD missions ahead of B-52 strikes over Vietnam. An F-111 would go ahead of the strike, flying very low to avoid detection by enemy radar, then climb to gain enough height to be able to bomb enemy radar or air defence installations before dropping back down below the minimum height for radar detection.

Another new feature of the F-111 was its crew escape system. Rather than individual ejector seats, the pilot and weapons officer, who sat side by side, were ejected from the aircraft in a capsule that incorporated floatation units in case of a water landing. The concept of an escape capsule has been experimented with on other aircraft, but has never really caught on.

Entering front-line service in 1968, the F-111 was certainly an advanced aircraft but suffered from a number of defects with the engines and wing

MODERN AIR-LAUNCHED WEAPONS

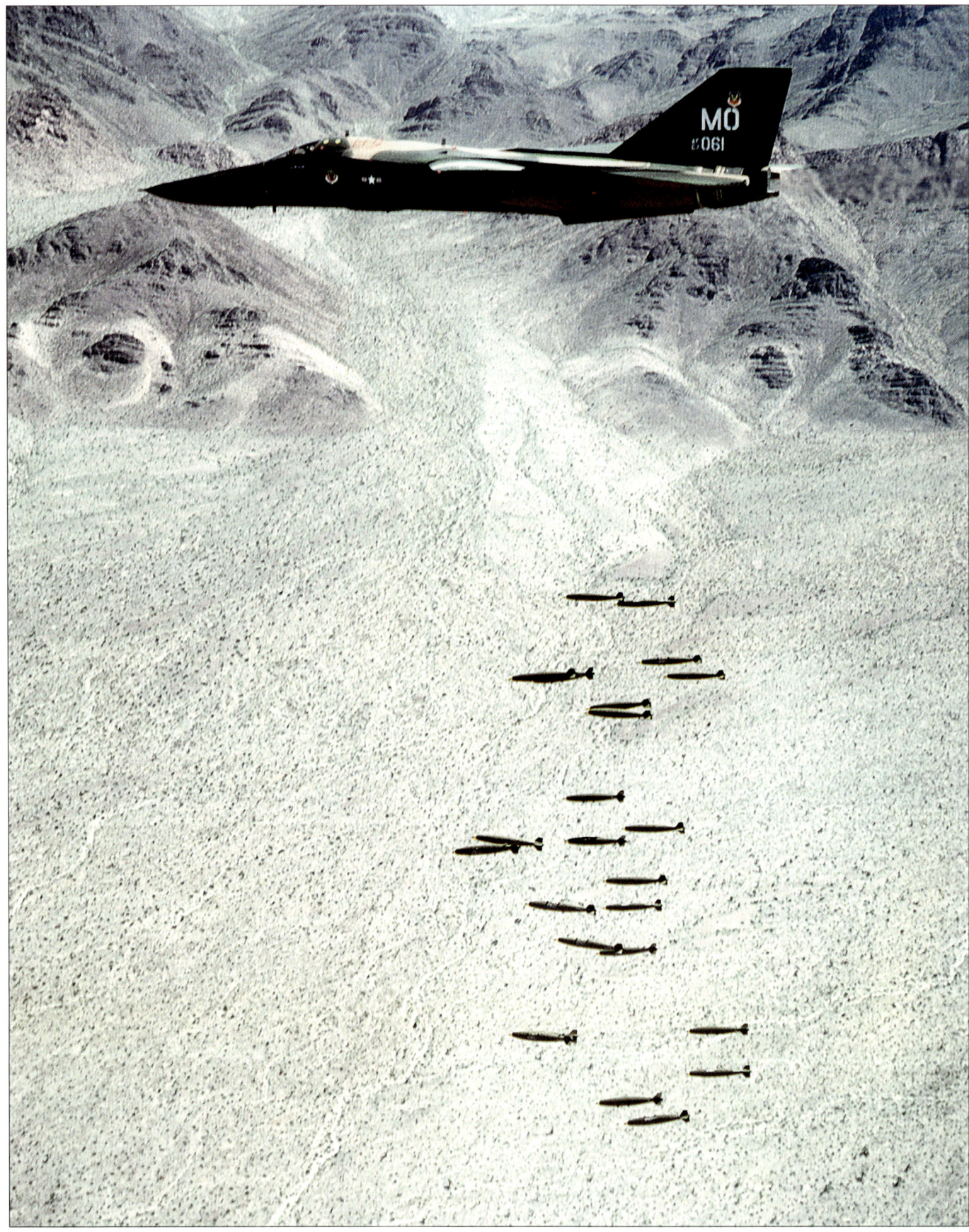

F-111

The integration of laser-guided munitions aboard the F-111 allowed the aircraft to truly realize its potential towards the end of its long career. F-111s employed guided bombs against Libya in 1986 and during the Gulf War in 1991.

LOAD 3 — Precision Strike

1 2x AIM–9P Sidewinder
2 4x GBU–15

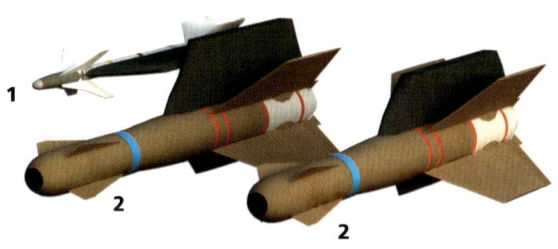
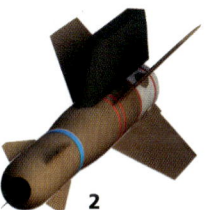
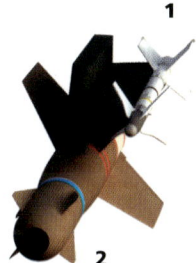

machinery. These defects led to three aircraft being lost during the first month of combat testing, none of them to enemy action. It was another three years before the Aardvark was ready to begin combat operations.

Once these early problems were ironed out, the F-111 proved itself a highly effective strike platform, capable of carrying 1814kg (4000lb) of ordnance internally and 14,290kg (31,500lb) on its four wing pylons. Its

Left: An F-111 dropping Mk 82 low-drag bombs on a test range in the United States. The Aardvark's low-level penetrator role is obvious from its camouflage pattern.

operational radius was also greater than the F-4 Phantom, which provided much of the U.S. strike capability.

Receptive to Modifications

The F-111 was gradually updated during its long service life. It is generally easier to upgrade a larger aircraft than a small one without degrading capabilities or reducing range by taking up fuel space with additional systems, and the F-111 proved receptive to modification. Among the distinct models were the cancelled F-111B naval fighter, and the F-111C, which was constructed for export to Australia.

A series of upgraded models, not all of them successful, led to the F-111F, which carried a laser designator and forward-looking infrared sensors for the precision-strike role. In 1986, F-111Fs based in England carried out a strike against targets in Libya, as part of a dispute over the Gulf of Sidra off the Libyan coast and in retaliation for Libyan support for anti-U.S. terrorism. Refused overflight permission by European nations, the strike force was forced to make a 2100km (1300-mile) detour each way, necessitating tanker support for much of the mission. The strikes were launched against airfields

MODERN AIR-LAUNCHED WEAPONS

and military barracks, along with national air defences, using carrier-based aircraft as well as the F-111 force. The latter dropped a mix of laser-guided and so-called dumb bombs. Most of the gravity bombs hit their targets; virtually all the laser-guided weapons were successful. One F-111 was lost.

During the 1991 Gulf War F-111s were found to be ideal platforms for 'tank plinking' missions using laser-guided bombs. Aardvarks also carried out a range of strike missions against rear-area targets. Suppression of enemy air defences was highly successful, and the Iraqi air force was more or less driven from the skies, so the F-111s were able to operate with relative impunity.

An enlarged version of the F-111, designated FB-111, was developed for use by U.S. Strategic Air Command. This was a true bomber, rather than a strike aircraft, and was equipped to carry nuclear bombs and the AGM–69 SRAM, allowing a measure of standoff capability. The FB-111 was capable of carrying two missiles internally and two under each wing.

Electronic Warfare Platform

The final incarnation of the F-111 family, designated EF-111A Raven, was an electronic warfare platform introduced in the 1970s. The last of these aircraft was retired in 1998. The strike and bomber versions have also ended their service lives; the FB-111 was replaced in the bomber role by the B-1B Lancer, while the F-15 Strike Eagle took over the medium-range strike niche from the F-111. The

Below: A fully loaded F-111 banks over England. Had the Cold War gone 'hot', the Aardvark would have undertaken low-level penetration and strikes against advancing Soviet forces and their logistics chain.

F-111

LOAD 4 — Anti-Shipping Strike

1 4x AGM–84 Harpoon

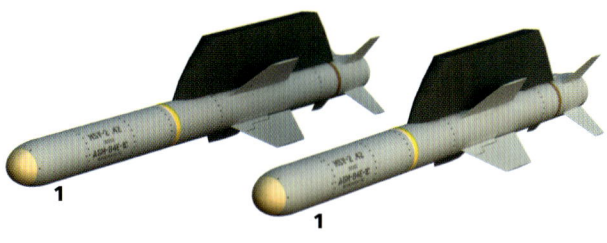

LOAD 5 — SEAD

1 2x AIM–9 Sidewinder
2 4x AGM–88 HARM

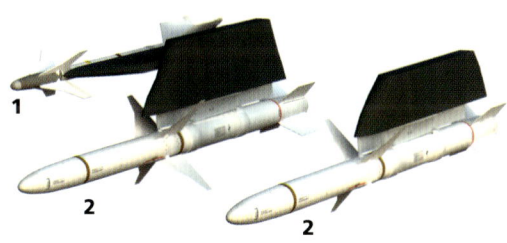
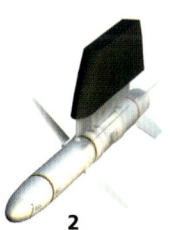
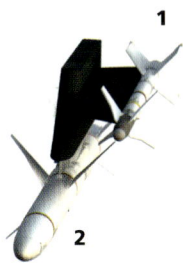

F/A-18 Hornet was chosen to replace Australia's F-111Cs. Thus the venerable F-111 has come to the end of its long life. However, its influence was considerable. A rash of 'swing-wing' designs followed its lead, and terrain-following radar has become standard on strike aircraft and even on some missiles.

Right: An F-111 undergoes munitions loading as part of Operation Desert Shield in 1991. The Gulf War, last operational deployment for the Aardvark, was a very different conflict to its Vietnamese debut.

MODERN AIR-LAUNCHED WEAPONS

B-1B Lancer

The B-1B is an advanced strategic bomber that was originally conceived to replace the B-52 fleet in U.S. inventory. After a long and difficult development history it emerged as a rather different aircraft than was first planned. Although intended for the strategic nuclear-strike role, the B-1B has found a niche as a high-performance conventional bomber, often undertaking strike missions that would normally be associated with a smaller aircraft. It is the last variable-geometry ('swing-wing') aircraft in U.S. service.

Targeting pods
The addition of a targeting pod carried under the B-1B's nose enables it to undertake precision-strike missions. GPS-guided weapons can also be launched. Although originally conceived as a strategic bomber, the B-1B has thus evolved into a multi-mission platform capable of precision-strike and even close-support missions.

Internal weapons bay
The three weapons bays can carry a range of ordnance. Weapons are carried on racks or rotary launchers that fit inside the bay and can be swapped out to accommodate other weapons. Additional weapons could theoretically be carried externally but this is not a normal procedure for the B-1B.

Speed and stealth
The Lancer's engines are located close to the fuselage and blended into the wing-root area. This not only avoids interference with the variable-geometry wing but also reduces the engines' radar return. The Lancer carries no defensive weapons, relying instead on speed, stealth and electronic countermeasures.

B-1B LANCER

LOAD
1
Precision Area Attack

1 60x GBU–38 JDAM

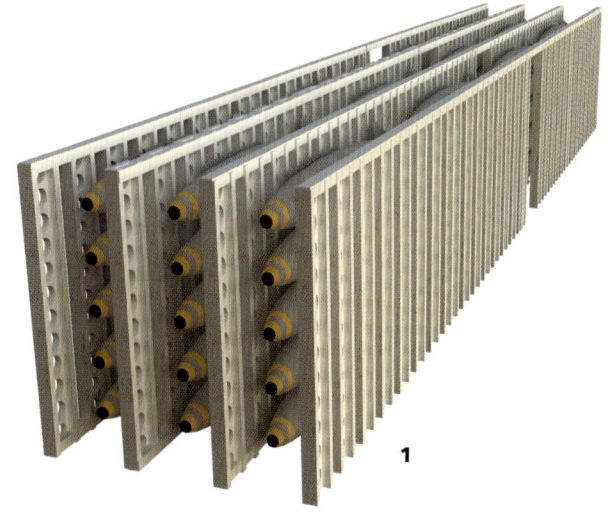

LOAD
2
Standoff Precision Attack

1 18x AGM–158 JASSM

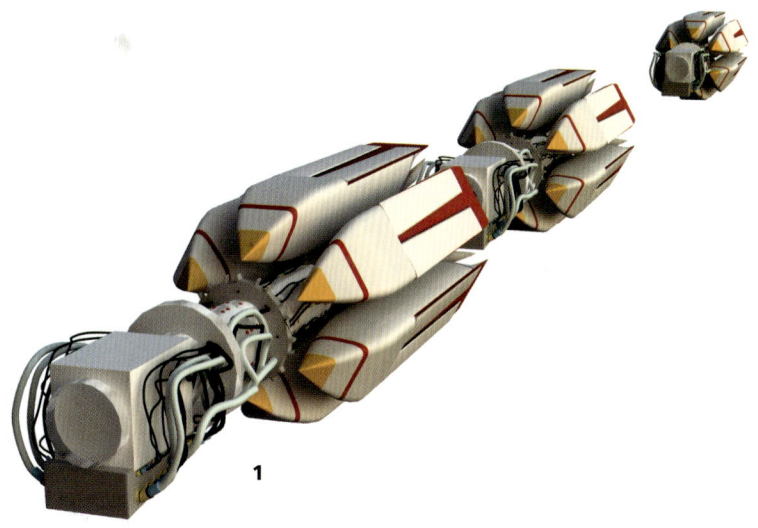

LOAD
3
Infrastructure Strike

1 18x AGM-86C cruise missile

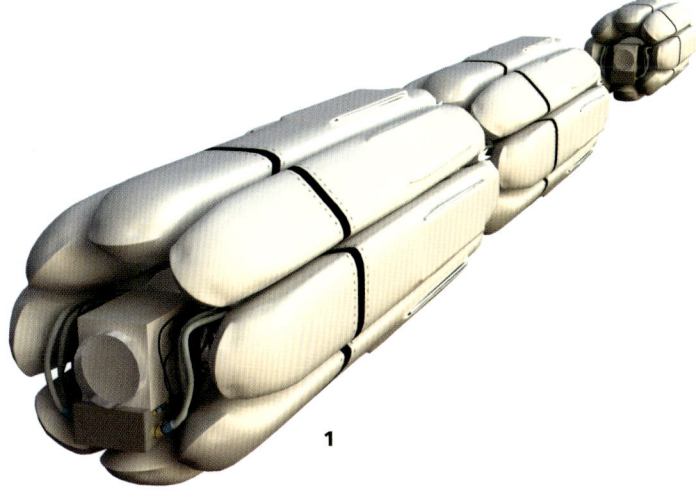

MODERN AIR-LAUNCHED WEAPONS

Above: A Joint Air-to-Surface Standoff Missile (JASSM) is loaded into a B-1B's weapons bay. The first JASSM launch from a Lancer took place in August 2006.

When the aircraft that became the B-1B was first conceptualized, a large bomber force capable of carrying nuclear weapons deep into an enemy heartland was considered essential to deterrence. The likely opponent was the Soviet Union, which had strong air defences consisting of interceptor aircraft and missile batteries.

For a time, the ability to fly high and fast was sufficient to ensure penetration to the target area, but the development of missiles that could threaten high-flying bombers forced a rethink of this strategy. A move towards low-level penetration ensued. Using this strategy, the bombers would cruise at high level to a point just outside enemy radar range then dive to low altitude, penetrating the enemy's defences at low level and high speed.

Low-level penetration enabled the bombers to place terrain obstacles between themselves and enemy radar installations, and vastly shortened the engagement distance that could be achieved by surface-to-air (SAM) missile sites even if the bomber were detected. Radars aboard interceptors would be less effective due to 'ground clutter' and the bomber's high speed would hopefully carry it quickly out of range of any defensive unit that tried to respond. It might be possible to return to a more fuel-efficient higher altitude once past the thickly defended border zones.

Nuclear Questions

The B-52, envisaged as a high-level bomber, was not well suited to low-level penetration, so a replacement seemed desirable. However, there were serious questions about the need for a nuclear bomber. Land-based and submarine-launched ballistic missiles offered the ability to carry out the same missions with less risk of interception. Although a bomber could be used more than once, many cynics saw nuclear bombing missions as one-way trips, making the bomber

Area Denial

If enemy forces can be denied use of a route or area, or simply driven from it, then the task of friendly ground forces becomes that much easier. The two weapons of choice for this mission are air-scattered mines and cluster bombs. Both are delivered from very similar dispensers and can make use of wind-corrected munition dispenser (WCMD) technology. This uses inertial navigation, assisted by the GPS system, to guide the dispenser to the target area despite the effects of wind.

Cluster bombs are used for a direct attack, offering saturation coverage of the target area. Against 'soft' targets cluster munitions are extremely lethal, which can make the target area untenable. However, once the attack is over there is no lasting threat, unless the enemy can be convinced that a follow-up strike is likely.

Mines, on the other hand, continue to be a threat once they are deployed. An air-dropped minefield cannot be concealed as the weapons remain above ground, so it is unlikely to surprise an alert enemy. However, it makes an effective deterrent once in place and could be delivered directly onto a target unit if desired.

As an alternative to cluster bombs, carpet-bombing with large quantities of conventional bombs is also effective. Again, this is unlikely to be a lasting deterrent to hostiles entering the area unless it is believed that the attack will be repeated. Once the effects of a cluster bomb or carpet-bombing attack have been demonstrated, the threat can be enough to cause the enemy to vacate the area.

This threat can be implied, for example, by reconnaissance overflights, or overt, for example, by dropping leaflets stating that a given area will be attacked in the near future. This could potentially cause enemy forces to decamp rather than face aerial bombardment, achieving military objectives by the use of a threat rather than action and saving lives in the long run.

A technician prepares to load JDAM GPS-guided bombs onto a B-1B. Most strikes against targets in Afghanistan during the Global War on Terror were made by B-1B and B-52 bombers.

MODERN AIR-LAUNCHED WEAPONS

LOAD 4 **Low-Level Area Denial**

1 30x CBU–103 Wind-corrected munitions dispenser

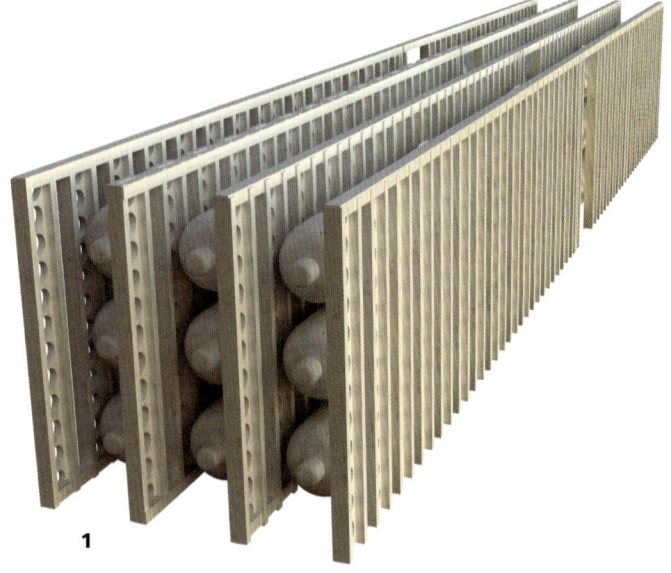

LOAD 5 **Infrastructure Strike II**

1 12x AGM-154C JSOW

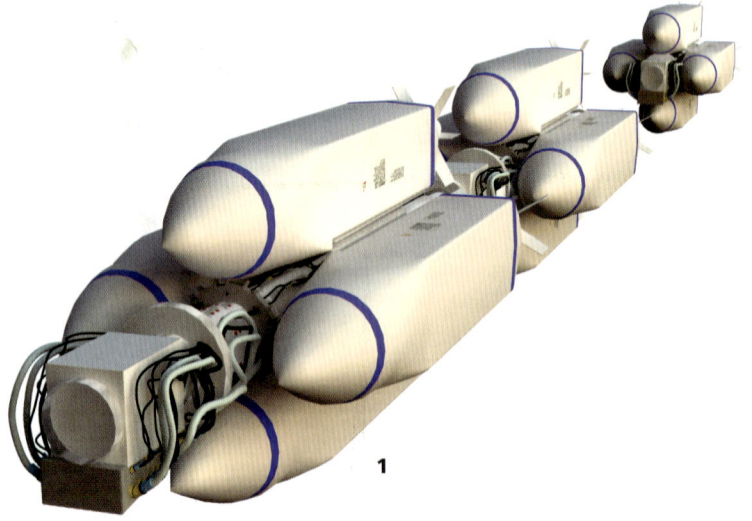

little more than a slower and more expensive missile with a crew aboard.

As a result, the B-70 programme, which was meant to produce a suitable high-speed, low-altitude penetrator, was subject to delays and repeated studies to determine its viability. In 1977 the project, which had been renamed B-1A some years before, was cancelled. The project was restarted under the B-1B designation, however, as a result of a changing air-defence environment. Improved Soviet missile and interceptor technology meant that the B-52 force, even using air-launched cruise missiles, was likely to become ineffective in the nuclear deep-strike role.

Deep Strike and Conventional

The B-1B had slightly different design requirements from the A model concept, such as a lower top speed during the penetration phase of a mission. It was also conceived in the light of shifting defence priorities. Up until that point the overriding U.S. concern was the ability to fight a major war against the Soviet Union and its Warsaw Pact allies, in Europe and along the sea lanes between U.S. and European ports. Forces dedicated to this narrow mission brief were unsuitable for use in other theatres and against other opponents.

For this reason, the B-1B Lancer was required to undertake both the deep-strike nuclear-bomber role and also be capable of undertaking conventional operations. The end of the Cold War and changes in the global

B-1B LANCER

security environment meant that the B-1B eventually gave up its nuclear role, becoming a conventional strike aircraft. A series of upgrades, notably the Conventional Mission Upgrade Programme, have allowed the B1-B to keep pace with changing weapons technology and to mature into a devestatingly lethal strike platform.

Depending on its mission, the B-1B can carry a range of ordnance in its three internal bays and six external hardpoints, all of which are located under the fuselage. The Lancer was designed with the capability to fire air-launched cruise missiles and the AGM–69 short-range attack missile. The latter was retired from service but

Above: A B-1B approaches a tanker with its fuel port open. The already impressive range of these aircraft is enhanced by mid-air refuelling, making crew endurance the only practical limit on mission duration.

the ALCM was developed into a conventional standoff weapon capable of delivering a range of warheads,

MODERN AIR-LAUNCHED WEAPONS

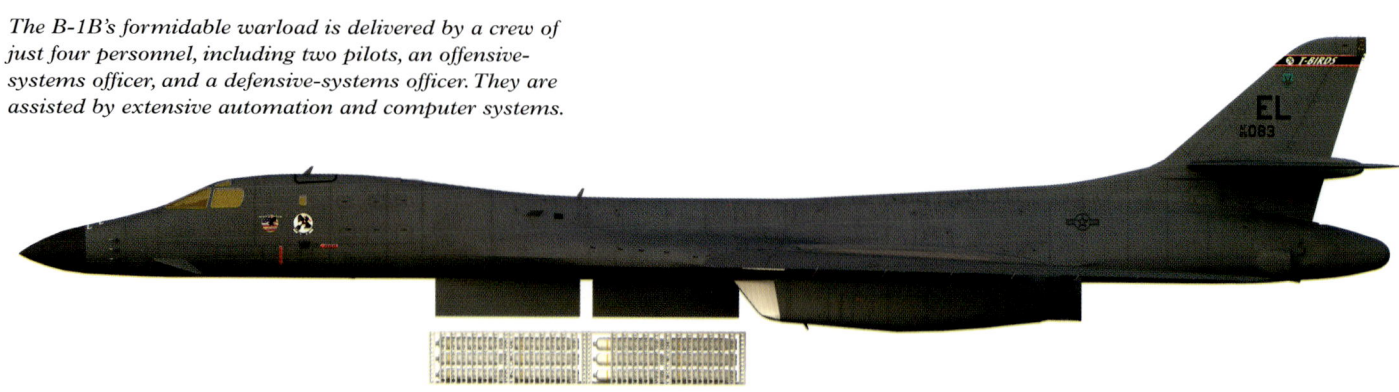

The B-1B's formidable warload is delivered by a crew of just four personnel, including two pilots, an offensive-systems officer, and a defensive-systems officer. They are assisted by extensive automation and computer systems.

LOAD 2

Air-Dropped Minelaying

1 30x CBU–89 GATOR mine (delivered from SUU-64 tactical munitions dispenser)

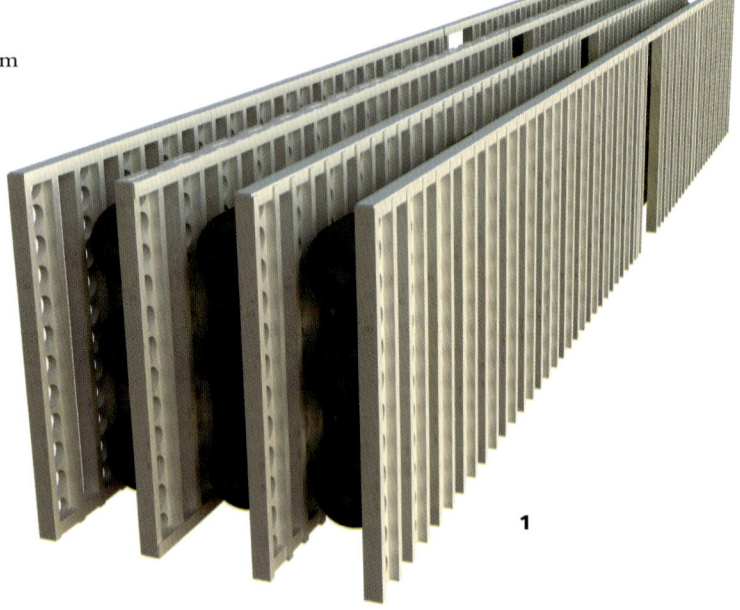

including penetrators for 'bunker-busting' operations. As a bomber rather than a strike aircraft, the B-1B was not originally equipped with a designator for laser-guided weapons, though a pod-mounted designator system is now being integrated as part of the upgrade programme, and laser-guided munitions have been used against enemy troops in Afghanistan.

The Lancer normally uses GPS-guided weapons for the precision-strike role. These would normally be 24 GBU-31 910kg (2000lb) bombs or other weapons in the JDAM family. Alternatively 24 AGM-158 JASSM standoff missiles or 12 AGM-154 JSOW weapons can be carried for a standoff precision strike. The B-1B can also function as a traditional bomber, dropping unguided munitions for area-denial or rear-area strike missions. A typical payload for this mission might be up to 84 225kg (500lb) Mk82 bombs or 30 guided or unguided dispensers for cluster munitions or mines. Naval mines can also be carried.

The B-1B served with U.S. Strategic Air Command (SAC) in the nuclear bomber role from 1986 through to the disbandment of SAC in 1992. The move to conventional operations permitted participation in operations in Iraq in the late 1990s, though unguided weapons were used at this time. Over the Balkans, and during the 2003 invasion of Iraq, GPS-guided weapons were employed, mainly 910kg (2000lb) JDAM bombs.

The Lancer continues to evolve. In March 2008 it became the first aircraft to attain supersonic speeds using a blend of traditional and synthetic aviation fuel. The arrival of the GBU-38, a smaller GPS-guided bomb, enables the B-1B to undertake close air support missions using precision-

B-1B LANCER

delivered weapons on coordinates supplied by ground troops.

There are still doubts as to whether the B-1B is really necessary in the U.S. inventory. Its speed and stealthiness compared to the B-52, and its potent electronic warfare package, make it a highly survivable platform but critics suggest that the small B-2 Spirit fleet can handle 'top-end' tasks while the B-52 is better suited to the 'bomb-truck' workhorse role. However, the B-1B is faster than either of these aircraft and carries a larger payload than the B-2. It also requires much less maintenance support than the B-2.

This combination of factors has ensured that there is still a place for the B-1B in the U.S. arsenal. It is able to deal with time-sensitive missions that might be beyond the capabilities of a B-52 force, and its long range enables it to operate from distant bases. The ability to perform as a close air-support platform is a useful secondary capability that could never have justified the initial cost of developing the aircraft but represents the way that modern air forces wring every possible scrap of utility out of platforms that have already been paid for.

Above: This composite image shows a real B-1B with an artist's representation of its weapons capacity laid out before it. As this clearly demonstrates, it can carry a total of 55,000kg (125,000lb) of varied ordnance.

The future of the B-1B depends not so much on its ability to find a new role in the changing strategic environment (it has already done that) but whether the financial benefits of removing it from service outweigh the utility it has demonstrated. The huge development cost has already been paid and the aircraft are in service. The next few years will show whether or not they can earn their keep.

MODERN AIR-LAUNCHED WEAPONS

B-2 Spirit

The B-2 Spirit is a unique 'stealth bomber' designed to penetrate heavily defended areas and strike at targets that other aircraft simply cannot reach. It is the most expensive combat aircraft ever built, with a distinctive 'flying-wing' shape. The combination of this shape and the advanced materials used in its construction results in an extremely low radar cross-section.

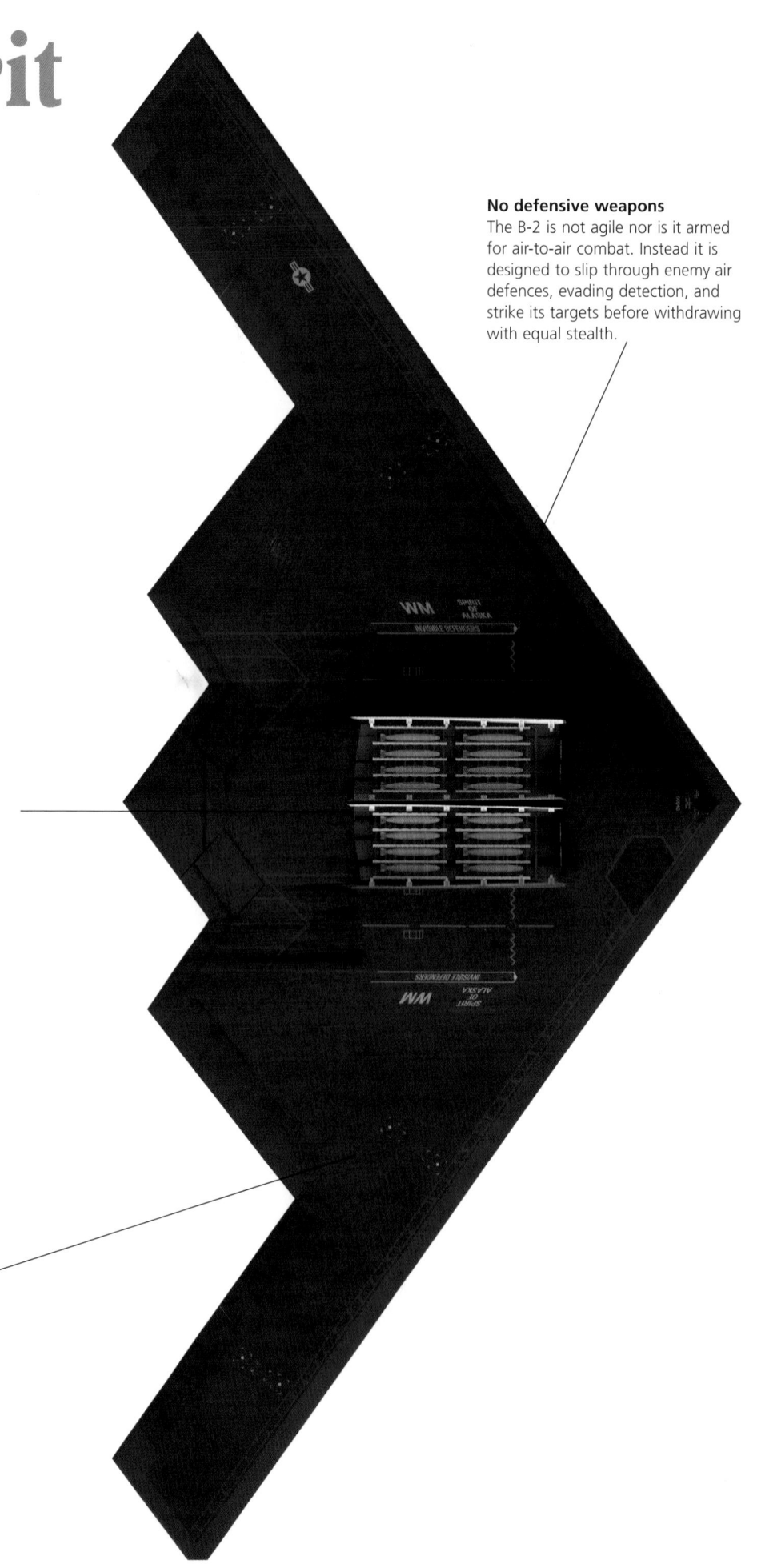

No defensive weapons
The B-2 is not agile nor is it armed for air-to-air combat. Instead it is designed to slip through enemy air defences, evading detection, and strike its targets before withdrawing with equal stealth.

Internal weapons bay
All weapons are carried in an internal bay; there are no external hardpoints. The B-2 is the only aircraft that can carry large standoff weapons internally and thus maintain its stealthy profile.

Stealthy penetrator
The B-2's unusual 'flying-wing' shape minimizes radar return by eliminating perpendicular surfaces. Engines, weapons and crew areas are blended into a smoothly curved surface. Thermal signature from the engines is hidden by the rear edges of the wing surface.

B-2 SPIRIT

The B-2 is not a particularly fast nor manoeuvrable aircraft, defending itself primarily by evading detection and therefore avoiding being attacked. The outer skin has a coating that absorbs radar energy rather than reflecting it, and the engines, which provide a strong return to enemy radar, are positioned as deep within the aircraft as possible to reduce their signature. Their exhaust fumes are vented through a trough designed to reduce their thermal emissions by a combination of air cooling and heat-absorbent material.

The B-2 was conceived during the Cold War and was intended to penetrate Soviet air defences to deliver nuclear weapons. It first flew in 1989, by which time its intended role was about to disappear. Funding such an ambitious and hugely expensive project had always been a controversial issue, and with the end of the Cold War it was perhaps inevitable that the originally planned force of 133 aircraft would be greatly reduced. In the end, 20 aircraft were built and entered service with the U.S. Air Force in 1997.

Resolving Technical Issues

The development process was a long one because several technical problems had to be resolved along the way. A shift in emphasis from high- to low-level penetration necessitated a redesign and pushed costs even higher. In part, the immense development cost resulted not from work on the aircraft itself but on the computer-

Above: The B-2 is 'low-observable' rather than invisible to radar or thermal sensors. It can be detected, though only at very short range. It can of course be spotted visually, but the chances of a patrolling fighter being able to make an interception are minimal.

aided design and manufacturing systems used for the project. Compartmentalization of the project, deemed necessary for security, also drove up the cost.

The B-2 is also extremely expensive to operate, requiring roughly twice as much maintenance time as a B-52 or B-1B. Air-conditioned hangars are necessary to prevent degradation of the aircraft's stealth capabilities due to weathering effects on the skin. A portable hangar system was developed to allow forward basing, and a new radar-absorbent

MODERN AIR-LAUNCHED WEAPONS

LOAD 1   Conventional Bomber

1 Up to 80 Mk82 JDAM

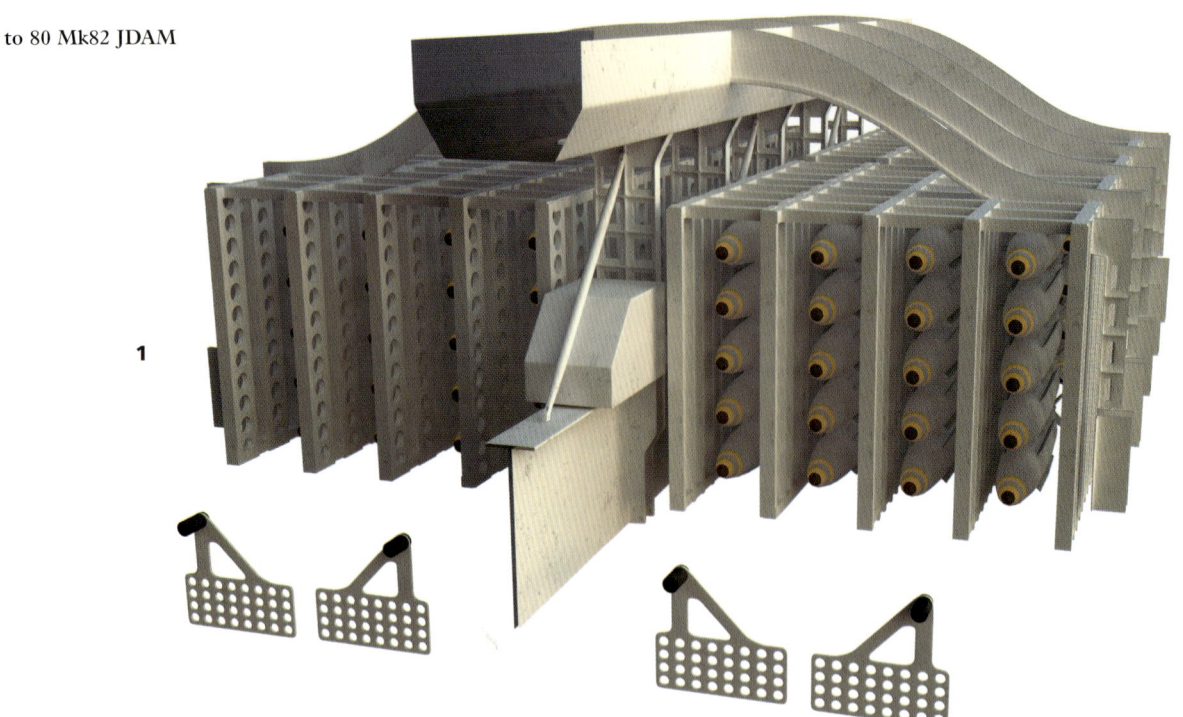

B-2 SPIRIT

The B-2 Spirit's distinctive profile has no fins or other large, flat surfaces that provide a strong radar return.

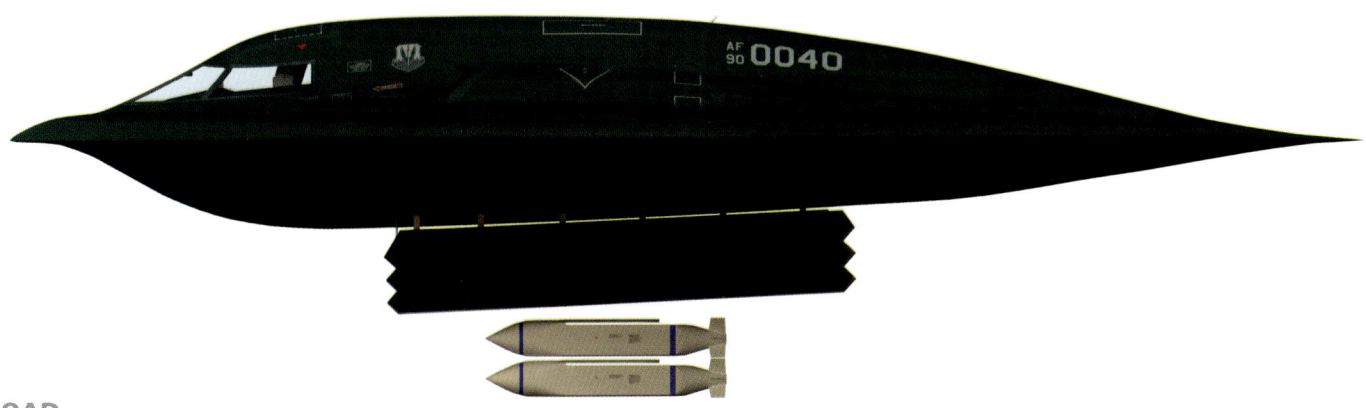

LOAD

2 **Standoff Precision Strike**

1 12 x AGM–154C JSOW
(unitary penetrator variant)

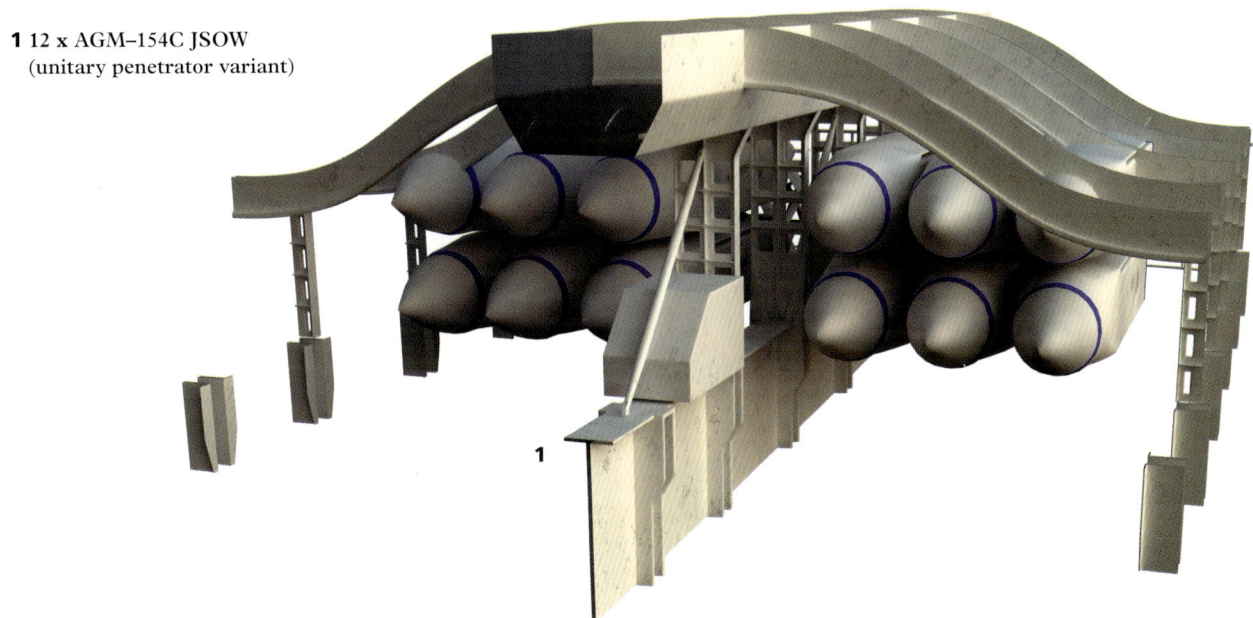

coating has been developed that does not degrade so readily.

Although the cost of the B-2 is enormous, its capabilities are arguably impressive enough to justify this. A USAF study suggested that a pair of B-2s could perform the tasks that would normally be assigned to 75

Left: The B-2 is a complex, sophisticated aircraft. It requires comprehensive ground support, which makes forward deployment difficult. Its long range enables it to carry out most missions from its home base.

other aircraft. This incredible capability is the result of a combination of range, payload and survivability. Since the B-2 can slip through most air defences completely undetected, SEAD and fighter escort missions may be unnecessary, which in turn reduces the need for support aircraft such as tankers and electronic warfare platforms.

The use of precision weaponry enables targets to be reliably destroyed with a small number of weapons, where previously several strikes might be needed before success was achieved. This is in addition to the capability to reach targets that would require prohibitively high losses to attack if non-stealthy aircraft were to be deployed.

The B-2 has no external hardpoints because this would interfere with its stealth characteristics. All weapons are carried in two internal bays, which collectively can hold 18,144kg (40,000lb) of ordnance. This can

MODERN AIR-LAUNCHED WEAPONS

Standoff Precision Strike

The ability to strike a small target from a great distance allows difficult missions to be carried out with minimal risk to aircraft. The mission consists of three phases: conveying the weapon to launch point; the weapon's own flight to the target area; and terminal attack manoeuvres.

The initial launch point may or may not be within enemy-controlled airspace, depending on the weapon to be used. Delivery by a high-performance aircraft or stealthy platform is desirable if the launching aircraft is likely to meet resistance but, in the case of very long-range weapons, delivery could in theory be carried out by any aircraft. A 'cargo/bomber' concept has been explored with this option in mind but, at present, the weapon is likely to be delivered by a warplane.

Once released, the weapon may glide or make a powered flight to the target area using a combination of inertial navigation and GPS assistance. The same method may be used for terminal attack, or other systems, such as thermal seeking, may be substituted to provide greater accuracy.

The AGM-154 Joint Standoff Weapon (JSOW) is an example of this type of standoff precision weapon. Capable of delivering either a two-stage penetrator bomb or submunitions for area effects, JSOW is a glide weapon that must be launched from fairly close to the target area (28km/15nm at low altitude, 74km/40nm for a high-altitude launch). This makes it possible to undertake precision strike missions without getting close to a heavily defended target. A powered version is under development, which may extend the weapon's range out to 222km (120nm).

Standoff weapons of this sort are highly suitable for SEAD missions and strikes against warships. Not only does the range of the weapon assist in aircraft survivability, but its small size makes the weapon harder to intercept or shoot down, offering improved chances of success over an attack by aircraft that must close to launch shorter-range weapons.

Technicians aboard USS Enterprise *prepare an AGM-154 JSOW for transport up to the flight deck. Loading and support operations are made more difficult by the cramped confines of an aircraft carrier.*

B-2 SPIRIT

Above: A B-2 Spirit retracts its landing gear after takeoff. One of the challenges the B-2's designers faced was to find space for all systems within the wing/fuselage with a minimum of protrusions and corners.

include nuclear and conventional weapons, and also naval mines. Weapons are carried in a pair of bomb-racks and a rotary launcher, which can carry a range of weaponry.

In the nuclear strike role, a B-2 can carry up to 16 of either the freefall nuclear bombs or the B61-11 nuclear penetrator munition. This is designed to penetrate deeply into the ground before detonating, increasing the chances of destroying a bunker or missile silo. A similar capability is offered by the GPS-guided Massive Ordnance Penetrator (MOP) weapon. The B-2 can carry one of these huge weapons in each of its two bays.

Missiles and Other Weaponry

For the standoff strike role, the B-2 can carry up to 16 AGM-129 cruise missiles or Joint Standoff Weapons while 16 GPS-guided 910kg (2,000lb) JDAM bombs can be carried for precision-strike missions. This number will soon be increased to 80 by modifications to the bomb racks. Guided and unguided munitions dispensers can be used to deploy cluster bombs and air-scattered mines. Further upgrades to the targeting and delivery system will allow the B-2 to carry a mix of weapon types and to attack moving targets with the Small Diameter Bomb.

The B-2 arrived too late to enter service in its intended role, but has

MODERN AIR-LAUNCHED WEAPONS

LOAD 3 — Cluster Bomb

1 36x CBU–87

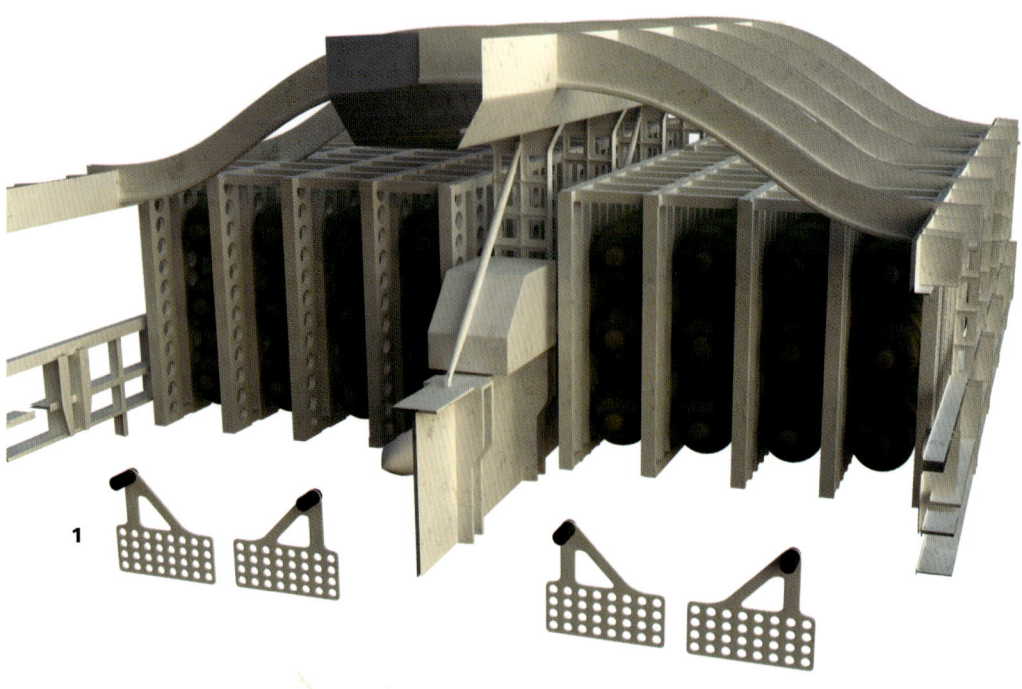

taken part in three campaigns as a conventional bomber and strike platform. In 1999, B-2s made a 35-hour non-stop round trip from their base in the USA to strike targets in Kosovo. They were the first U.S. aircraft to use the JDAM family of weapons in the Balkans. B-2s deployed to Diego Garcia for operations against Iraq in 2003, though some aircraft continued to operate out of their home base in the USA. B-2s have also operated over Afghanistan. None have ever been lost to enemy action, though one was destroyed as the result of an accident during takeoff at Guam.

Specialist Maintenance

Operating from a home base to strike targets on the other side of the world is inefficient in many ways, but the length of time spent getting to and from the target is less significant than the maintenance time required between sorties. The specialist facilities necessary for this maintenance, and the need to maintain suitable security around this highly valuable aircraft, somewhat offset the disadvantages of a long flight to and from the target area.

The B-2 has a range without refuelling of 11,110km (6,000nm), extended to 18,520km (10,000nm) with a single mid-air refuelling. It is theoretically capable of refuelling several times, but the endurance of the two-member crew is a practical limit on the length of any given operation.

The B-2 is operated only by U.S. forces and will probably never be offered for export. There are few likely opponent nations that possess air defences sufficiently capable to challenge the B-2, and many critics state that its huge operating cost is not justified by any current or foreseeable threat. For this reason, among others, a proposal by manufacturers Northrop to build another 20 B-2s at a reduced cost was not taken up by the U.S. government.

However, the few aircraft that did make it into service are sufficiently useful that they are likely to be kept in the arsenal for some time. Upgrade programmes have already given the B-2 improved radar, communications and instrumentation, and it seems likely that a future derivative of the B-2 may be built. This hypothetical aircraft could benefit from the immense funding already sunk into the B-2 project and, if it were evolutionary, and not revolutionary as the B-2 was, might be far less expensive to develop while still remaining at the cutting edge of stealthy strike capability.

Right: Mk84 bombs are loaded aboard a rotary launcher prior to commencing a mission. However impressive an aircraft's capabilities may be, in the final analysis it is a delivery systems for weapons rather than a weapon in its own right.

B-2 SPIRIT

MODERN AIR-LAUNCHED WEAPONS

F-35A/B/C Lightning II

The F-35 Lightning II is a single-seat multi-role aircraft with three variants available. The F-35A is a relatively conventional aircraft, while the F-35B is capable of short takeoff and vertical landing operations. The F-35C is a carrier-capable variant. All versions are 'stealthy' and are derived from the Joint Strike Fighter (JSF) project which, in turn, had its origins in earlier projects implemented from 1992 onwards. The project officially began in 1996. A demonstrator aircraft was flown in 2000, with the F-35 making its first flight in 2006.

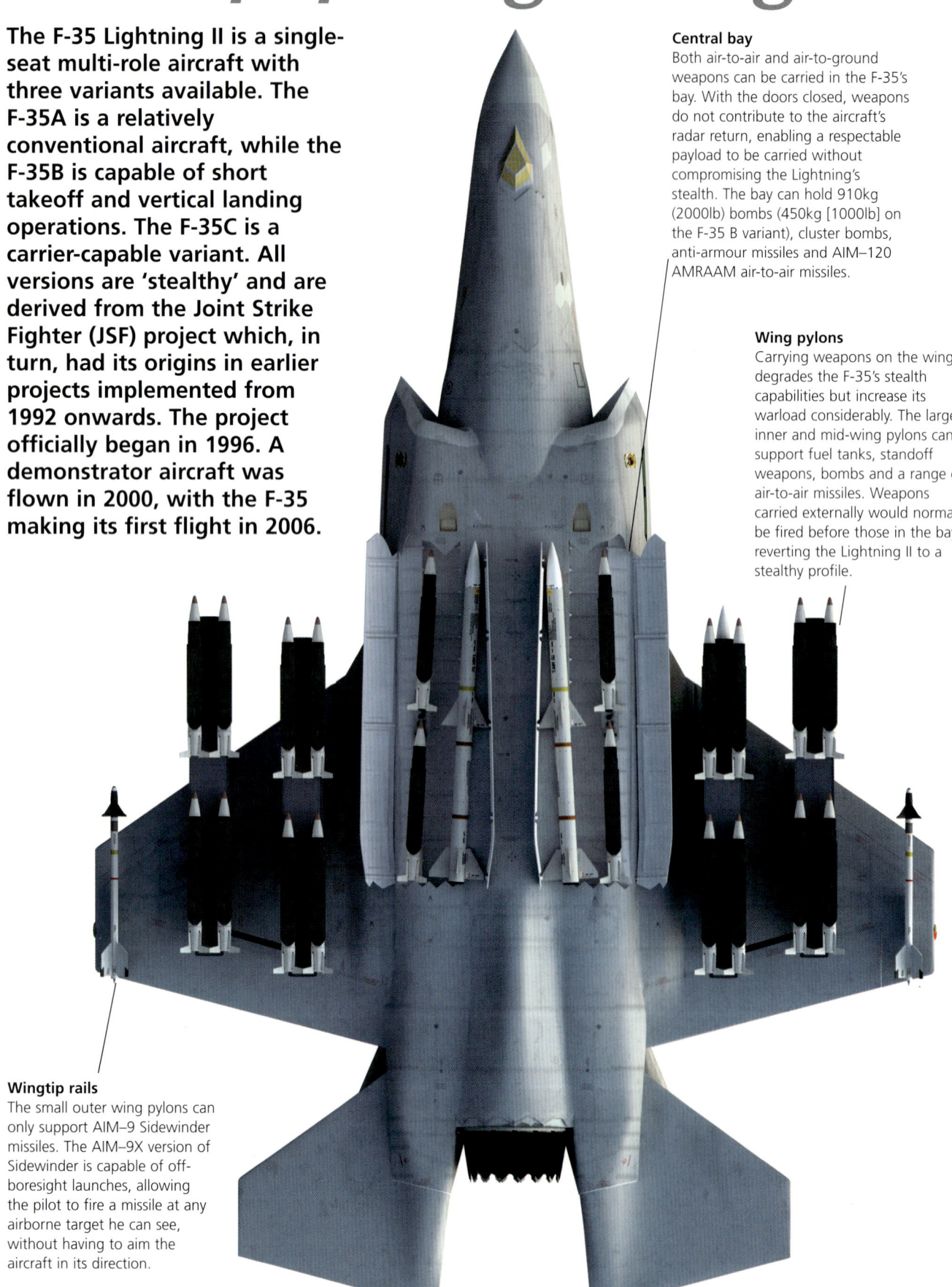

Central bay
Both air-to-air and air-to-ground weapons can be carried in the F-35's bay. With the doors closed, weapons do not contribute to the aircraft's radar return, enabling a respectable payload to be carried without compromising the Lightning's stealth. The bay can hold 910kg (2000lb) bombs (450kg [1000lb] on the F-35 B variant), cluster bombs, anti-armour missiles and AIM–120 AMRAAM air-to-air missiles.

Wing pylons
Carrying weapons on the wings degrades the F-35's stealth capabilities but increase its warload considerably. The large inner and mid-wing pylons can support fuel tanks, standoff weapons, bombs and a range of air-to-air missiles. Weapons carried externally would normally be fired before those in the bays, reverting the Lightning II to a stealthy profile.

Wingtip rails
The small outer wing pylons can only support AIM–9 Sidewinder missiles. The AIM–9X version of Sidewinder is capable of off-boresight launches, allowing the pilot to fire a missile at any airborne target he can see, without having to aim the aircraft in its direction.

F-35A/B/C LIGHTNING II

LOAD 1

Anti-Armour (UK)

1 2x Brimstone
2 2x AIM–132 ASRAAM

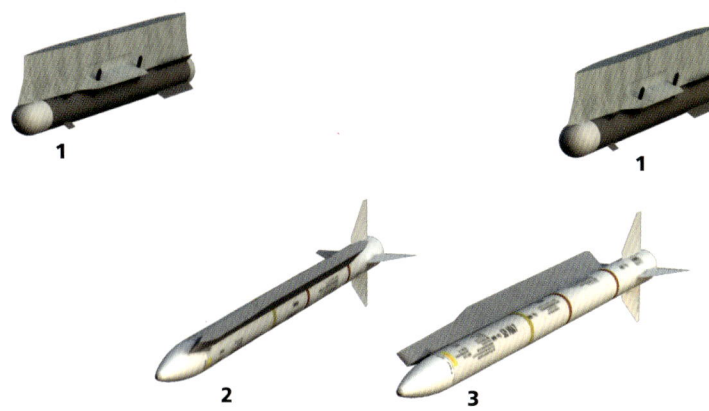

LOAD 2

Ground Attack

1 2x AIM–9 Sidewinder
2 2x Mk84 JDAM

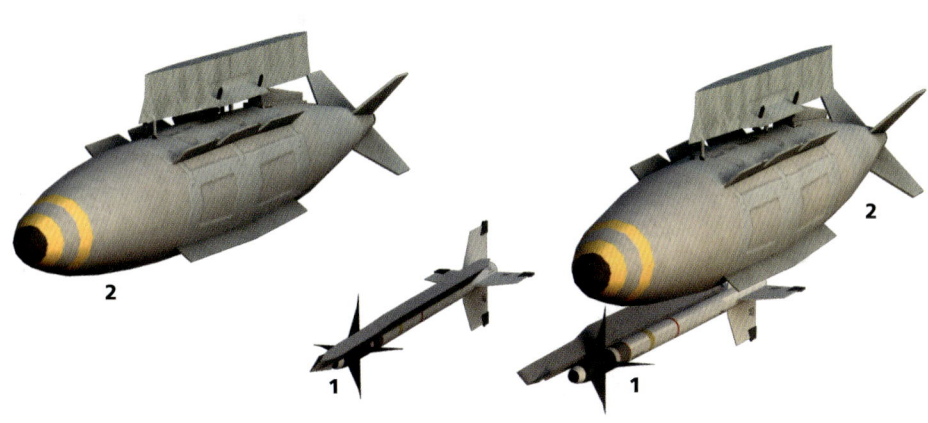

LOAD 3

Standoff Strike

1 2x AGM–154C JSOW
2 2x AIM–120 AMRAAM

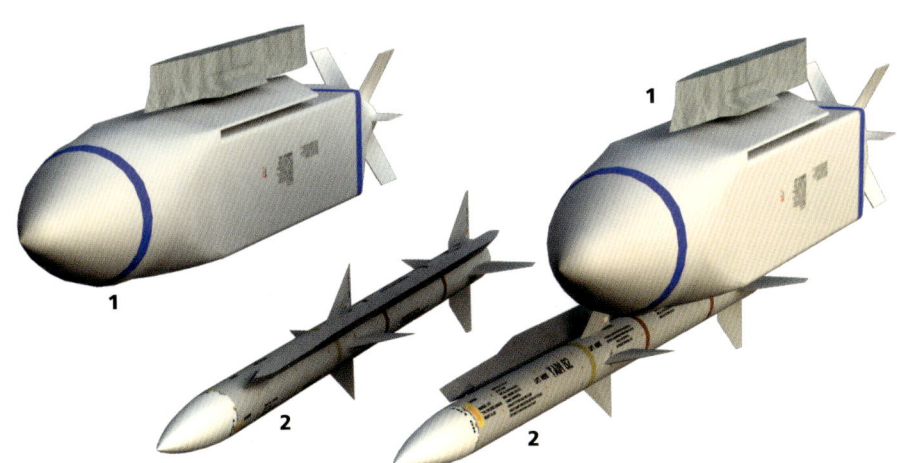

101

MODERN AIR-LAUNCHED WEAPONS

A side view of the F-35 shows the aircraft with its weapons bay doors open and no stores on the wings. The Lightning's silhouette is characteristic of the 'fifth generation' of combat aircraft, which incorporate low-observable technologies. Note the lack of sharp angles as compared with earlier generations of combat aircraft.

LOAD 4 Low Level General Purpose

1 2x CBU–103 wind-corrected munitions dispenser
2 2x AIM–9 Sidewinder

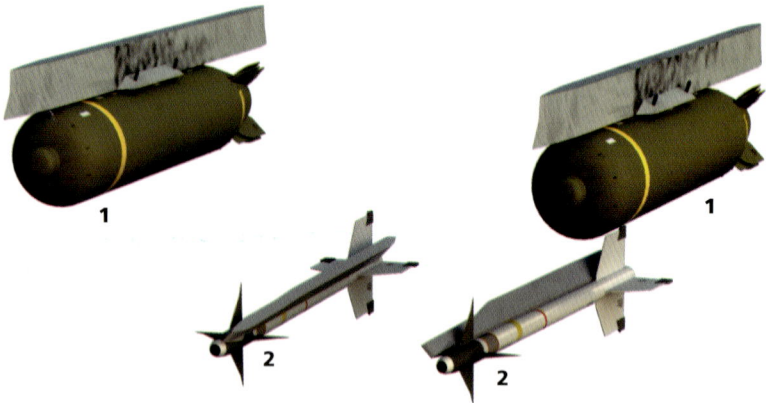

The JSF project was aimed at creating a family of closely related aircraft that could fill a range of niches in the inventory of the U.S. Air Force, Navy and Marine Corps, as well as the armed services of other countries, notably the UK. The aircraft created by this project would eventually be the replacement for a number of designs in current use, including the A-10, F-16, Harrier and F/A-18 A-D models.

There are many advantages to be gained from a 'family' approach rather than a range of designs, especially in terms of spares availability and maintenance expertise. Lessons learnt by Navy crews can be implemented on Air Force bases, improving efficiency and mission-capability, while costs can be kept down by reducing the need to maintain inventory of many different kinds of spares.

The F-35 was the result of an international project, and was intended from the outset to be attractive as an export unit. The design had to be sufficiently flexible to meet the needs of users who might envisage very different roles for the aircraft. The U.S. Air Force and other air forces desiring a land-based aircraft required a high-capability strike platform with good air-to-air performance, while the U.S. Navy needed the same in addition to the ability to operate from large aircraft carriers. Other navies, using much smaller carriers, required additional capabilities including the ability to take off and land in a very short space.

Lift Fan System

Using a Short Takeoff and Vertical Landing (STOVL) aircraft aboard a small aircraft carrier is not unprecedented; the Royal Navy and U.S. Marine Corps have used Harriers this way for many years and a similar aircraft, albeit using a different technical approach, was developed for the Soviet Navy. The F-35B uses a lift system that has more in common with this aircraft, the Yakovlev 141 'Freestyle', than with that of the Harrier.

F-35A/B/C LIGHTNING II

The Yakolev aircraft design bureau provided technical assistance during the development of the F-35B, which uses a lift fan located in the forward part of the fuselage and a thrust-deflector to redirect engine thrust downwards at the rear of the fuselage. Balance is provided by smaller thrust nozzles in the wings. The development of this system caused delays and considerably increased the cost of the project.

However, it was not desirable for all F-35s to have the same capabilities. The thrust vectoring system necessary for STOVL capability was omitted from the conventional F-35A because it represented a needless expense for users not requiring a STOVL aircraft. Nevertheless, all variants are closely similar and share most components.

The F-35 is a stealthy aircraft, though slightly less so than the larger F-22 Raptor. The A version is capable of speeds of 2000km/h (1200mph) and internally mounts a 25mm GAU-12 cannon. The B and C versions of the F-35 can carry a 25mm cannon in a pod if necessary, but do not have integral gun armament. A similar pod may in future be used to carry other systems for reconnaissance or specialist mission profiles.

The C version, designed for the U.S. Navy's carriers, is almost identical to the F-35A but has a strengthened undercarriage and internal structure to withstand catapult launches and arrested landings. Folding wingtips are necessary for hangar operations, and the F-35C has slightly larger wings and control surfaces to allow a low-speed approach for a carrier landing. This has the side effect of increasing range and payload.

The B version sacrifices fuel and some space in the weapons bay to make room for the lift fan. Range and payload are both somewhat reduced, though general capabilities are much the same as other variants. The payload reduction is fairly small – the F-35A and C can carry four GBU-39 Small Diameter Bombs per bay, while the B variant can carry three.

Located in front of the undercarriage, 910kg (2000lb) of

Below: An F-35 with some of the weapons it can carry laid out on display. The gun (centre) is mounted internally on the F-35A and can be carried in an external pod aboard the B and C variants.

MODERN AIR-LAUNCHED WEAPONS

LOAD 5

Non-Stealthy Long Range Standoff Strike (UK)

1 4x AIM–132 ASRAAM
2 2x 1816l (480gal) fuel tank
3 2x Storm Shadow

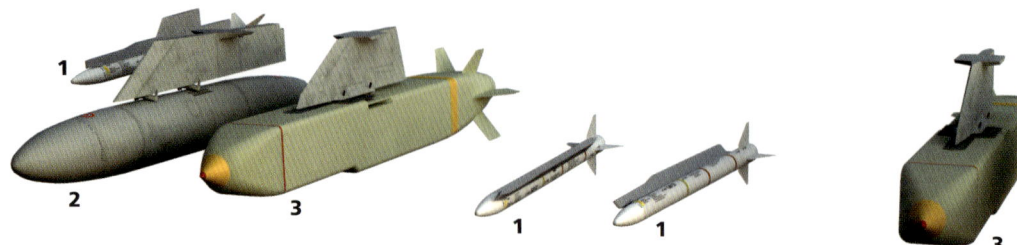

LOAD 6

Air to Air

1 2x AIM–9 Sidewinder
2 8x AIM–120 AMRAAM

LOAD 7

Non-Stealthy Ground Attack

1 2x AIM–9 Sidewinder
2 6x Mk–84 JDAM
3 2x AIM–120 AMRAAM

F-35A/B/C LIGHTNING II

ordnance can be carried in the F-35A's two internal bays. Each bay contains two hardpoints, which can mount the same or different weapons. All versions can carry a range of weapons internally, including JDAM GPS-guided bombs, JSOW standoff weapons, the Paveway family of laser-guided bombs, wind-corrected munitions dispensers for cluster bombs and mines, and Brimstone anti-armour missiles. For air-to-air combat the F-35 carries Beyond-Visual-Range missiles such as AIM–120 AMRAAM and 'dogfight' missiles such as AIM–9 Sidewinder.

There are four underwing pylons plus two wingtip missile rails for additional stores. However, carrying external stores increases the radar cross-section of the Lightning II, making it much easier to detect. If this is not a concern, however, range can be extended with external fuel tanks and a variety of additional ordnance can be carried. This includes large weapons, such as the Storm Shadow and JASSM standoff missiles, as well as other weapons like the AIM–132 ASRAAM air-to-air missiles. It is envisaged that the F-35 will fly with a mixed air-to-air and air-to-ground armament much of the time, though it can be reverted to a pure fighter or strike/close support role without much difficulty.

Above: One of the development and demonstration aircraft, at the time designated X-35C, flying in the early stages of the project. Concerns about excessive drag and weight necessitated modifications before the final F-35 design emerged.

MODERN AIR-LAUNCHED WEAPONS

LOAD 8 — Non-Stealthy Multi-Mission

1 2x AIM–9 Sidewinder
2 22x GBU–39 Small Diameter Bomb
3 2x AIM–120 AMRAAM

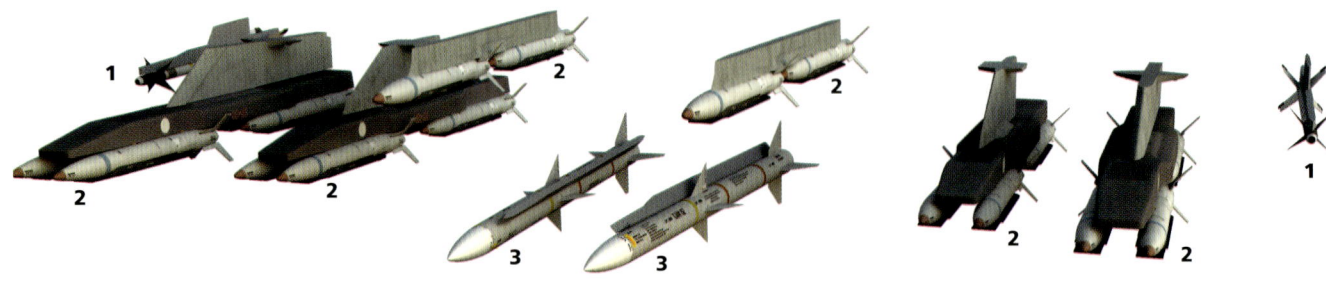

LOAD 9 — Standoff Hard-Target Precision Strike

1 2x AIM–9 Sidewinder
2 2x 1816l (480gal) fuel tank
3 2x AGM–158 JASSM

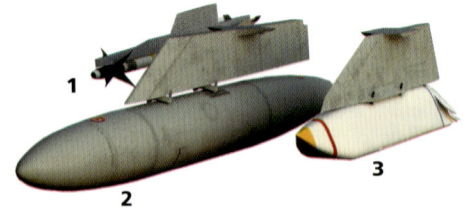   

The primary developer and main intended user of the F-35 is the USA, but the funding and development process involved the UK, Italy, the Netherlands, Australia, Canada, Denmark, Norway and Turkey. Large purchases by these nations will make the F-35 the world's most numerous fighter even before additional export sales are generated. Some nations plan to buy one variant, while others intend to operate F-35As from land bases and deploy F-35Bs aboard their aircraft carriers. Interest in the export version has been indicated by a number of potential users who were not involved in the development process but intend to purchase the aircraft 'off the shelf'.

One advantage enjoyed by F-35 pilots is the ability to use High-Off-Boresight (HOBS) weapons such as the AIM–9X Sidewinder. These weapons are aimed and locked by looking at the target rather than pointing the missile at it, enabling 'over the shoulder' dogfight missile attacks against targets outside the frontal arc of the F-35. This negates the requirement to manoeuvre into a suitable position before launching a weapon and could revolutionize air-to-air combat, enabling engagement of targets that would once have been impossible to hit without a lengthy period of hazardous manoeuvring.

Untested in Combat

The F-35 is just beginning its career, and is yet to be tested in combat. In theory, its stealth and agility will give it enormous advantages over the current generation of fighters. In fact, it has been suggested that it is as much as four times as effective. With so many potential users, it is only a matter of time before the Lightning sees combat, quite possibly against its own kind.

Laser-Guided Weapons

Most laser-guided weapons are designed to seek a specific frequency of laser light reflecting from the target. So long as the laser continues to shine on the target (known as 'painting' or 'lasing' the target), the weapon will guide itself to an impact very close to this point. Typical accuracy is within 3m (10ft) of the aim point.

Laser guidance has advantages and disadvantages. The laser beam can be defeated by smoke or bad weather, and must be kept aimed at the target while the weapon is en route. This requires the designator to remain in the vicinity and to retain line-of-sight to the target, which can be hazardous.

A laser-guided weapon can be switched from one target to another, or to a point on the ground close to a target that has become obscured for some reason. This allows a stream of weapons to be launched at short intervals and to be guided to a succession of targets by transferring the laser spot to the next as each is destroyed. Such a method works best with powered weapons, though there is a limit to how much a bomb can manoeuvre without losing the ability to reach the target. However, laser-guided bombs can be lofted rather than dropped, which gives them considerable momentum and the ability to function as unpowered glide missiles to some extent. To loft a bomb, a fast-moving aircraft pulls up from low altitude and releases the weapon in an upwards direction. This enables it to clear obstructions while keeping them between the aircraft and the target's air defences.

Some aircraft can self-designate, painting the target for their own bombs, but 'buddy-lasing' is also possible. A different aircraft (or a helicopter, or ground troops equipped with a designator) paints the target while the launching aircraft turns away to return to base or seek other targets.

Two missiles are in the air, both launched by the lead plane. One homes in on the lead plane's designator while the wingman uses 'buddy lasing' to guide the second missile. He then launches his own missiles, guiding one himself and handing the other off to his flight leader.

MODERN AIR-LAUNCHED WEAPONS

AV-8B Harrier II

The AV-8B Harrier is a unique single-seat strike aircraft capable of V/STOL (Vertical/Short Takeoff and Landing) operations. Thrust from its engine is delivered through controllable nozzles, allowing the Harrier to operate in very confined areas, from damaged runways, or off the deck of ships. This ability to hover or use vectored thrust instead of aerodynamic lift to take off gained the Harrier its nickname 'Jump Jet'.

Gun pods
The Harrier has two pods in the underside of the forward fuselage. A 25mm cannon is normally mounted in the port pod; the starboard pod carries 300 rounds of ammunition for it.

Wing pylons
The Harrier's six wing pylons can carry rockets, bombs, cluster munitions and missiles for ground attack, including laser-guided bombs and anti-radar missiles. Short- and medium-range air-to-air missiles can also be carried. The inner and middle pylons can accommodate up to four external fuel tanks.

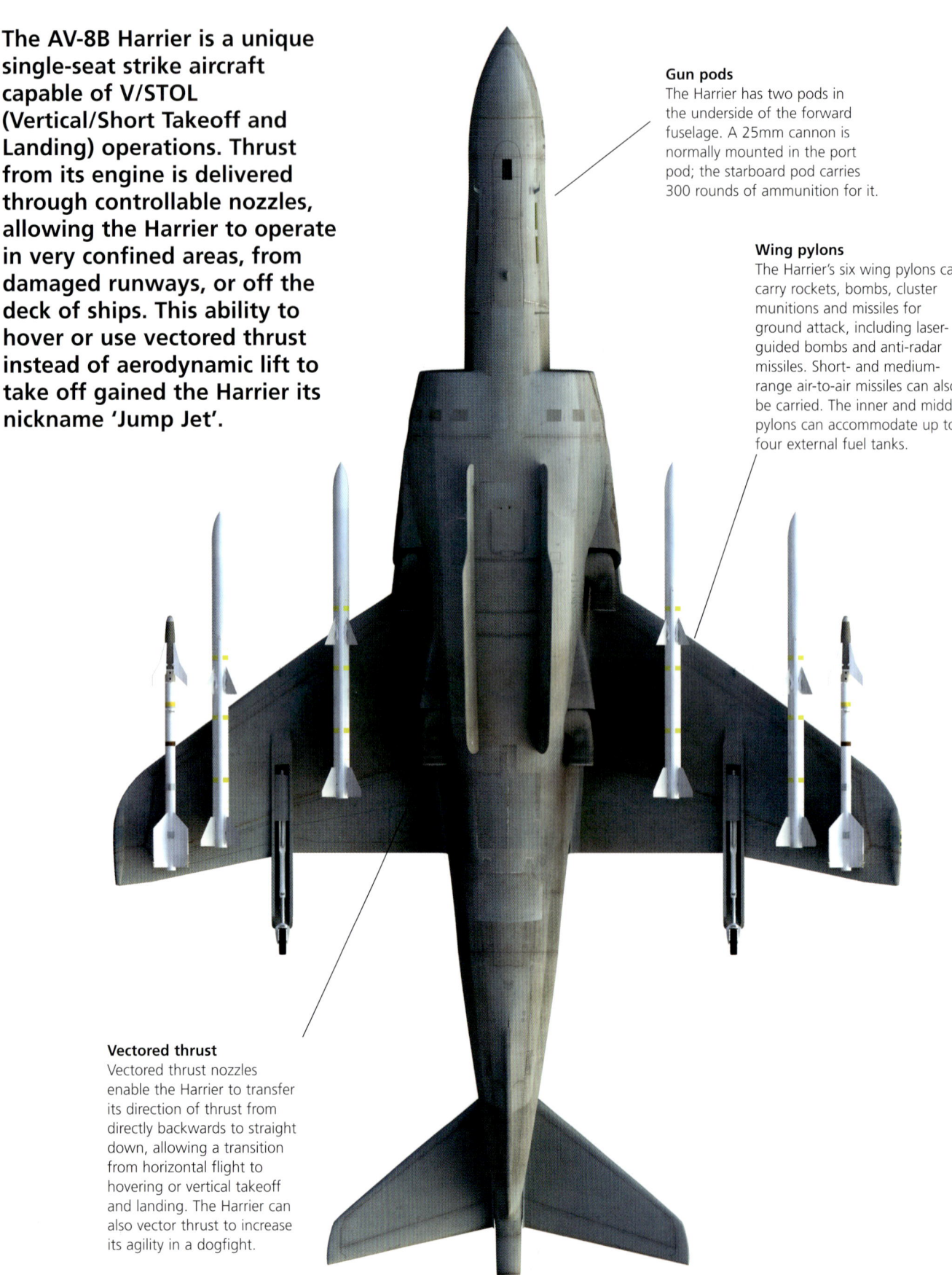

Vectored thrust
Vectored thrust nozzles enable the Harrier to transfer its direction of thrust from directly backwards to straight down, allowing a transition from horizontal flight to hovering or vertical takeoff and landing. The Harrier can also vector thrust to increase its agility in a dogfight.

AV-8B HARRIER

LOAD 1
Air to Air

1 2x AIM–9 Sidewinder
2 4x AIM–120 AMRAAAM

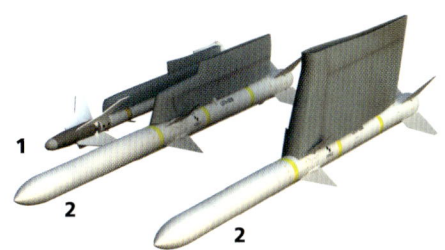

LOAD 2
Anti-Armour

1 1x LITENING targeting pod
2 4x AGM–65E Maverick
3 1x AIM–9 Sidewinder

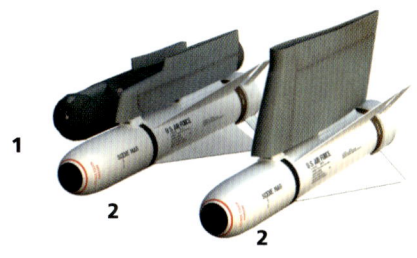
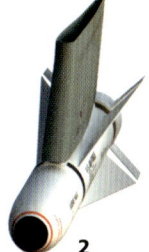

LOAD 3
Close Air Support

1 4x Mk82 unguided bomb
2 2x LAU–68 rocket pods

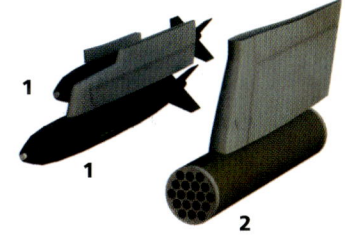

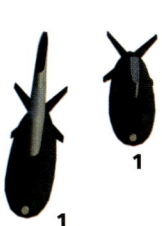

MODERN AIR-LAUNCHED WEAPONS

Above: U.S. Marine Corps Harriers fly here with wing tanks but no external weapons during Operation Desert Shield. Ferry missions between bases are flown without weapons where no threat is anticipated.

The Harrier has a long history. It was developed from a pre-production aircraft, the Kestrel, which first flew in the early 1960s. By the end of the decade this design had matured into the early-model Harrier adopted by British and U.S. forces. Its features fulfilled a number of needs. The U.S. Marine Corps needed a strike aircraft that could support their operations without relying on shore bases or a full-sized aircraft carrier, while the rough-field capability of the Harrier was attractive to forces expecting to fight a major war in Europe.

It was assumed that in the event of a major European war, NATO airfields would be attacked and possibly put out of action early in the conflict. Fast jets need a long, smooth runway from which to operate. However, the Harrier could not only use whatever undamaged section remained, but could even operate from a forest clearing if necessary. The threat of chemical-weapon attacks against airfields made dispersal and concealment an effective way to keep at least some air power operable. Although this capability was never called upon in the way it was originally envisaged by its designers, it has resulted in an aircraft with the ability to operate from forward bases in the most primitive conditions.

The Harrier's vectored thrust can be used to shorten its takeoff distance, but for vertical takeoff or landing it must operate with a reduced load. It is entirely possible for a Harrier to make a conventional rolling takeoff with a full load, and then land vertically after expending its stores. Hovering in a combat zone is extremely hazardous, but vectored-thrust capability does allow the Harrier to perform manoeuvres that other aircraft cannot achieve. By altering the pitch of the thrust nozzles, known as Vectoring in Forward Flight (VIFF), a Harrier can rapidly decelerate or increase its rate of turn. This can throw off an opponent who has an advantageous position, but it is not a manoeuvre that can be routinely used in combat.

AV-8B HARRIER

Close Air Support

It is not possible for air forces to completely defeat the ground forces of an enemy, nor to take and hold ground. The close air support mission is as close as they come to achieving this. By attacking enemy forces in contact with friendly troops, aircraft can function as 'flying artillery' and directly influence the land battle. They can often hit positions that are out of reach of ground units, removing a threat or obstacle.

In recent times, the close air support mission has been widened; heavy bombers can now dump large quantities of GPS-guided bombs on top of enemy troops in close proximity to friendlies. However, this is unusual. For the most part the close air support mission remains the task of relatively small aircraft coming in low, and using the traditional weapons of guns and rockets, plus small bombs and perhaps short-range guided missiles.

Guided weapons are not always cost-effective for close air support missions, as the time from launch to impact is usually very short. This limits the usefulness of guidance and thus it is the judgement and skill of the pilot or weapons officer that determines the effect of a strike. Close air support missions are hazardous for aircraft since they must come down low, risking ground fire as well as contact with the ground. There is also very little time to identify targets, increasing the risk of 'blue-on-blue' or 'friendly fire' incidents. Here again, the skill of personnel is of paramount importance.

Strafing rockets have been a favourite CAS weapon for several decades. Powerful enough to affect a range of targets yet light enough to be carried in large numbers, rockets are normally launched in a 'ripple' from pods, striking ahead of the aircraft. They are aimed in much the same way as a fixed forward-firing gun, with the aircraft diving towards the target and 'walking' the impact points across it.

Pods of 70mm (2.75in) rockets are loaded aboard a US Marine Corps F/A-18 Hornet. Rockets are an excellent weapon for Close Air Support, enabling a single aircraft to engage several targets or to attack an 'area' target such as a concentration of enemy vehicles or infantry.

MODERN AIR-LAUNCHED WEAPONS

AV-8B HARRIER

The AV-8B Harrier is an extremely versatile aircraft, chosen by the US Marine Corps for its ability to provide both air defence and close support for amphibious operations. When necessary, it can also carry out precision strikes against land targets or enemy warships threatening the task force.

LOAD 4 — Precision Strike

1 1x AIM-9 Sidewinder
2 4x GBU-16
3 1x LITENING targeting pod

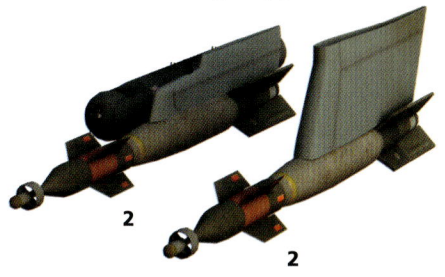

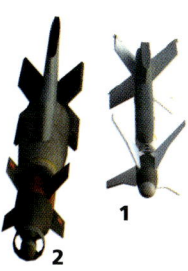

The Harrier was gradually updated and developed into a number of versions optimized for different roles. This eventually led to the current Harrier II, which has been extensively redesigned and represents a second generation of the original aircraft, with better electronics, payload and performance than earlier models. Reliability and safety have also been improved. The Harrier was at one time notorious in U.S. Marine Corps circles as an accident-prone aircraft.

Left: A U.S. Marine Corps Harrier lands on USS Iwo Jima. *Harriers are ideal aircraft to operate from smaller flight decks; recovery of an aircraft that can land vertically is far simpler than one that arrives at high speed.*

This was due, at least in part, to the difficulty of performing hovering and vertical landing or takeoff manoeuvres. There is little margin for error aboard an essentially stationary aircraft, and a fairly minor problem with engines or thrust control, or a pilot error that might be of little consequence under other circumstances, can lead to a catastrophic crash. Experience has improved expertise in both operating and maintenance, largely eliminating faults that led to earlier crashes.

The Harrier II mounts a 25mm GAU-12 cannon internally, with 300 rounds. Three pylons on each wing and one under-fuselage mount carry 6000kg (13,235lb) of stores including rockets, missiles and bombs. This is reduced to 1815kg (4000lb) if a vertical takeoff is necessary. Range is fairly short but, with the capability to replace up to four pylons' weapons with drop tanks, not a serious issue.

In keeping with one of its originally envisaged roles, the Harrier is an excellent close-support aircraft. It can carry pods each containing 19 70mm strafing rockets, cluster bombs, napalm canisters or unguided 'iron' bombs. These weapons are all highly effective from low level, and for a more general ground-attack role the Harrier can carry AGM-65 Maverick missiles and laser-guided bombs. AGM-84 Harpoon missiles are available for the

MODERN AIR-LAUNCHED WEAPONS

LOAD 5 — Precision Strike II

1 1x LITENING targeting pod
2 2x AGM–65E Maverick
3 2x GBU–16
4 1x AIM–9 Sidewinder

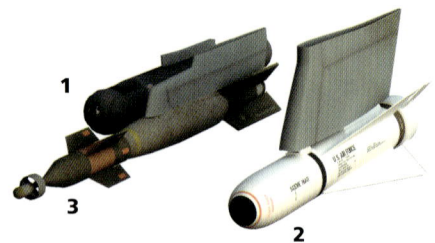
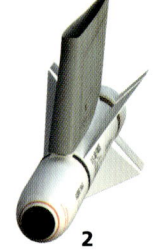
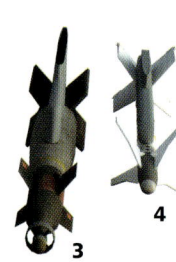

LOAD 6 — Anti-Shipping Strike

1 2x AIM–9 Sidewinder
2 2x 1135l (300gal) fuel tank
3 2x AGM–A4 Harpoon

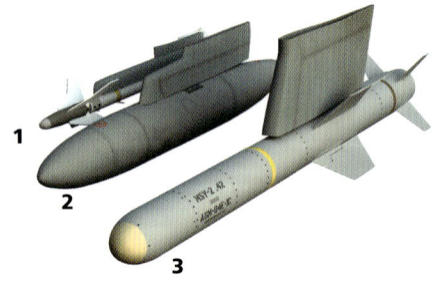
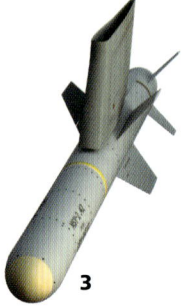

LOAD 7 — General Support

1 2x AIM–9 Sidewinder
2 2x LAU–68 rocket pod
3 2x Mk83 unguided bomb

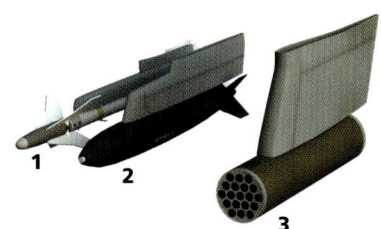

AV-8B HARRIER

anti-shipping role and although the Harrier is not ideally suited to the SEAD role it can carry anti-radiation missiles.

The AV-8B is not a high-performance air-superiority fighter but, for the fleet-defence role, it can carry short-range missiles, such as Sidewinder or ASRAAM and medium-range AMRAAM or similar missiles. The Harrier was designed to operate from small carriers that might not carry any other type of fixed-wing aircraft and thus must rely on their AV-8Bs for defence as well as attack.

British Harriers (of an earlier generation than the Harrier II) performed successfully in air-to-air combat against Argentinean jets during the 1982 Falklands conflict. The British Sea Harriers were only armed with Sidewinder missiles and guns; more recent versions can engage from beyond visual range.

British Harriers also operated in a ground-attack role over the Balkans and in Iraq, and have more recently been deployed in Afghanistan in combat against the Taliban. Operating in an environment where enemy air defences consist mainly of small arms and shoulder-fired missiles, the Harrier supported ground troops with guided weapons as well as rockets. These weapons are especially useful against dispersed personnel targets because they possess sufficient power to affect a group of personnel even if they are under cover, but can be carried in great enough quantities to engage multiple targets.

Above: A U.S. Marine Corps Harrier makes a rolling takeoff from USS Bataan. *Although the Harrier can take off vertically, it uses a lot of fuel and greatly restricts the payload that can be carried. A short rolling takeoff using conventional lift is more efficient.*

During the 1991 Gulf War, Harriers were based much further forward than other U.S. air assets. Most operated from land bases while a proportion were based offshore. This enabled Harriers to respond quickly to requests for air support or the notification of a target. As a result, on average, missions undertaken were relatively short in duration. There were 3380 sorties that took up a total of 4083 flight hours, with an average turnaround time of 23 minutes.

Operational Advantages

The ability of the AV-8B to deliver air support at short notice, after minimal delay from request to commencement of attack, is a by-product of the aircraft's impressive short-field capability. During later operations in Iraq, U.S. Marine Corps Harriers operated from runways that other jets simply could not have used. At times they flew from sections of highway.

The ability to fly slowly or hover was particularly useful when carrying out reconnaissance over built-up areas. The Harrier pilots were able to undertake accurate attacks or execute the handing off of targets even in close proximity to friendly troops or other non-combatants.

The Harrier is in service with the U.S. Marine Corps as well as the armed forces of Great Britain, India, Spain and Italy. Upgrades are still ongoing at the time of writing. The Harrier II received LITENING pods to allow laser guidance of weapons, and there are plans to add the capability to programme and launch GPS-guided weapons to the existing Harrier fleet. However, it is likely that the AV-8B will be replaced by a version of the F-35 Lightning, an aircraft that offers similar V/STOL capability and can therefore fill the same operational niche.

115

MODERN AIR-LAUNCHED WEAPONS

Tornado

The Panavia Tornado is a twin-engine multi-role combat aircraft with variable-geometry wings. It was designed by an international consortium to meet the needs of several air forces, and after a difficult development period eventually went into service with Great Britain, Germany and Italy. Saudi Arabia later ordered a force of Tornados but was not part of the original programme.

Targeting pods
The Tornado has been upgraded with a Forward-Looking Infrared system and improved avionics. It can also utilize a range of pod-mounted systems, including laser guidance for weapons, and a range of reconnaissance systems.

Fuselage
The Tornado has four under-fuselage weapon stations. These can carry medium-range air-to-air weapons or air-to-ground ordnance including cruise missiles and runway-denial weapons. Either one or two (depending on the variant) 27mm cannon are also mounted in the fuselage.

Pivoting pylons
The two pylons on each wing pivot to maintain orientation as the Tornado's wings are swept. These pylons can accommodate fuel tanks, air-to-air and air-to-ground or anti-radar missiles, anti-ship missiles and bombs.

TORNADO

LOAD 1 — Anti-Armour

1 11x Brimstone
2 4x AIM–132 ASRAAM

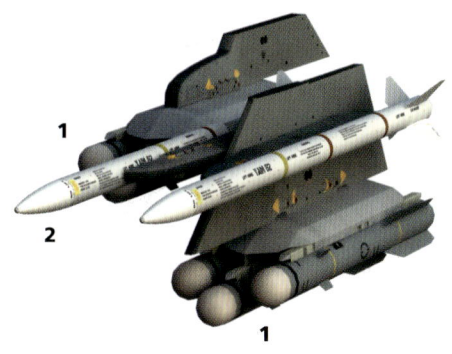

LOAD 2 — Precision Strike

1 2x GBU–24
2 2x 1552l (410gal) fuel tank
3 1x LITENING targeting pod

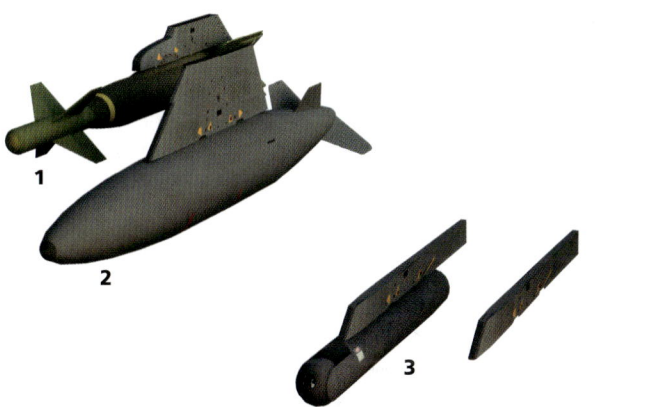
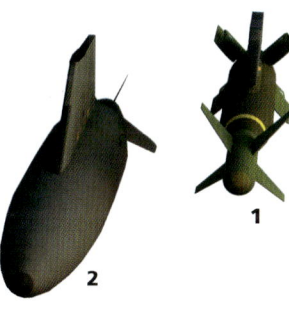

LOAD 3 — Runway Denial

1 4x AIM–132 ASRAAM
2 2x 1552l (410gal) fuel tank
3 2x JP233 munitions dispenser

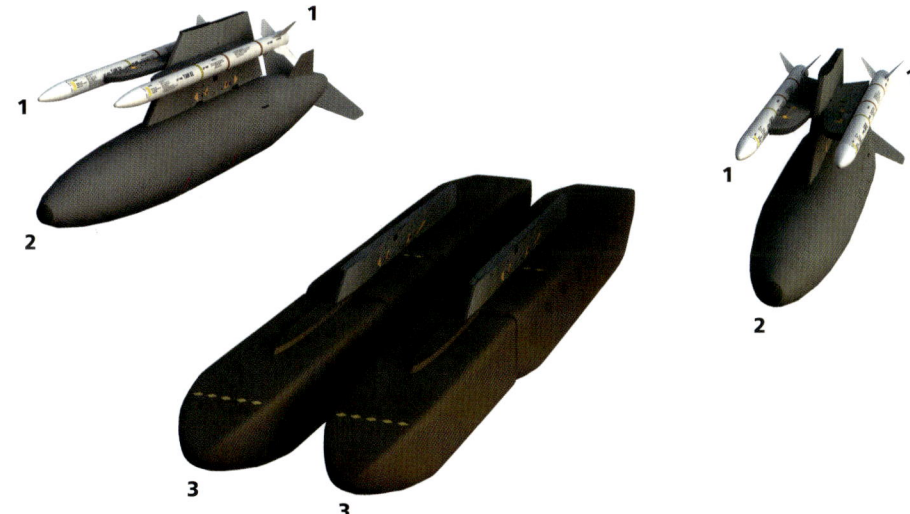

MODERN AIR-LAUNCHED WEAPONS

Offensive Counter-Air Operations

Counter-air operations are aimed at limiting or eliminating the enemy's capability to make use of air power, either offensively or defensively. Counter-air operations may include escort missions and interceptions of enemy aircraft, as well as attacks on their bases or supply depots.

Ground-attack missions can be used in three ways in a counter-air context: attacks on grounded aircraft themselves; on their support facilities; or on the runways they are intended to use. Aircraft are easy enough to destroy if they can be caught in the open, but once dispersed around an airbase in protected waiting areas (revetments) they make more difficult targets. Similarly fuel, ammunition and maintenance facilities can be protected by thick concrete, earth and sandbags, making their destruction a challenge.

However, aircraft for the most part need a smooth runway in order to take off and land. This is by definition a large and fixed surface, which is relatively easy to hit even without guided weapons. Craters in the runway can make it unusable until they are filled in, reducing the momentum of enemy air operations. Any explosive warhead can achieve this, though weapons that penetrate the ground and then explode are more effective.

For this purpose, specialist runway-denial weapons have been developed. These generally deploy submunitions including a combination of cratering warheads and mines to interfere with attempts to deal with the damage. International bans on anti-personnel mines made these weapons illegal but the concept remains viable.

Airfields can be harassed in various ways, for example, using standoff missiles delivering cluster bombs. These pose relatively little hazard to hardware but can make it impossible for ground crews to work, either on aircraft or to fill in the craters made by bombs hitting the runway.

An RAF Tornado releases thermal decoy flares during a combat mission over Iraq. Even with the Iraqi air force largely suppressed, man-portable infrared-seeking missiles remained a threat to Coalition aircraft operating at low altitude.

TORNADO

The Tornado was conceived out of two independent programmes. Britain and France began developing a variable-geometry aircraft in 1965, while Belgium, Canada, Germany, Italy and the Netherlands began seeking a replacement for their F-104 fighters in 1968. French withdrawal from the Anglo-French project caused Britain to join what became known as the Multi-Role Combat Aircraft (MRCA) project in 1968.

Although Canada and Belgium pulled out of the project in 1969 and the Netherlands later curtailed its involvement, the remaining three partners saw the project to completion, with a prototype flying in 1974. From the outset, the Tornado was designed with flexibility in mind, enabling it to carry out a range of missions. It was originally envisaged that there would be a single-seat fighter version and a two-seat strike variant, but eventually all Tornado versions emerged as two-seaters. However, several distinct variants have since been created, all based on a common airframe.

Drawing on earlier Anglo-French studies, the Tornado was designed for all-weather operation. It had variable-geometry wings to allow the best possible performance at all attitudes and in all conditions. With the wings forward, the Tornado benefits from maximum lift, which allows a shorter takeoff and landing run, allows

Below: A German Tornado armed with HARM anti-radiation missiles flies over the Balkans during Operation Allied Force. Its mission is to retaliate against Surface-to-Air missiles that fire on Allied aircraft.

MODERN AIR-LAUNCHED WEAPONS

LOAD 4

SEAD

1 5x ALARM
2 4x AIM–132 ASRAAM

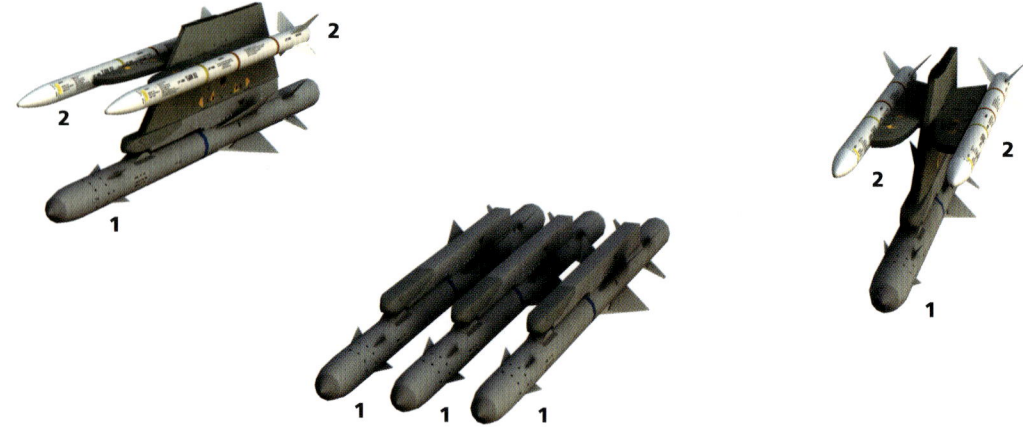

LOAD 5

Anti-Shipping Strike

1 2x Kormoran
2 2x 1552l (410gal) fuel tank
3 4x AIM–132 ASRAAM

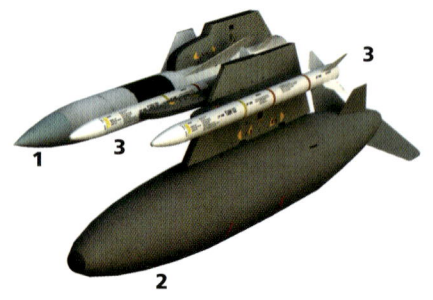
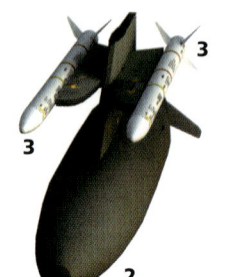

LOAD 6

Multi-role Strike

1 6x Brimstone
2 4x AIM–132 ASRAAM
3 4x GBU–12
4 1x LITENING targeting pod

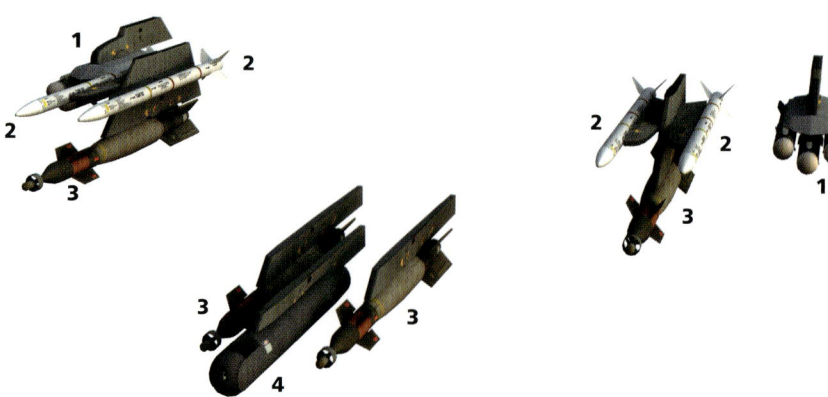

TORNADO

Above: A U.S. Air Force KC-10 Extender tanker aircraft refuels an RAF Tornado over Iraq. Tanker support extends combat radius and loiter time, enabling aircraft to remain on call longer for time-critical missions.

economical cruising and improved accuracy with unguided weapons by permitting a lower attack speed. Sweeping the wings back reduces drag at high speeds and permits a higher top speed. This was considered important for the air-defence mission, where Tornados might be required to intercept potentially hostile aircraft as early as possible.

The twin engines of the Tornado enable it to reach a top speed of Mach 2.2 at high altitude. At sea level, maximum speed is Mach 1.2. The engines are located within individual cells to improve resistance to damage, and are very robust. The airframe is built around a titanium wing box, giving great structural strength, and was designed with ease of maintenance in mind. It has more than 350 access panels, which can either be removed or swung out of the way on hinges.

The first Tornados entered service in 1980, and production continued until 1998. During this time several versions emerged. The GR1 was optimized for ground attack and close support, with GR1A versions being developed for the reconnaissance role. The GR1B was intended for long-range anti-shipping strikes. A mid-life upgrade programme created the GR4, an updated strike version.

The GR4 is capable of using GPS and laser-guided weapons and has been configured to accept future weapon systems into its electronics package. The crew of two, a pilot and a weapons officer, have multi-function displays in addition to a digital map system, plus a FLIR system that projects directly onto the pilot's head-up display.

Tornado ECR for SEAD

Germany and Italy operate a specialist SEAD version, the Tornado ECR. This aircraft carries specialist electronics designed to locate and identify enemy radar emissions, and can then attack them with AGM-88 anti-radiation missiles. German ECR variants were initially equipped with infra-red reconnaissance systems, but it was decided that this secondary role was not an effective use of SEAD aircraft.

MODERN AIR-LAUNCHED WEAPONS

A Tornado carrying two Storm Shadow cruise missiles plus external fuel tanks. Sidewinder missiles are also carried for self-defence, but it is preferable for strike aircraft to evade enemy contact and to avoid fighting their way through wherever possible.

LOAD 7 **Cruise-Missile Delivery**

1 2x Storm Shadow
2 4x AIM–132 ASRAAM
3 2x 1552l (410gal) fuel tank

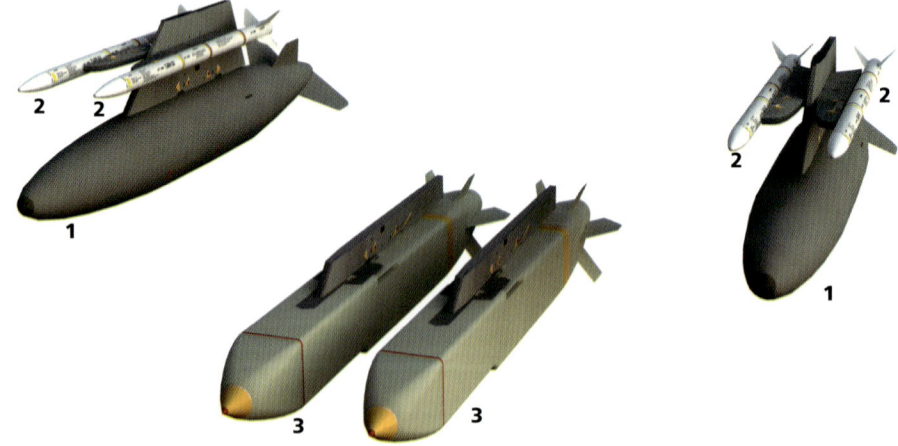

The Tornado ADV (Air Defence Variant) is a dedicated long-range interceptor with electronics and weapon system optimized to this mission. It is fundamentally a specialist aircraft derived from a multi-role platform. The original models were designated F2 (F1 was the prototype). A modified version of the F2 served as a testbed for various experimental technologies, including helmet-mounted systems and holographic heads-up displays. Tornado F3s featured improved propulsion and cockpit systems. About one-quarter of those manufactured are configured as trainers, but they still retain full combat capability.

Respectable Agility

The Tornado usually carries one or two 27mm cannon (depending on configuration; some versions have no cannon armament) as a back-up weapon. It is not a dogfighter, though its agility with the wing in mid-swept position is respectable. Its primary air-to-air weapons are medium-range radar-guided missiles, in keeping with its original mission of intercepting Soviet bombers. It can carry four AIM–9 Sidewinder or ASRAAM short-range missiles plus four Skyflash or AIM–120 AMRAAM for air-defence operations.

In the ground-attack role, the Tornado can carry a wide variety of ordnance. A range of anti-radar and anti-ship missiles are available, plus Storm Shadow cruise missiles. The Brimstone anti-armour weapon and laser-guided bombs allow precision attacks, while freefall (unguided) ordnance includes cluster bombs and runway-denial systems. Some aircraft carry a LITENING targeting pod, and sidewinders may be carried for self-defence or targets of opportunity.

TORNADO

The Tornado was customized in answer to the requirements of its operators during the Cold War. The Air Defence Variant was intended to convey missiles to a launch point as quickly as possible, while the ground-attack version was designed with low-level penetration raids in mind. This capability has proven useful in recent conflicts, notably the 1991 Gulf War, enabling the Tornado to penetrate air defences in a manner that would normally require a much more stealthy aircraft. However, low flight makes an aircraft vulnerable to short-range weapons, such as guns and man-portable missiles. Once Iraqi air defences were suppressed the Tornados reverted to less hazardous medium-altitude attacks.

Tornado Sees Action

The Gulf War was the first conflict in which the Tornado saw action. In the early stages of the conflict, Tornados carried out an offensive counter-air campaign, attacking air bases with bombs and runway-denial weapons. An inability to use laser-guided munitions was rectified by the deployment of designator-equipped Blackburn Buccaneers, which allowed the Tornado force to make precision strikes. Tornados helped enforce no-fly zones after the war, and on several occasions engaged air-defence installations that had fired on Allied aircraft.

In the Balkans conflict of the late 1990s, Tornados engaged air defences in the former Yugoslavia using anti-radiation missiles, and self-designated precision munitions for the first time. This was the last active deployment for the GR1 version; it was GR4s that took part in the renewed conflict in Iraq. These aircraft launched a number of Storm Shadow cruise missiles against Iraqi targets, which was a role that the original designers are unlikely to have anticipated. Tornados have also deployed to Afghanistan to support ground forces there.

Although production of the Tornado has ceased, mid-life upgrade programmes have been undertaken and will allow examples to continue operating for some years yet. In 2004, Italian Air Force Tornados began receiving improved electronics and the capability to use GPS and laser-guided bombs, while Tornados in Saudi Arabian service began an upgrade programme in 2008.

It is expected that Italian Tornados will be replaced by the F-35 Lightning II. British Tornado F3s are destined for retirement in 2011, but the Tornado will continue to serve in the interdiction/strike role. The RAF's GR1s were upgraded to GR4 capability from 1998–2003. These aircraft are expected to remain in service into the 2020s.

Left: *An RAF Tornado flies with its wings swept back. Few such 'swing-wing' designs are still deployed, yet the Tornado remains a very respectable combat aircraft even after 30 years in service.*

MODERN AIR-LAUNCHED WEAPONS

EF2000 Typhoon

The EF2000 Typhoon is a twin-engine multi-role combat aircraft designed to meet the needs of several European air forces. It is capable of fulfilling both the air-superiority and ground-attack roles either as a dedicated platform or in a 'swing-role' configuration, which allows it to switch between combat modes in the middle of a mission. Typhoons intended for combat operations are single-seat aircraft, but a two-seat trainer version is available.

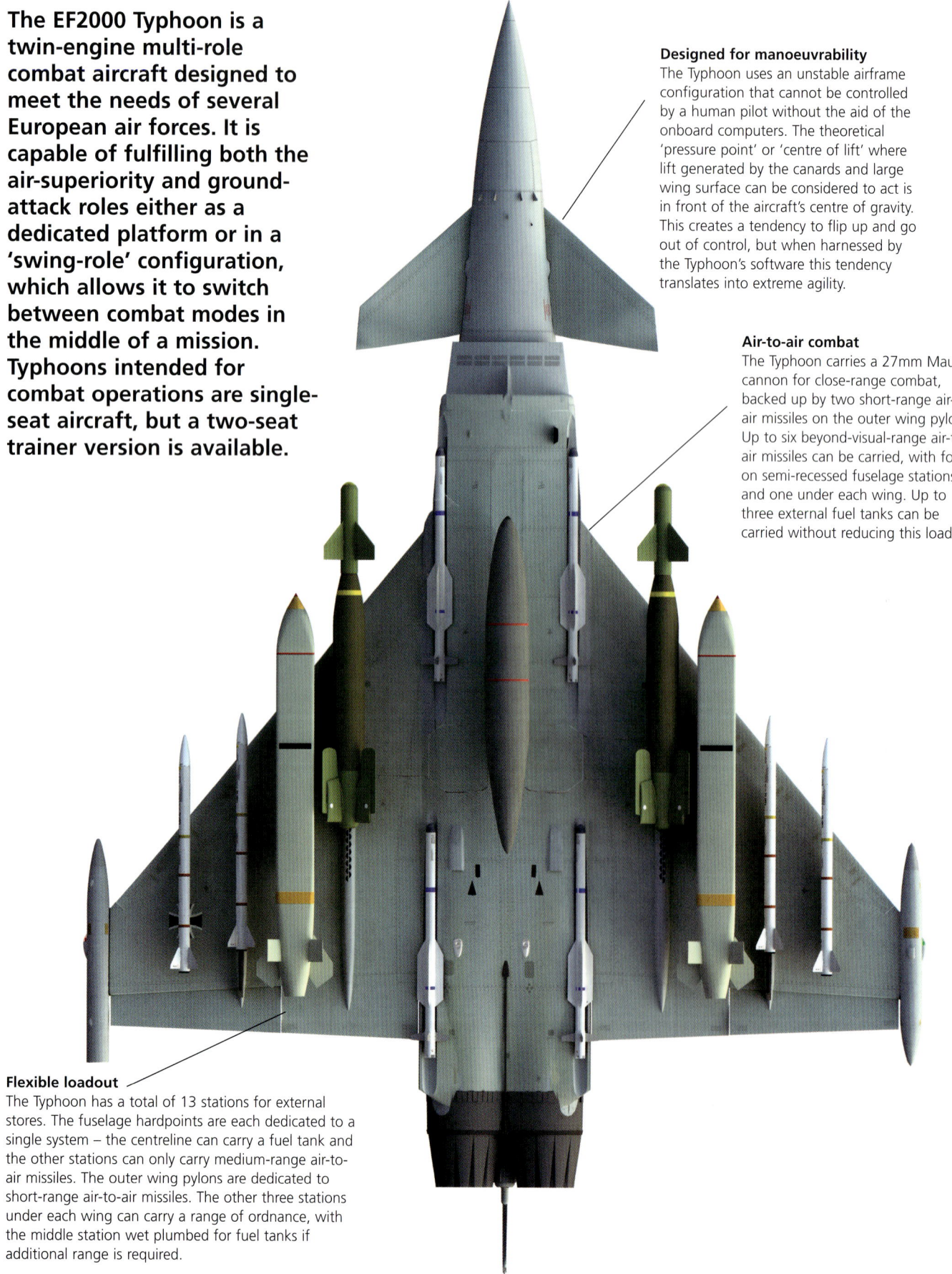

Designed for manoeuvrability
The Typhoon uses an unstable airframe configuration that cannot be controlled by a human pilot without the aid of the onboard computers. The theoretical 'pressure point' or 'centre of lift' where lift generated by the canards and large wing surface can be considered to act is in front of the aircraft's centre of gravity. This creates a tendency to flip up and go out of control, but when harnessed by the Typhoon's software this tendency translates into extreme agility.

Air-to-air combat
The Typhoon carries a 27mm Mauser cannon for close-range combat, backed up by two short-range air-to-air missiles on the outer wing pylons. Up to six beyond-visual-range air-to-air missiles can be carried, with four on semi-recessed fuselage stations and one under each wing. Up to three external fuel tanks can be carried without reducing this load.

Flexible loadout
The Typhoon has a total of 13 stations for external stores. The fuselage hardpoints are each dedicated to a single system – the centreline can carry a fuel tank and the other stations can only carry medium-range air-to-air missiles. The outer wing pylons are dedicated to short-range air-to-air missiles. The other three stations under each wing can carry a range of ordnance, with the middle station wet plumbed for fuel tanks if additional range is required.

EF2000 TYPHOON

LOAD 1 — Swing Role

1. 2x GBU–24
2. 4x IRIS–T
3. 4x AIM–132 ASRAAM
4. 2x Storm Shadow
5. 1x 1000l (264gal) fuel tank
6. 2x ECM pod

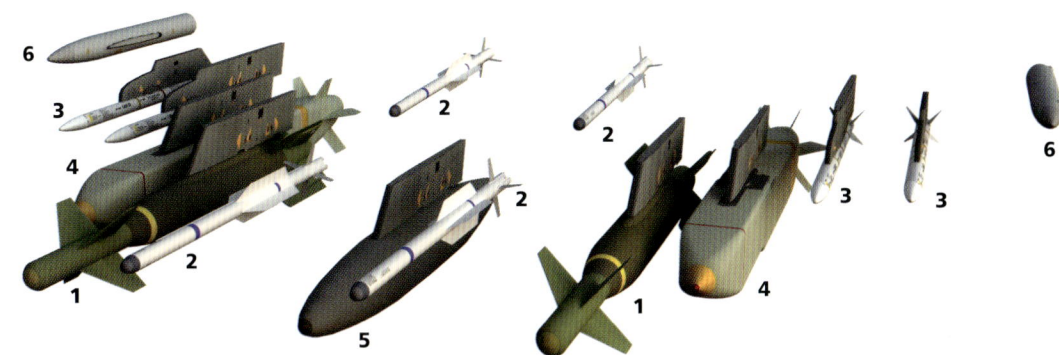

LOAD 2 — Swing Role II

1. 2x GBU–24
2. 4x Meteor
3. 4x AIM–132 ASRAAM
4. 2x Storm Shadow
5. 1x 1000l (264gal) fuel tank
6. 2x ECM pod

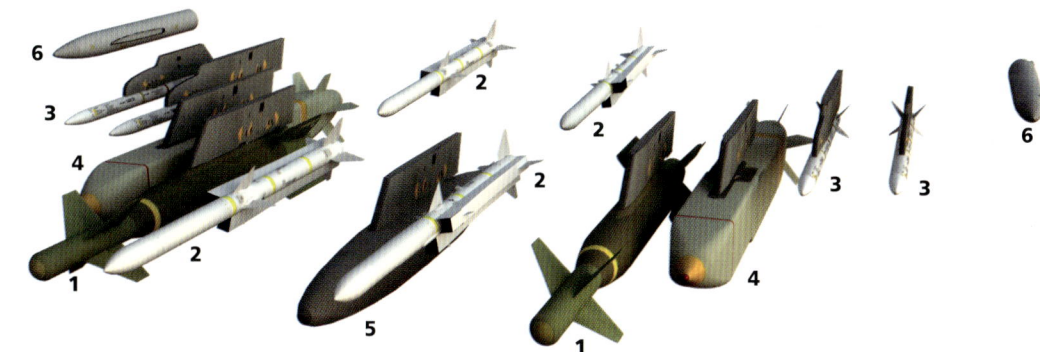

LOAD 3 — Air Superiority

1. 6x IRIS–T
2. 2x AIM–132 ASRAAM
3. 3x 1000l (264gal) fuel tank
4. 2x ECM pod

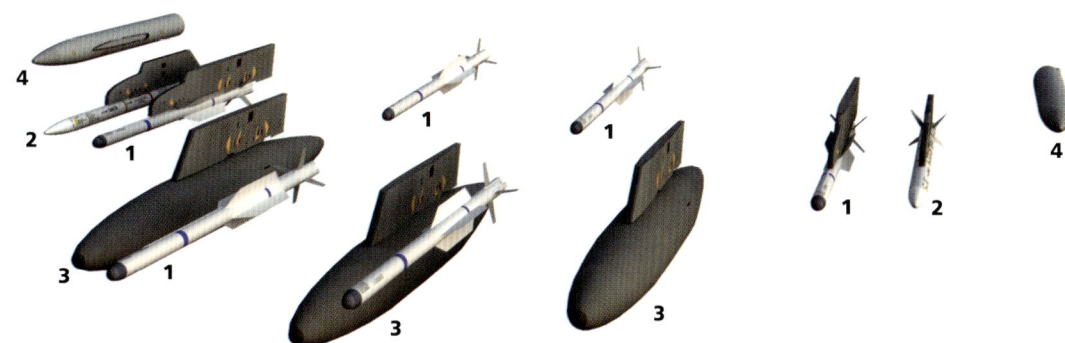

MODERN AIR-LAUNCHED WEAPONS

Above: Despite its small dimensions the Typhoon can carry a tremendous array of weapons, often in the same loadout. Its capability to switch rapidly between roles, possibly during a mission, makes it attractive in a world of tightening budgets.

The Typhoon is built by an international consortium involving companies based in four different European nations. It is in service with the air forces of Austria, Germany, Italy, Spain and the United Kingdom, and has attracted interest from nations within and outside of Europe. Some potential users have requested a carrier-capable version, which may or may not be feasible. An aircraft of this kind would have to compete with the broadly similar French Rafale for customers, and such a limited market might not justify the costs incurred in developing a carrier-capable version.

In order to meet the requirements of several operators, the Typhoon had to be an extremely flexible aircraft. But flexibility was one of the key requirements of the nations involved, so this was not a serious obstacle. No air force has a budget as large as it would like, so the concept of a single aircraft that could be transferred from one role to another as needed made good sense in an era of increasingly stringent defence budgets.

Multi-role capability

By equipping both strike and air-superiority squadrons with the same aircraft, air forces can make significant savings. In addition, enabling common training of ground crews, rather than requiring personnel to become acquainted with different aircraft saves not only money but time. Spares availability and procurement are also simplified, and there are cash savings possible in larger orders of aircraft and spares rather than small-volume purchases of different systems to support a range of aircraft.

The disadvantages of using aircraft with multi-role capabilities can be a reduced performance in one or all roles and an excessively high price tag. This meant that the design process was not an easy one, though it was assisted by an arrangement whereby each nation bought aircraft in tranches. Each tranche could incorporate upgrades and refinements made as a result of experience with earlier production aircraft.

The end result of the process was an extremely agile aircraft capable of reaching supersonic speeds without the use of afterburners, known as 'supercruise'. However, this is not possible when flying with external fuel tanks or bulky stores under the wings.

The delta-wing configuration, with a foreplane rather than a tailplane, drew on previous European experience with aircraft of this type, offering good lift and agility plus low drag at high speeds. To improve agility, the configuration is designed intentionally to be aerodynamically unstable.

Although not specifically a 'stealth' aircraft, the Typhoon incorporates a number of features designed to reduce its radar cross-section. The engines, a major source of strong radar return, are concealed by the fuselage shape and positioning of their intakes, while the shape of wings and other major surfaces is designed to reduce return. Some weapons are carried in recessed mounts, reducing the amount of radar energy they reflect, and energy-absorbent coatings are used on many surfaces.

Along with advanced radar, which includes an automated emission-reduction system, the Typhoon uses a passive infrared search and tracking system, enabling the aircraft's crew to scan for targets and threats without emitting detectable radar pulses. The range of an infrared system is less than that of radar, but the stealth benefits of low emissions are considerable. The same system can also be used to assist in the ground-attack mode.

The pilot is assisted by an advanced fly-by-wire system that accepts voice commands in addition to manual inputs. The system alerts the pilot when there is a risk of control loss, and in some circumstances can effect an automatic recovery. Many critical functions are accessed using fingertip controls located on the stick and throttle, including weapons and defensive-systems activation. The cockpit and controls were also designed to help the pilot remain conscious and functioning through sustained high-g manoeuvres.

Below: A Typhoon flying with a reduced warload. It is, of course, not necessary to load up every pylon. Fewer external stores means less drag, with consequent savings in fuel or an increase in combat range without the need to carry external fuel tanks.

MODERN AIR-LAUNCHED WEAPONS

LOAD 3

Air Superiority II

1 6x AIM–120 AMRAAM
2 2x AIM–132 ASRAAM
3 3x 1000l (264gal) fuel tank
4 2x ECM pod

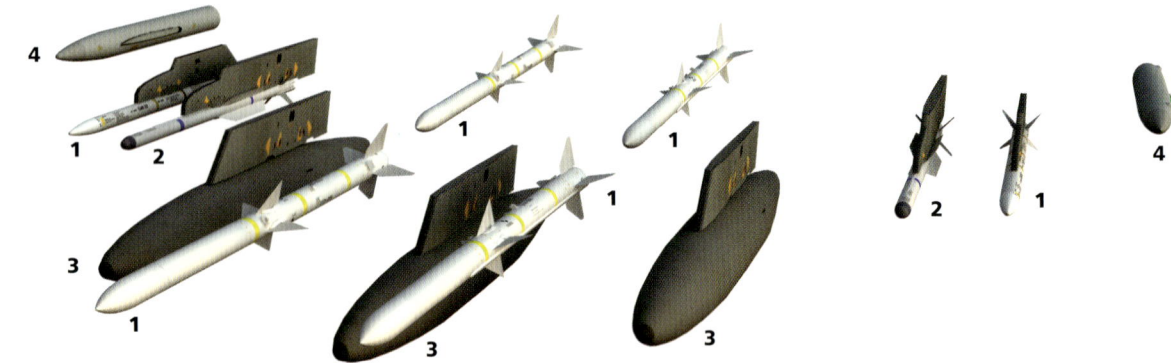

LOAD 4

Air Interdiction

1 2x AIM–132 ASRAAM
2 4x GBU–24
3 4x IRIS–T
4 1x LITENING targeting pod
5 2x ECM pod

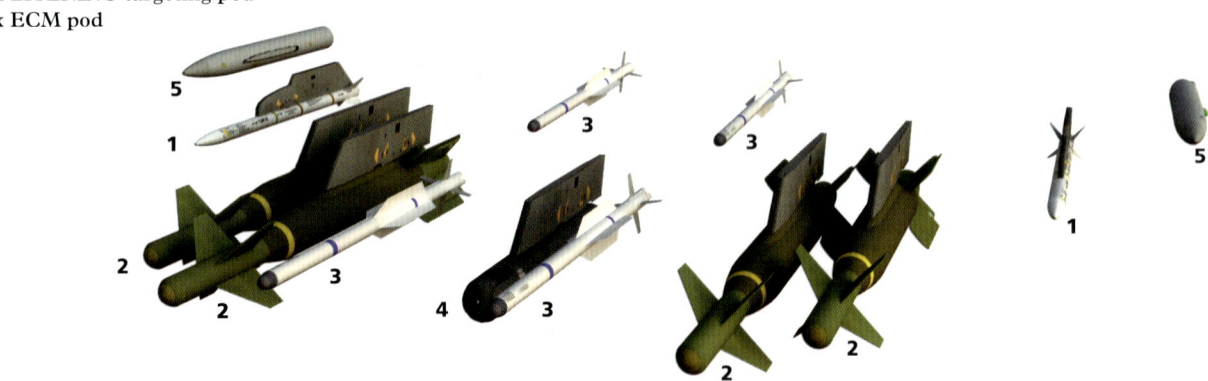

LOAD 5

SEAD

1 2x AIM–132 ASRAAM
2 2x ALARM
3 2x GBU–24
4 4x IRIS–T
5 2x ECM pod

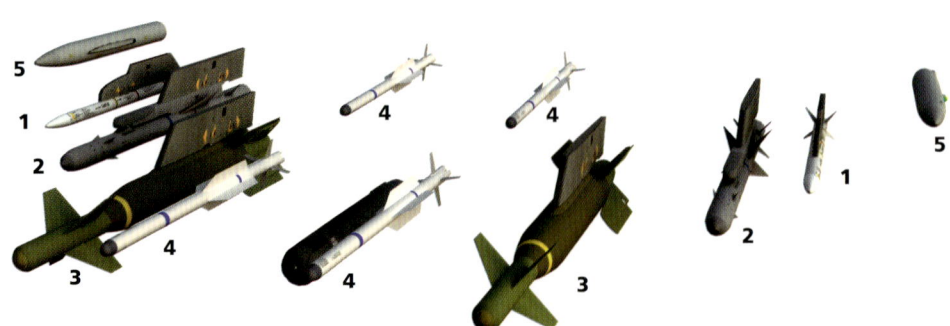

EF2000 TYPHOON

The Typhoon has 13 hardpoints for weapons or other stores – four semi-recessed fuselage stations and a centreline mount, plus four pylons under each wing. For air-to-air combat it can carry short-range and beyond-visual-range missiles plus its 27mm cannon. Short-range missiles can be launched 'off-boresight', i.e. without aiming the aircraft at the target. Coupled with its impressive manoeuvrability, this provides significant advantages in a dogfight.

For the strike role, the Typhoon can carry a range of weapons including AGM–84 Harpoon and anti-radiation missiles for anti-ship and SEAD missions respectively. Other standoff weapons include Storm Shadow cruise missiles and Brimstone anti-armour weapons. The Paveway family of laser-guided bombs are used with the LITENING targeting pod, and JDAM GPS-guided munitions can also be used. By carrying up to three fuel tanks instead of weapons (one on the centreline and one under each wing), the Typhoon's range can be improved.

Export successes

Typhoons are produced using a workshare arrangement based on the number of aircraft purchased. There are four production facilities, including one each in Germany, Italy, Spain and the UK. Each builds a different set of parts, but the final assembly of aircraft destined for each country is handled by its own plant. This arrangements spreads out the economic benefits, in terms of skills, technology and jobs, between the participating countries.

The Typhoon has no combat history as yet, but performance in exercises and evaluation flights seems very promising. Eurofighters have defeated F-15s, F-16s, F/A-18s and Mirage F-1s in exercise, often without sustaining any losses even when outnumbered. RAF Typhoons have conducted successful interceptions of foreign aircraft (a Russian Tu-95) in the air-defence role, and have been deployed to the Falkland Islands where they replaced a force of Tornados previously stationed there. Italian Typhoons have been operationally deployed to enforce airspace sovereignty over Albania. However, the only real trial of a combat aircraft is actual warfare, and this is yet to take place involving a Typhoon.

The Typhoon is just beginning its career and is likely to remain in service, with upgrades, for many years to come. Exports to countries outside the four manufacturing nations have already been made, with Austria and Saudi Arabia taking deliveries. Other interested nations may include Japan, India, Greece, Canada and Denmark. The main competitor in this field is the F-35 Lightning II. The F-22 Raptor is subject to an export ban and in some ways is made less attractive by the fact that it is a dedicated air-to-air platform. For tis reason, the Typhoon may represent a better all-round investment.

Above: This Typhoon is armed for ground attack, with six laser-guided bombs. Medium-range air-to-air missiles are not carried, though short-range weapons are. The latter produce little drag and are useful for self-defence; the benefits of omitting them from a warload are usually negligible.

MODERN AIR-LAUNCHED WEAPONS

The Typhoon is clearly a dogfighter, with canards for manoeuvrability and a bubble cockpit to improve the pilot's field of view. Its small size is an asset in a close-in fight, but does not preclude carrying large missiles and other bulky ordnance.

LOAD 6 — Maritime Strike

1 2x AIM-132 ASRAAM
2 4x Harpoon
3 4x IRIS-T
4 3x 1000l (264gal) fuel tank
5 2x ECM pod

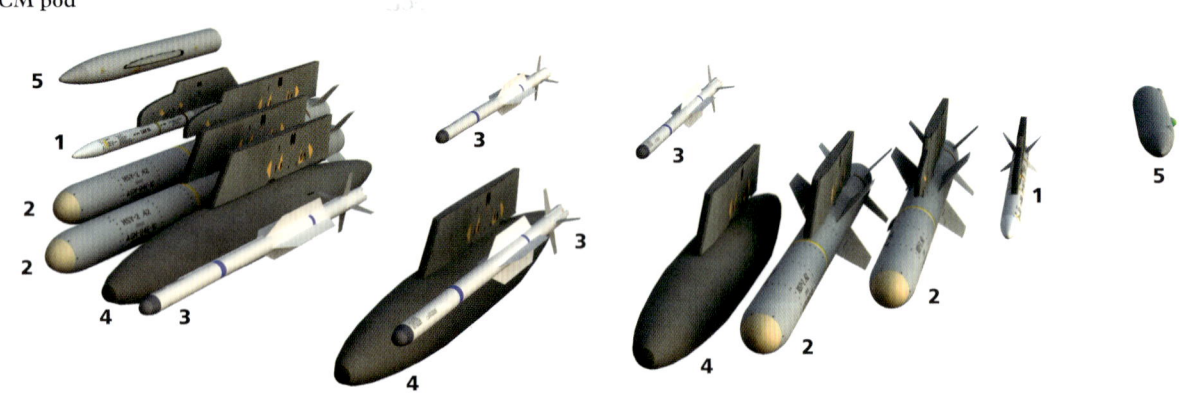

LOAD 7 — Close Air Support

1 18x Brimstone
2 2x AIM-132 ASRAAM
3 4x IRIS-T
4 1x 1000l (264gal) fuel tank
5 2x ECM pod

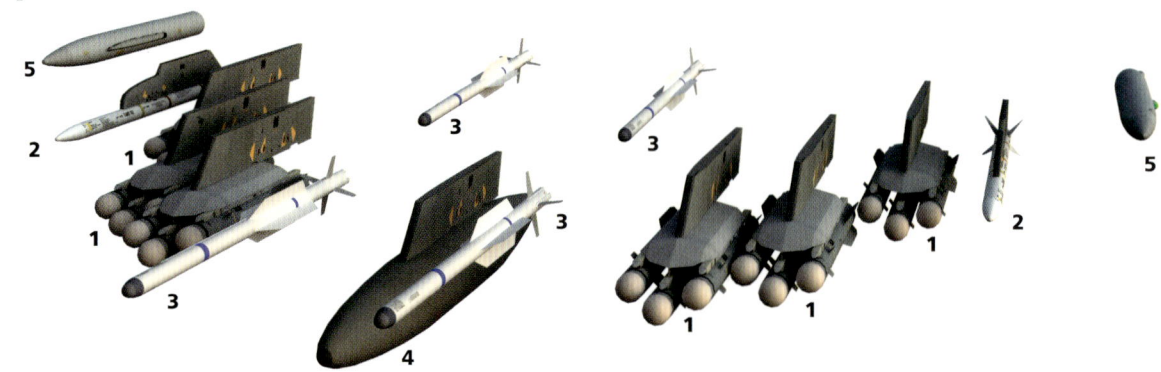

EF2000 TYPHOON

Swing-Role Mission Profile

It is not always possible to predict exactly what a given aircraft will be called upon to deal with in the course of a mission, or what sort of targets of opportunity may arise. This is especially true of aircraft carrying out long missions or held 'on call' to support friendly forces. The Eurofighter's 'Swing Role' configuration is designed to allow extreme flexibility, albeit at the cost of carrying less of any given weapon type than a plane configured for a particular mission.

A Eurofighter taking off in Swing-Role configuration carries a fuel tank and its internal gun in addition to external stores. It can undertake lengthy missions or loiter for a considerable time whilst awaiting instructions, and can fall back on its 27mm cannon once other stores are expended. However, it is more likely that the Typhoon would switch to other roles or return to base once its stores for a given mission were expended. For example a Eurofighter than had expended its ground-attack weapons could switch to flying top cover for other aircraft, perhaps swapping roles with those that had expended their ordnance.

For air-to-air combat the Eurofighter carries four Beyond-Visual-Range and four 'dogfight' missiles, enabling it to fight its way to a target or engage in ad-hoc interceptions. Ground-attack capability against a range of targets is provided by missiles and laser-guided bombs. These weapons might represent overkill against some targets, but the point of this configuration is that it can deal with whatever it encounters.

In addition to the capability to engage a range of targets, this configuration allows flexibility and redundancy to be built into a strike package. The loss of one or more aircraft en route to the target weakens the strike as a whole, but cannot eliminate capability in any one area. Thus the strike package cannot be 'mission killed' by the loss of all aircraft carrying a critical weapon system.

Using a mulitrole configuration such as this makes it possible to switch a strike package to different objectives, possibly against an entirely different type of target, mid-mission. Aircraft that have expended their ground attack weapons can then be retasked to join the counter-air mission before returning to base. Flexibility of this sort is highly useful in a rapidly changing battle environment.

Typhoons on a training mission, carrying centreline fuel tanks and short-range air-to-air missiles only. The Typhoon uses an integrated Armament Control System to monitor its weapon status and handle all aspects of weapon selection and launch.

MODERN AIR-LAUNCHED WEAPONS

Rafale

The Rafale is a delta-wing single-seat multi-role combat aircraft. It is carrier-capable and is small enough not to require folding wings for carrier operations. Although an empty Rafale is a little heavier than an F-16, its maximum takeoff weight is considerably greater, enabling it to carry more fuel and ordnance. The Rafale is in service with the French air force and navy, and has been offered for export.

Fuselage mounts
The Rafale mounts a 30mm cannon in its fuselage and in addition has six fuselage hardpoints (five on the naval version). These can carry a wide range of weapons including cruise missiles and even a nuclear missile in addition to the same stores as the wing pylons.

Wing stations
There are three pylons under each wing plus wingtip rails for short-range 'dogfight' air-to-air missiles. The three main pylons can accommodate a range of weapons including guided bombs, anti-ship missiles and air-to-air missiles. Unguided bombs and rockets can be carried, but would not normally be deployed by this aircraft.

External fuel capacity
The Rafael's centreline station and the inner two of its wing pylons are 'wet plumbed', meaning that they can carry external fuel tanks. If larger tanks (2000L [530gal] instead of 1050L [280 gal]) are used, three can be carried, on the centreline and inner wing pylons.

RAFALE

LOAD 1 — Air Superiority

1 2x AIM–132 ASRAAM
2 5x AIM–120 AMRAAM
3 2x 2000l (528gal) fuel tank

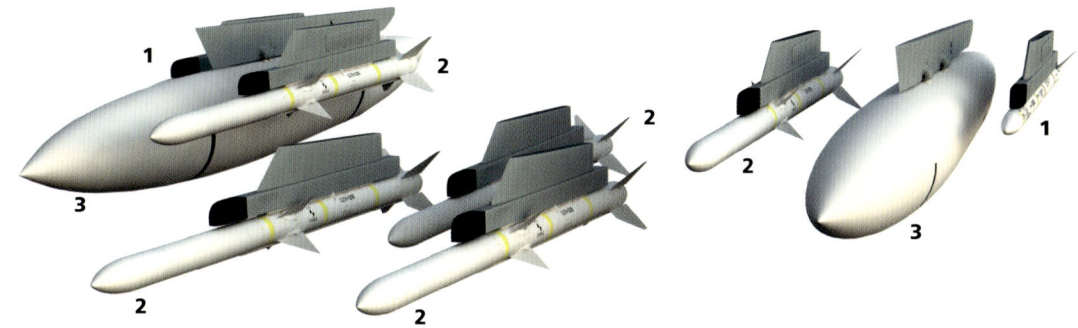

LOAD 2 — Multi-role

1 4x AIM–132 ASRAAM
2 2x AIM–120 AMRAAM
3 4x AGM–65 Maverick
4 1x 3000l (792gal) fuel tank

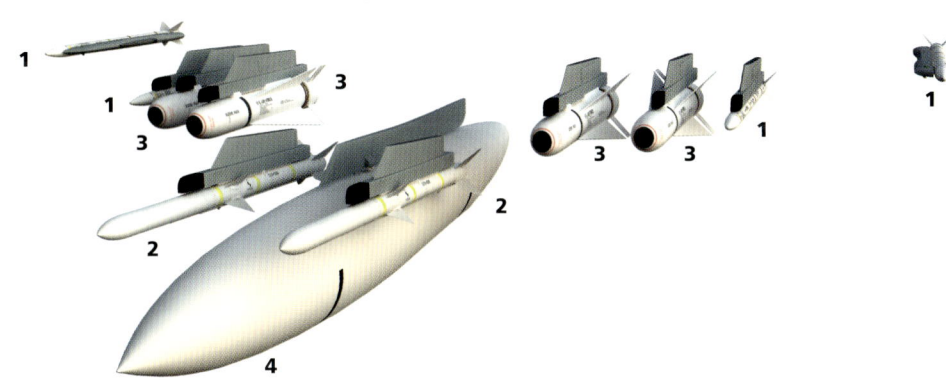

LOAD 3 — Precision Strike

1 4x AIM–132 ASRAAM
2 5x GBU–12

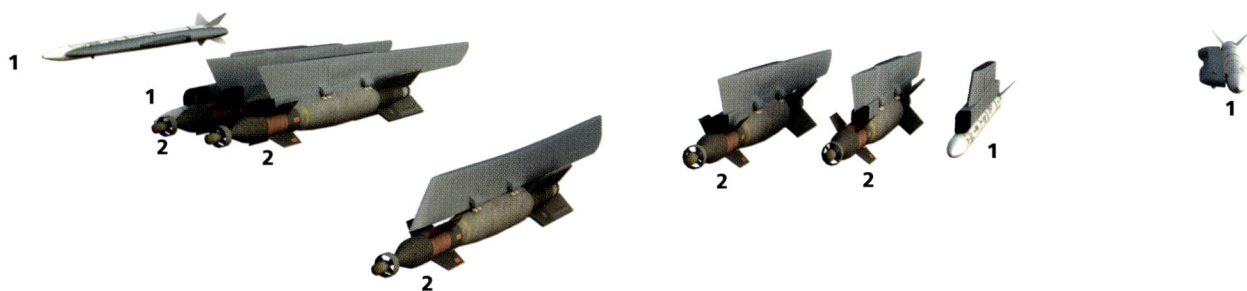

MODERN AIR-LAUNCHED WEAPONS

Above: A Rafale in flight carrying three external fuel tanks. This reduces the amount of pylon space for weapons, but there is still room for three Brimstone anti-armour weapons under each wing.

French defence planners recognized a need for a single aircraft that could replace several existing designs. The Navy needed a carrier-capable aircraft to replace its Super Etendard attack jets and its Crusader fighters. The Air force required a replacement for the Jaguar for the strike role and the Mirage 2000 for air defence. The new design also had to be capable of reconnaissance, strike and interdiction missions with guided, unguided and nuclear weapons where necessary.

First flying in 1986, the Rafale entered service in 2000. Like many such aircraft, it is produced in batches, with improvements incorporated into aircraft produced later. The F1 batch was delivered as an air-superiority platform, with the intention to later upgrade these aircraft to full capability. F2 models were delivered with air-to-ground missile capability, and F3 aircraft were delivered with full capability from the outset.

Later models are able to make use of a range of equipment pods, including the Damocles laser-designation pod, which can also carry infrared systems. Advanced radar and reconnaissance pods can be carried by F3 models, with the capability to pass data back to a ground station in near real time. Rafales are also equipped for buddy-refuelling, allowing a longer-range mission to be carried out without the use of vulnerable tankers.

Rafale Variants

There are two Rafale variants; Rafale C and M. The designation D was used during development to indicate the 'somewhat stealthy' characteristics of the aircraft, but production models are designated Rafale C. This is the standard multi-role version used by the French air force. The carrier-capable model is designated Rafale M.

RAFALE

A two-seat version also exists, designated Rafale B, and is largely identical to the C model. Unusually, a large proportion of Rafales in service are two-seat B models. Many prospective missions are long or complex, or both, making it necessary for a second member of the crew to carry some of the workload. A two-seat naval version, designated first BM and then N, was postulated but was never built.

The Rafale's control system uses a Hands-on-Throttle-and-Stick (HOTAS) system, with an advanced cockpit display and touch-sensitive screens. Control is also assisted by helmet-mounted systems. The cockpit layout allows for a larger display in the same space, because there is no need to make space for switches around the display screen. The onboard radar system can track up to eight targets simultaneously and automatically prioritizes targets and threats to assist the pilot's decision-making process. It is backed up by a thermal search and tracking system.

Defensive Counter-Air Operations

Ideally an enemy air force will be defeated in its own airspace, by offensive action. However, this is not always feasible. Defensive counter-air capabilities include all measures taken to prevent enemy aircraft penetrating friendly airspace and carrying out their missions.

The first requirement is detection, which ideally occurs as early as possible. Airborne radar systems Airborne Early Warning (AEW) aircraft can often detect and track targets from greater ranges than their ground-based equivalents due to their elevated position. This makes them prime targets for the enemy's fighters, but AEW platforms are normally deployed deep in friendly airspace where they can be protected by fighters.

Early detection gives a good chance of early fighter interception. If a standing combat air patrol (CAP) is maintained, these aircraft can be directed to intercept the intruders more quickly than fighters that must take off and gain altitude before beginning their transit to the combat area. The delay is even longer if unprepared aircraft must be armed and fuelled before the mission begins.

If interception is impossible, it is still sometimes possible to pursue the retiring strike force and attack it. This does not protect a target that has already been attacked but it does inflict casualties on the enemy force and may reduce confidence in their ability to carry out future missions, which contributes to the counter-air campaign.

In the meantime, the defence of the target falls upon missile and possibly gun emplacements on the ground. Some air defence sites are primarily

The new generation of 'swing-role' fighters are meant to switch between strike and defensive counter-air roles at need. Once this Rafale has expended its bombs it can protect other strike platforms with its medium- and short-range air-to-air missiles.

concerned with Area Defence, using medium- or long-range weapons to attack enemy aircraft moving into the defended zone. Area defence may cover the region around a specific target or can be deployed on a route that hostiles are likely to take, either to or from the target.

Point-Defence, as the name suggests, is concerned with the defence of a specific point. Short-range missiles and guns are used for this mission, attacking enemy aircraft as they come in close to make their attack. Many point-defence weapons cannot hit high-flying aircraft but are effective against any target that comes in low to make an attack. Ground troops can use small arms and support weapons in a point-defence mode, though this is mainly effective against helicopters.

MODERN AIR-LAUNCHED WEAPONS

RAFALE

The small size of the Rafale is apparent in this side view. Modern designers can cram enormous capability into a small airframe. Coupled with precision-guided weapons, this makes for an extremely cost-effective package.

LOAD
 Anti-Shipping Strike

1 2x AIM–132 ASRAAM
2 4x Exocet
3 2x AIM–120 AMRAAM
4 1x 3000l (792gal) fuel tank

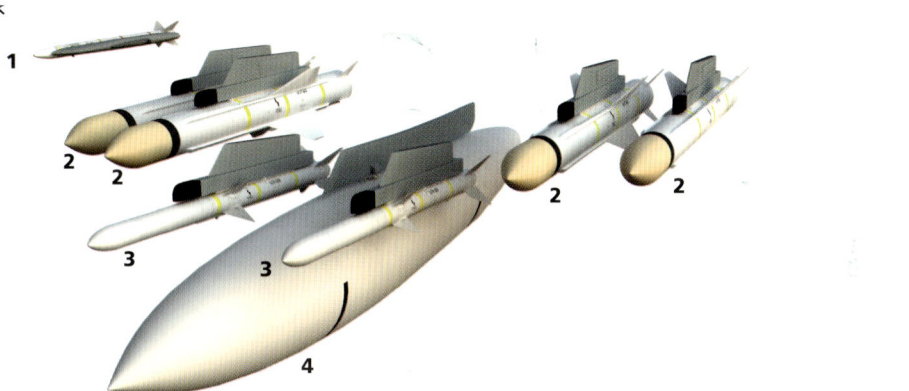

The light weight of the Rafale combined with its powerful engines enable it to use very short runways, reportedly needing as little as 400m (1300ft) to take off. Landing speed is also low, which is a big advantage for carrier operations. The delta wing and forward canard arrangement allows for very high agility, with the aircraft able to pull up to 11gs in an extreme manoeuvre, and stay airborne at speeds as low as 100 knots (115mph). The aircraft is designed to routinely handle 9g to –3g stresses and remain under control. It can reach Mach 2 at altitude. The Rafale mounts a 30mm cannon plus 14 hardpoints for weapons and stores: four under the fuselage, two on the centreline, three under each wing and a set of wingtip missile rails. The naval M version has one less hardpoint. For the air-to-air role, a range of missiles can be carried including ASRAAM, Sidewinder and Magic Infra-red guided short-range weapons, and Meteor, MICA and AMRAAM beyond-visual-range missiles.

Left: This dramatic underside view shows the flexibility of the Rafale's warload. In addition to air-to-air missiles and external fuel it still manages to carry six laser-guided bombs for precision-strike missions.

Ground-attack weapons include anti-radiation missiles for the SEAD mission, anti-ship missiles, anti-runway weapons and the Sagem AASM, a modular precision-guided bomb using GPS guidance and can also carry a thermal terminal seeker for greater accuracy. The Rafale can also carry out a nuclear strike with ASMP standoff missiles or launch conventional cruise missiles.

Discreet, not Stealthy

The Rafale is not a 'stealth' aircraft as such. Instead its designers describe it as 'discreet'. A combination of low

137

MODERN AIR-LAUNCHED WEAPONS

emissions, small size and techniques to reduce radar return combine to make it difficult to detect compared to earlier generations of fighters. However, its approach to stealth is an active one, making use of local territory to avoid detection where possible. An advanced terrain-following system allows high-speed flight at 30m (100ft), with the aircraft pulling up to 5.5gs in order to make best use of terrain cover.

The Rafale may also carry an active-cancellation system. This system automatically transmits a low-powered radar pulse almost identical to one striking the aircraft, but out of phase with it so that any return is cancelled out. This highly complex technology is very much in its infancy, but if it is successful it will go a long way towards making an aircraft invisible to radar.

The naval version of the Rafale was the first to enter service, as the replacement of France's ageing force

Below: Despite a passing similarity to the F-16 Fighting Falcon, the Rafale belongs to an entirely new generation of fighter aircraft with vastly greater capabilities.

RAFALE

LOAD 5
Anti-Shipping Strike (short range)

1 2x AIM–132 ASRAAM
2 4x Penguins

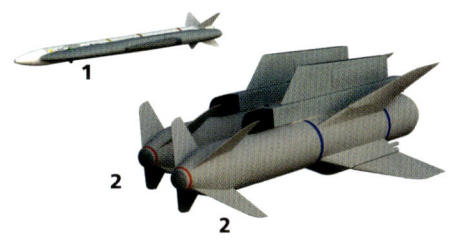
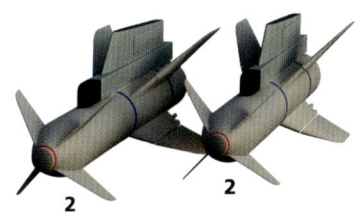

LOAD 6
SEAD

1 2x AIM–132 ASRAAM
2 5x ALARM
3 2x AIM–120 AMRAAM

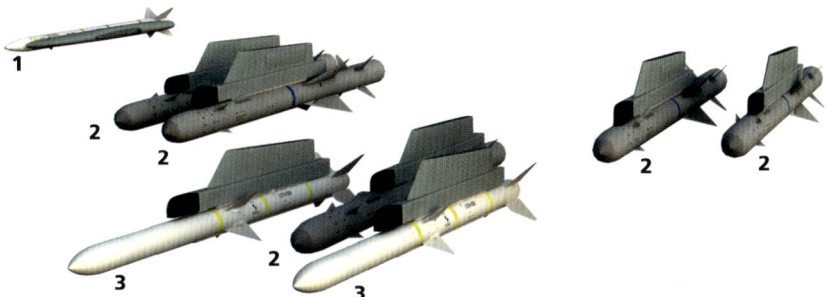
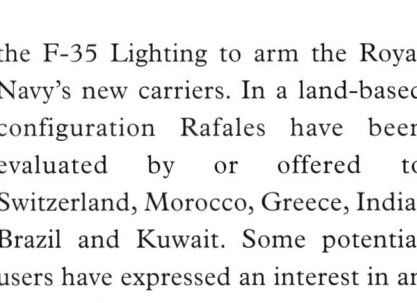

of carrier aircraft had become urgent. Although the official entry-to-service date was in 2000, it was not until 2004 that the force became fully operational. In the interim, Rafales flew escort and support missions over Afghanistan as part of an operational evaluation programme. The F1 versions then in use were not able to employ air-to-ground weapons, so were restricted to a fairly passive role.

A hurried conversion programme enabled a small force of Rafales to drop laser-guided bombs, though they had to rely on designation by other aircraft, including designs that the Rafale had been introduced to replace. In 2007, this force carried out its first strike missions, in support of Dutch troops fighting in Afghanistan.

Attracting Interest Abroad
In the international marketplace, the Rafale has been attracting considerable interest from various nations. As a carrier-capable fighter it has been considered by the United Kingdom as a possible alternative to the F-35 Lighting to arm the Royal Navy's new carriers. In a land-based configuration Rafales have been evaluated by or offered to Switzerland, Morocco, Greece, India, Brazil and Kuwait. Some potential users have expressed an interest in an upgraded version.

If such a variant is produced, this may become the new standard to which existing Rafales are upgraded. Whether or not this is the case, the Rafale is intended to arm the French air force and navy until at least 2040.

MODERN AIR-LAUNCHED WEAPONS

Gripen

The Gripen first flew in 1988 and entered service in 1997. It is a single-seat multi-role combat aircraft capable of cruising at more than Mach 1 without afterburners, and can carry both air-to-air and air-to-ground weapons plus anti-ship missiles. The Gripen is in service with the South African, Czech and Hungarian air forces in addition to that of its native Sweden. Sales have been made to the Royal Thai Air Force, with delivery scheduled for 2011. A two-seat trainer version is also available, which is identical in most ways to the combat variant but does not carry a cannon.

Canards
The Gripen's manoeuvrability is greatly enhanced by the use of forward canards, coupled with a design that exhibits 'relaxed stability'. Without constant corrections from the fly-by-wire system the Gripen will depart from stable flight. This makes the aircraft far more responsive to pilot commands and improves dogfighting performance.

Centreline station
The Gripen has seven external hardpoints: two wingtip stations; two pylons under each wing; and one on the centreline. Heavy loads restrict the aircraft's manoeuvring performance if they are carried under the fuselage rather than under the wings. Most commonly, a fuel tank is carried on the Gripen's centreline, though it can be dispensed with depending upon the mission.

Wing pylons
The outer wing stations can carry Sidewinder missiles, while the mid and inner pylons can accommodate a range of guided and unguided weapons, from cruise missiles to strafing rocket pods. Air-to-air and air-to-ground weapons can be mixed in the same loadout.

GRIPEN

LOAD 1
Multi-role

1 2x IRIS–T
2 2x AIM–120 AMRAAM
3 2x GBU–32 JDAM
4 1x 2271l (600gal) fuel tank

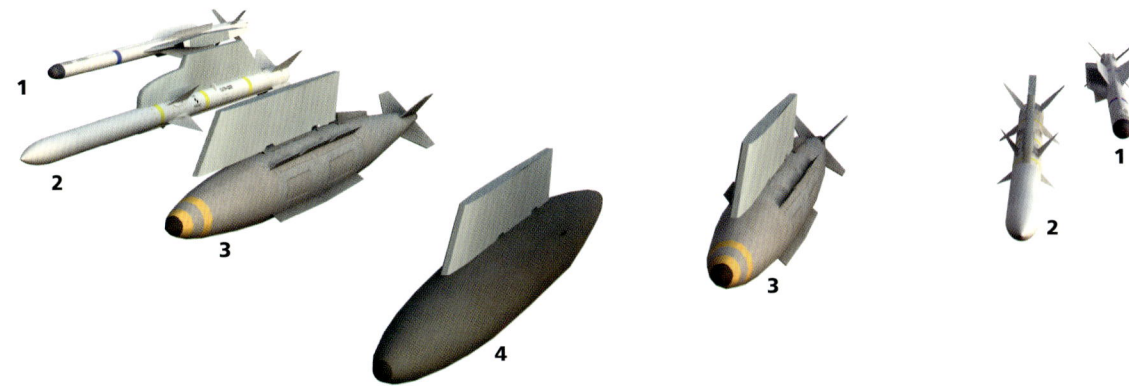

LOAD 2
Air Superiority

1 2x AIM–132 ASRAAM
2 4x Meteor BVRAAM
3 1x 2271l (600gal) fuel tank

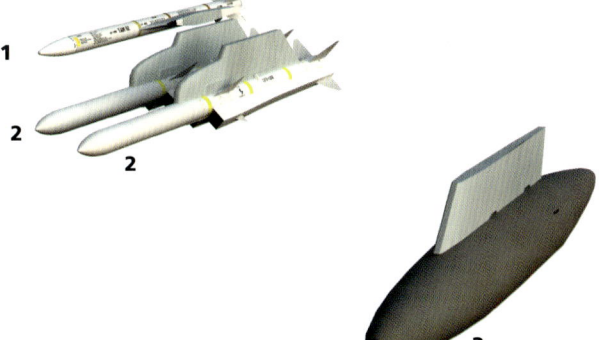
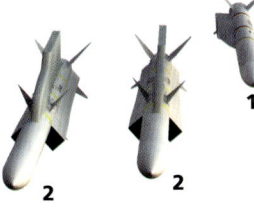

LOAD 3
Anti-Shipping Strike

1 2x AIM–9 Sidewinder
2 2x AIM–120 AMRAAM
3 2x RBS–15F
4 1x 2271l (600gal) fuel tank

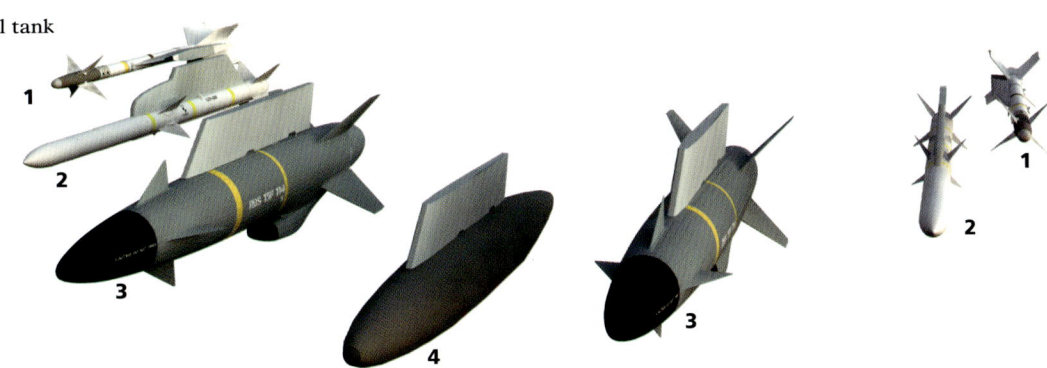

141

MODERN AIR-LAUNCHED WEAPONS

Above: The Gripen was designed from the outset to carry a range of weapons, using varied forms of guidance, and to swap between them without requiring reprogramming or hardware installation.

Sweden has a long history of armed neutrality, and produces a range of weapons and vehicles to secure its own defence. These are also offered for export, offsetting their development costs to some extent. It was such costs that caused the sudden cancellation of a light attack aircraft project in the middle of development. This placed the company responsible, Saab, in a difficult financial position and forced them to urgently find a new aircraft project that would attract government funding.

A single multi-role aircraft that could replace Sweden's existing fleets of Viggens and Drakens presented the only viable alternative. With defence spending under close scrutiny, it was necessary to offer a project that gave the maximum possible benefit from investment and building costs. Government specifications were stringent. The new aircraft had to be highly capable in the fighter, reconnaissance and attack roles, and foreign competitors would be allowed to bid for the contract.

Beating off rival bids to secure the contract, the Gripen emerged as an advanced delta-wing design with forwards canards to enhance and assist manoeuvrability. The airframe is as light as possible thanks to carbon-fibre materials being used wherever possible. A single engine design was chosen to keep weight and costs down, and flight testing showed that drag was significantly less than expected. This improves both flight and short-field performance, which means the Gripen is able to take off in a short distance and can use a reinforced road as a runway if necessary.

Makeshift Operation as Needed

The Gripen was conceived first and foremost to defend Sweden from invasion. Defence plans made provision for the fact that airbases might be destroyed or overrun, and required the Gripen to be able to

Sea-Skimming Anti-Ship Missile Attack

In many ways a warship is similar to a building or other land-based structure, and can be attacked in the same ways. However, ships have the ability to evade an attack, and often carry significant air defences, which can make a close-range attack suicidal. Guided weapons offer the ability to attack from outside the ship's lethal range, but some are more effective than others. GPS-guided weapons fly to a pre-set point rather than seeking a target; a moving ship may not be at the impact point when the weapon arrives. Laser-guidance is more capable against moving targets but, at sea, conditions are not always ideal for laser systems.

The weapon of choice for shipping strike is thus a self-guided missile, which seeks the target using either its thermal or radar signature. Launched from beyond visual range, the missile proceeds to the target area under its own internal guidance system. This generally uses inertial navigation and may be augmented by GPS guidance. The missile flies low to avoid detection for as long as possible, reducing the time available to the target for countermeasures or attempts to shoot down the missile. Its altitude is controlled by a radar altimeter, which measures the distance between the sea surface and the missile.

Once within attack range, the missile seeks its target using either active radar or passive thermal guidance. A missile using active radar guidance emits radar pulses that can be detected by the target, announcing its presence, while thermal guidance homes in on the heat signature of the vessel and does not produce emissions that can be detected.

Anti-ship missiles are designed to explode after penetrating a hull or superstructure, causing a blast effect inside the target for maximum destructive potential. This does not require such a robust weapon as the type needed for 'bunker-busting', because a modern warship's hull is rather less resilient than several feet of concrete. In fact, a 'bunker-buster' warhead might pass straight through a warship without detonating. This would cause a certain amount of damage but would probably be survivable. An internal explosion is far more likely to result in a sinking or, at the least, cripple the target.

Maritime strike missions are often carried out over considerable distances, making extra fuel tanks a necessity. This reduces warload, but makes it possible to dispense with vulnerable tanker aircraft for most missions.

MODERN AIR-LAUNCHED WEAPONS

Above: A Gripen flying without external fuel, carrying four AGM-65 Maverick missiles. The Maverick must be locked on to the target by the pilot but, once launched, it seeks the target without further human input, enabling the pilot to do other tasks.

operate from makeshift airstrips. Resupply might come from caches of pre-positioned stores or be delivered by a crew operating out of the back of a truck. In order to avoid being caught helpless on the ground, the Gripen was designed with a turnaround time of 10 minutes.

These features were designed to allow an embattled Sweden to keep fighting for as long as possible, but they are also attractive to potential operators overseas, who might wish to base their fighters well forward using rudimentary facilities, or who may find the fast turnaround extremely useful for high-tempo operations.

Having created an effective aircraft to provide the defence needs of its native country, the Gripen's designers set about incorporating improvements and modifications intended to make it attractive to international buyers. These include a retractable refuelling probe, NATO-standard weapons pylons and improved electronics. Reconnaissance and Forward-Looking Infrared (FLIR) pods were also integrated into the basic design along with refinements in pilot comfort.

The Gripen can achieve Mach 2 in 'clean' configuration (i.e. with no external stores) at high altitude, and around Mach 1.15 at low level. It is highly manoeuvrable at low and high speed, and can use its canards as air brakes during landing. All wheels of the undercarriage are braked, with an anti-skid system to reduce stopping distance on the ground. Indeed, Gripen pilots have carried out aircraft carrier landings in the simulator, despite the aircraft not possessing an arrester hook. This has never been attempted in real life, however.

Control uses a fly-by-wire system, with many functions accessed by buttons on the throttle and stick. The system is triply redundant and has a simple analogue back-up system in case the main system becomes inoperable. The fly-by-wire system compensates for the deliberate instability of the design, allowing the pilot to retain control while gaining the benefit of improved agility. The system can also help keep the aircraft under control if it has been damaged. The canards can be used as a replacement for disabled ailerons, and the system can correct for altered flight characteristics that have been brought about by damage.

The pilot has three multi-function displays plus a head-up display. Earlier models used monochrome displays but later Gripens have full-colour displays. These allow the pilot to quickly access data from flight systems as well as radar, infrared and a

GRIPEN

A Gripen with Taurus cruise missiles under the wings. Taurus is a fire-and-forget (i.e. self-guiding) cruise missile. It is an expensive weapon, intended for use against high-value and probably well-defended targets.

LOAD 4

Standoff Bunker-Busting

1 2x AIM–132 ASRAAM
2 2x Taurus KEPD 350
3 1x 2271l (600gal) fuel tank

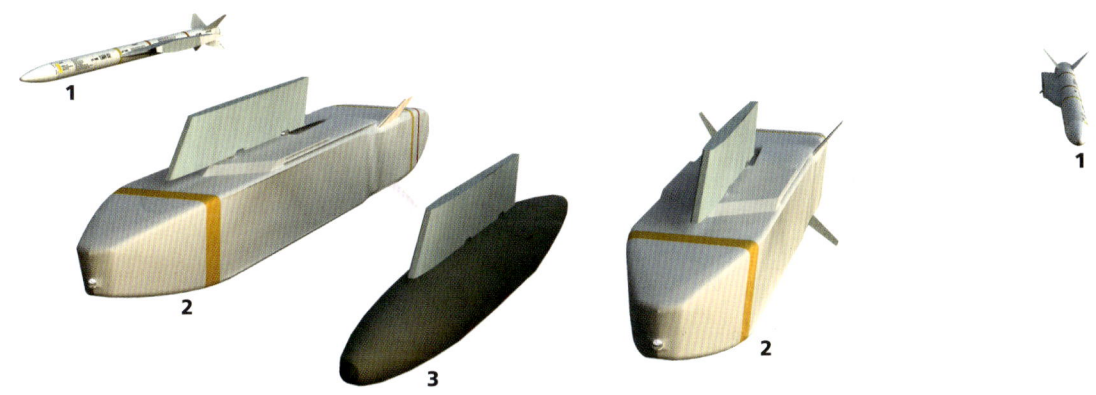

LOAD 5

Precision Strike

1 2x IRIS–T
2 4x GBU–12

MODERN AIR-LAUNCHED WEAPONS

reconnaissance pod, if one is carried. Cooperation between aircraft is improved by the use of Tactical Information Data Link System (TIDLS), which shares sensor information between aircraft via a secure radio link. Data is also transmitted to ground-based stations, allowing the mission to be evaluated in real time and updates sent back to the pilots if necessary. This ability to cooperate has a number of uses. The

most obvious is for one aircraft to provide radar data to others in the vicinity, ensuring that they are not detected by their emissions. Alternatively, one aircraft can use electronic countermeasures against a target while another tracks it, or radar data from several aircraft can be combined. This allows triangulation of a target or the cooperative use of different radar frequencies to defeat enemy jamming attempts.

The Gripen has seven external hardpoints for stores and weapons. In addition to a centreline pylon and wingtip rails there are two pylons under each wing. For the air-to-air role, the Gripen carries AIM–9 Sidewinder missiles on the wingtip rails and MICA or AIM–120 AMRAAM on the wings for beyond-visual-range engagements. Later versions are capable of using other missiles including Meteor and IRIS–T.

Ground-attack and anti-shipping weapons include the Taurus KEPD 350 standoff missile, RBS-15 radar/GPS-guided anti-ship missile and 225kg (500lb) laser-guided bombs. Unguided weapons including 225kg (500lb) mk8 bombs, cluster munitions and rocket pods can also be employed. A combination of ground-attack and air-to-air weapons can be accommodated, allowing a midair switch from air superiority to attack missions and back.

An Attractive Option

The Gripen has found favour with several buyers, but lost out to the F-16 in Poland and the EF2000 in Austria. Both deals involved either political or economic considerations as well as military ones. It remains an attractive option for many buyers, not least as it requires a smaller team of support personnel. The Gripen may find more buyers in future, probably among countries wishing to replace aircraft such as the Mirage or Mig-21.

Left: The Gripen was built with the export market in mind, and has already attracted overseas orders. Multi-role aircraft are a popular buy in today's defence marketplace.

MODERN AIR-LAUNCHED WEAPONS

Su-27/30/35 & Chinese variants

The Su-27 is a twin-engine, single-seat air-superiority fighter. It is extremely agile in flight and has become famous for performing manoeuvres such as the Cobra at airshows. The Su-27 is in service with several air forces worldwide and continues to be a strong competitor in the export fighter marketplace.

Canards
The Su-27 has spawned a number of increasingly sophisticated variants. Among the additional features of these aircraft are forward canards that enhance the aircraft's dogfighting performance and allow manoeuvres at extremely high angles of attack.

Defensive systems
The Flanker carries a multi-mode radar jammer in wingtip pods. This is backed up by a radar warning receiver and both thermal and radar decoy dispensers. The system is integrated to provide protection to other aircraft in the same formation.

Wing and fuselage hardpoints
In addition to its 30mm cannon the Su-27 has up to 10 external hardpoints, depending on the variant. Three pylons are located on each wing, with two on the engine intakes and two more on the centreline. These normally carry air-to-air weapons, though the aircraft can also carry guided and unguided air-to-ground weapons.

SU-27/30/35 & CHINESE VARIANTS

LOAD 1

Air to Air/Naval Interceptor

1 4x AA–11 (R73E)
2 6x AA–10 (R27)
3 Sorbtsiya ECM pod

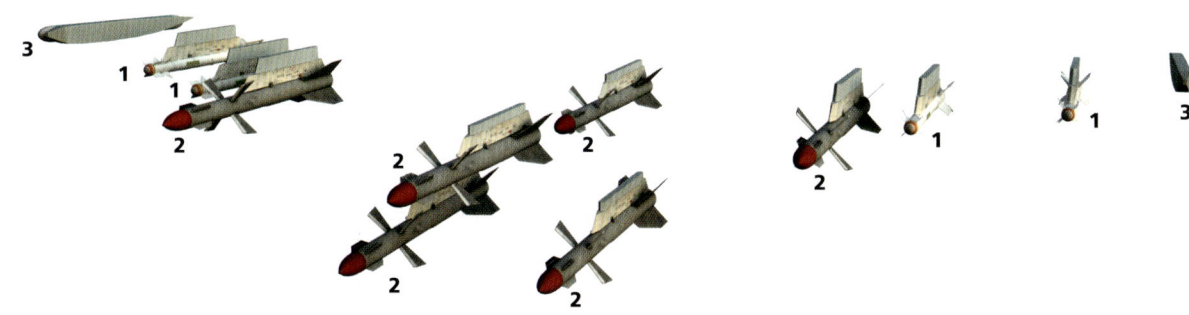

LOAD 2

SEAD

1 4x AA–11 (R73E)
2 4x Kh–31
3 Sorbtsiya ECM pod

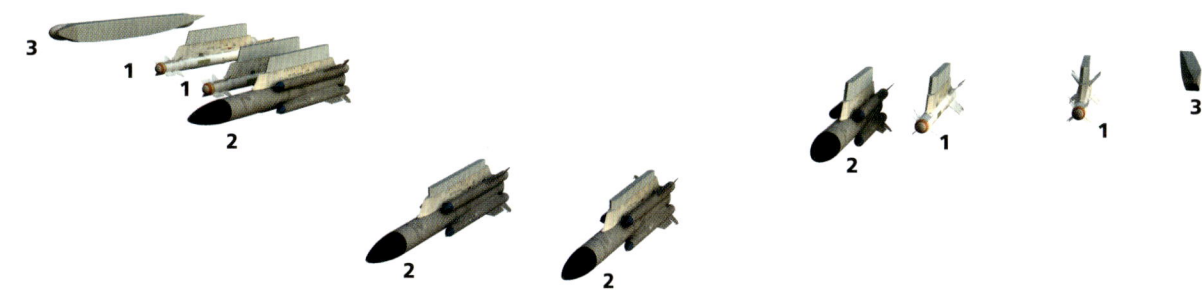

LOAD 3

Precision Strike

1 2x AA–11 (R73E)
2 4x KH–29
3 Sorbtsiya ECM pod

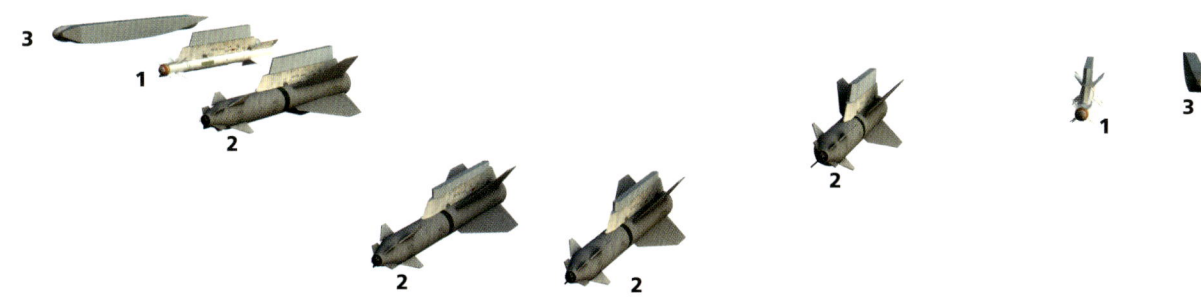

149

MODERN AIR-LAUNCHED WEAPONS

At the end of the 1960s, designers in the Soviet Union were tasked with creating an air-superiority fighter that could match the new generation of U.S. fighters then under development. The design requirements were tough, demanding not only Mach 2 or better performance but also extreme agility and excellent short-field performance. This would allow the new fighter to use rudimentary forward airstrips, keeping pace with an advancing ground campaign.

It was eventually decided that it would be far more cost-effective to build two different aircraft, each emphasizing some aspects of the original specifications. From this divergence came the relatively small and light MiG-29 and the larger, heavier Su-27, which first flew in 1977. This aircraft was given the NATO reporting name of Flanker, and entered service in 1982.

Small but agile

Despite its size the Flanker is a very agile aircraft, remaining stable and controllable even at very high angles of attack, i.e. when the aircraft's nose is well 'above' the direction of flight, such as in a hard turn at low speed. This is thanks partly to aerodynamics and partly to the quadruply-redundant fly-by-wire (FBW) system that controls the aircraft. The FBW system automatically corrects attempts by the pilot to pull excessive g forces or to perform manoeuvres that may result in a spin. Despite the limits imposed by the automatic systems the Flanker can perform manoeuvres at 9 to –3.5gs.

The Flanker's engines are both robust and reliable, and have proven capable of functioning normally even in very rough airflow. This permits extreme manoeuvres such as the Cobra, which might cause engine

Below: An Indian Air Force Su-30 takes part in Red Flag international exercises in the USA. Ironically, U.S. fighters are routinely used in the Red Flag exercises to simulate combatants; this aircraft may have flown against F-15s pretending to be Flankers.

SU-27/30/35 & CHINESE VARIANTS

The easiest ways to distinguish an Su-27 from a Mig-29, apart from size, are to look for the characteristic 'droop' of the Flanker's nose and the 'stinger' located between the engine exhausts.

LOAD 4 — Ground Attack

1 2x AA–11 (R73E)
2 4x S–8 rocket pod
3 4x KAB500L bomb
4 Sorbtsiya ECM pod

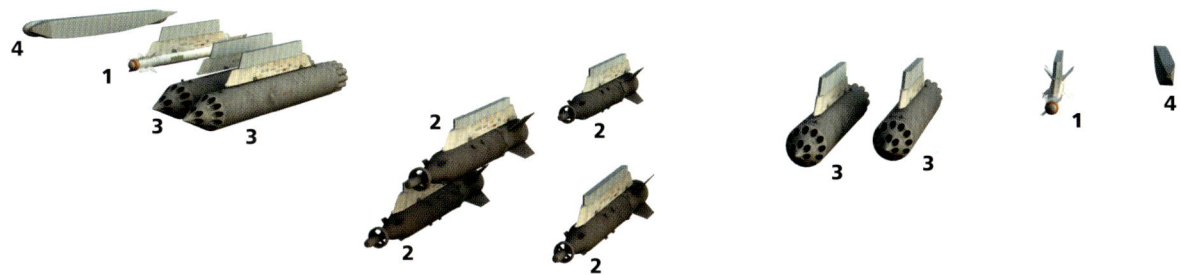

failure in another aircraft. Fuel economy at cruising speeds is sufficient to permit a good operational range, and the engines themselves are protected from damage as far as possible. They are placed as far apart as is practicable in a fighter, increasing the chance that one engine will survive any damage that cripples the other. Additionally, mesh screens placed over the intakes prevents ingestion of debris from a poorly prepared field.

The pilot is assisted in combat by a pulse-doppler radar system that grants look-down, shoot-down capability and can track 10 targets simultaneously while engaging two with missiles. The Flanker is also equipped with an infrared search-and-tracking system and a laser rangefinder.

NATO analysts designated the original prototypes as Flanker-A, and the early production model as Flanker-B. The designation Flanker-C was given to a combat-capable two-seat trainer version called Su-27UB by its designers. A naval version, with canard foreplanes and folding wings for carrier operations, was reported as Flanker-D in the West but is designated Su-33 in Russia.

The current standard version in Russian service is designated SU-27SM and incorporates upgrades including a higher payload and better electronics. However, a number of other members of the Flanker family have appeared over the years, some as export models and some as essentially new aircraft based on the Su-27 airframe. The Su-30 is a two-seat multi-role fighter/strike platform, while the Su-27IB or Su-34 is a two-seat strike version. Designated Flanker-E in the West, the Su-35 is an upgraded air-to-air model, while the Su-37 employs vectored thrust.

Missile Weaponry

The Su-27 carries a 30mm cannon and a mix of medium-range and short-range missiles for air-to-air combat. Missile targeting is assisted by helmet-mounted systems that allow a missile

151

MODERN AIR-LAUNCHED WEAPONS

LOAD 5
Cruise Missile Delivery

1 2x AA–11 (R73E)
2 4x KH–59
3 Sorbtsiya ECM pod

LOAD 6
Standoff Anti-Shipping Strike

1 2x AA–11 (R73E)
2 6x KH–31A
3 Sorbtsiya ECM pod

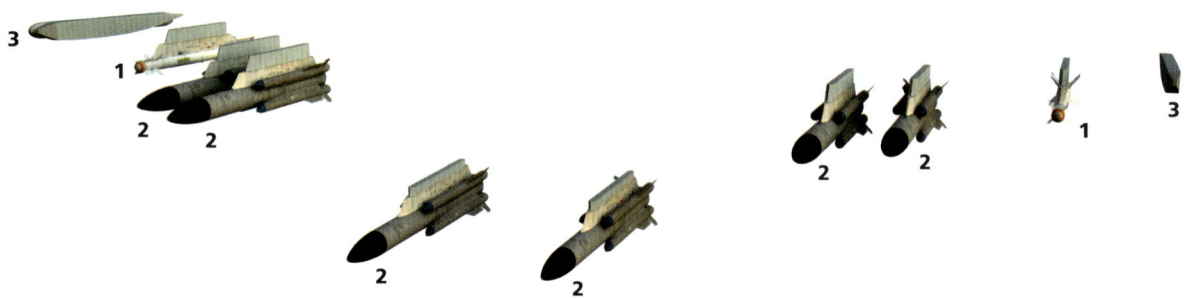

to be aimed off-boresight by looking at the target. The Flanker can also use a range of unguided ordnance including both freefall and retarded bombs, plus rockets and cluster munitions.

Flankers have been in front-line service with the Russian air force for years, but have seen little action. There are unconfirmed reports of Flankers flown by Russian pilots serving with the Ethiopian armed forces downing several (probably seven) Eritrean MiG-29s in 1999–2000. Ethiopian Su-27s have also carried out ground attacks against targets in Somalia.

Flankers are in service with several post-Soviet Union states, including Russia, Belarus, Kazakhstan, the Ukraine and Uzbekistan. In addition, many nations, such as Angola, Eritrea, Ethiopia, Indonesia, Malaysia, Venezuela and Vietnam, have taken delivery of small numbers. Other nations, such as Mexico, have given the Flanker consideration, but have not proceeded with purchases for various reasons.

The major export customers for the Flanker family are India and China. The Indian Air Force took delivery of a Flanker variant designated Su-30MKI (or Flanker-H in the West), which was redesigned as a multi-role platform with canards and vectored thrust for improved manoeuvring. The electronic and avionic systems were also upgraded. In addition to those bought from Russia, India acquired a license to build more Flankers in its own factories.

Right: The Su-30MKI, an Su-27 variant, forms the mainstay of the Indian Air Force's fighter fleet, and will do so for a considerable time to come. Production of new Flankers is still ongoing under license.

SU-27/30/35 & CHINESE VARIANTS

MODERN AIR-LAUNCHED WEAPONS

Bomb Flight Profiles

When a bomb is dropped from an aircraft, it proceeds forward at the same speed that the aircraft was travelling at, though gradually slowed by air resistance (drag). The bomb's initial downward velocity is zero if the plane was flying exactly level at the instant of release. If it were diving at the point of release the bomb will have some downward momentum; if the bomb is released in a climb then it will travel upwards for a time before gravity causes it to begin to fall.

Theoretically, the point of impact can be precisely calculated if the height, angle of dive or climb, and speed of the aircraft is known. However, in practice even a well-timed launch does not guarantee impact at the aim point. The primary reason for this is the effect of wind, which obviously becomes more pronounced the further the bomb has to fall. High-level bombing was found to be highly inaccurate during World War II for this reason, combined with the difficulty of accurately calculating a release point.

One way to improve accuracy is to dive towards the target. However, dive-bombing can only be carried out by relatively small aircraft and requires a predictable approach that makes the aircraft easy for ground fire to hit. A better option is to drop the weapon while flying at a low level, but this risks damage to the aircraft when the bomb detonates as it will strike the target almost directly under the plane. Retarded free-fall bombs solve this problem by deploying brakes to slow the weapon, retarding the trajectory down so that the aircraft can fly out of the blast zone. Retarded bombs dropped in this manner are not subject to significant wind effects and can be delivered with impressive accuracy.

Guided bombs can be 'lofted' in the general direction of the target by a low-flying aircraft, which pulls up, releases the weapon and then turns away towards safety. This allows a measure of standoff capability to be achieved with an unpowered weapon. The weapon can shorten its flight path once it begins terminal guidance, but it cannot extend its range. Thus bombs are usually lofted towards a point well over the target.

Using retarded bombs allows an aircraft to deliver its payload from low altitude, increasing accuracy. The bombs are slowed by air brakes or parachutes, enabling the aircraft to clear the danger zone before the weapons strike the ground.

SU-27/30/35 & CHINESE VARIANTS

LOAD 7 Iron Bomb

1 2x AA–11 IR Missiles
2 8x KAB500 bombs
3 Sorbtsiya ECM pod

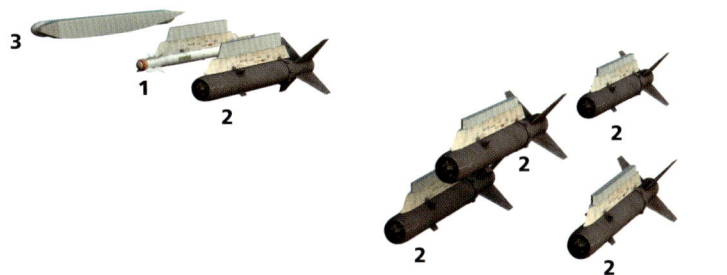
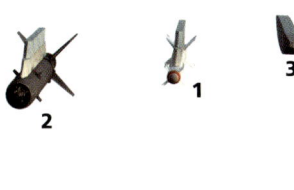

China was the first major overseas buyer of Flankers. After an initial buy of Su-27s, a series of improved versions were developed for offer to China. Some were successful, others less so. Chinese designers then created a variant of the Su-27 designated J-11B. This aircraft was largely the same but used Chinese electronics systems.

The J-11B led to a dispute between China and Russia, as the original contract included a clause whereby China would not export the Su-27. The J-11B was deemed by the Russian authorities to be a close copy and thus in violation of the agreement. Russia cancelled China's production license for the SU-27 and its variants and ceased delivering components. This did not prevent new negotiations for a naval version of the Flanker from taking place, but this deal fell through, not least due to Russian concerns that a cheaper locally produced version would soon find its way on to the international market.

The Flanker family is still in production, and will be India's primary air-superiority fighter for some years to come. In fact, projected manufacturing will not peak until 2017–18. The latest upgraded models are highly competitive in terms of both combat capability and export potential, so it is likely that the Flanker family has a long future. However, the Su-35BM model has acquired the nickname of 'the last Flanker', suggesting that the current models have moved so far from their origins as to be a wholly new aircraft.

Below: The latest Flander-A variants are so different from the original Flanker-A that they may be considered to be entirely different aircraft.

MODERN AIR-LAUNCHED WEAPONS

MiG-29/35

The MiG-29 Fulcrum is a twin-engine, single-seat fighter produced in land-based and carrier-capable variants. Primarily intended for the air-superiority role, the Fulcrum also has some ground-attack capability. It entered service with the Russian air force in 1983 and has since been widely exported.

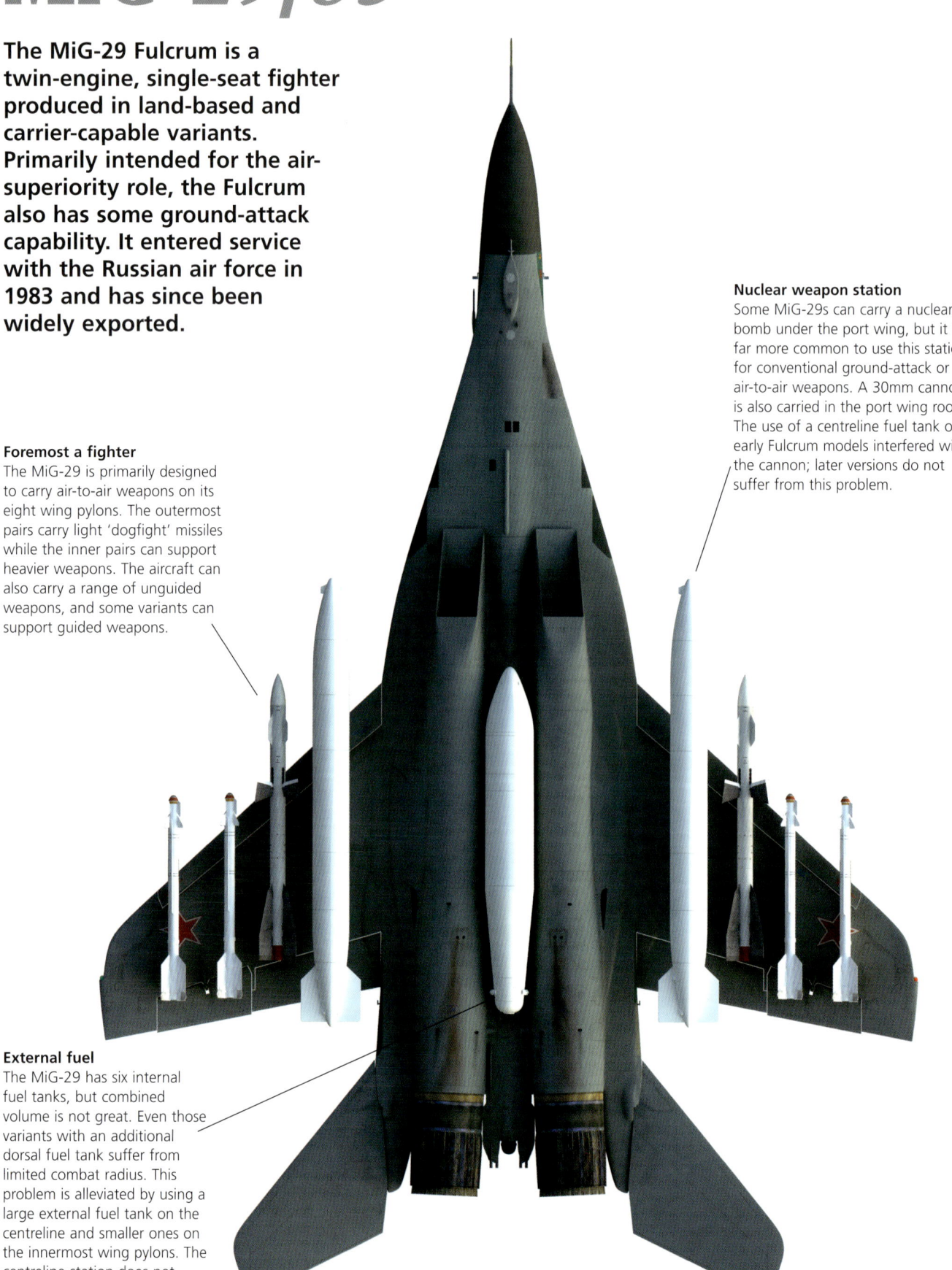

Nuclear weapon station
Some MiG-29s can carry a nuclear bomb under the port wing, but it is far more common to use this station for conventional ground-attack or air-to-air weapons. A 30mm cannon is also carried in the port wing root. The use of a centreline fuel tank on early Fulcrum models interfered with the cannon; later versions do not suffer from this problem.

Foremost a fighter
The MiG-29 is primarily designed to carry air-to-air weapons on its eight wing pylons. The outermost pairs carry light 'dogfight' missiles while the inner pairs can support heavier weapons. The aircraft can also carry a range of unguided weapons, and some variants can support guided weapons.

External fuel
The MiG-29 has six internal fuel tanks, but combined volume is not great. Even those variants with an additional dorsal fuel tank suffer from limited combat radius. This problem is alleviated by using a large external fuel tank on the centreline and smaller ones on the innermost wing pylons. The centreline station does not carry weapons.

MIG-29/35

LOAD 1
Air to Air

1 4x AA–11 (R73E)
2 4x AA–10 (R27)

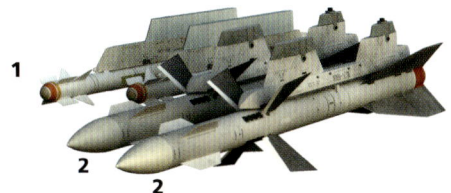
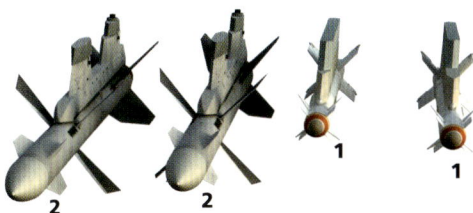

LOAD 2
Air-to-Air Extended-Range Interception

1 2x AA–11 (R73E)
2 4x AA–10 (R27)
3 2x 1500l (396gal) fuel tank
4 1x 1900l (502gal) fuel tank

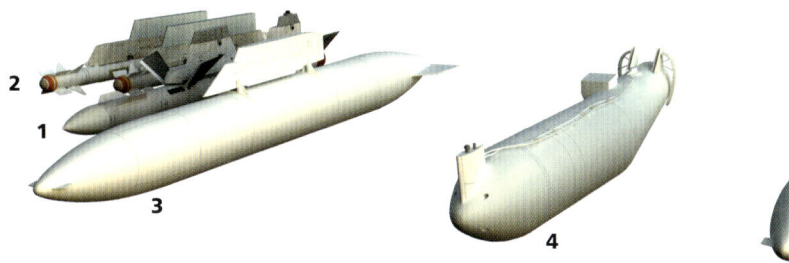
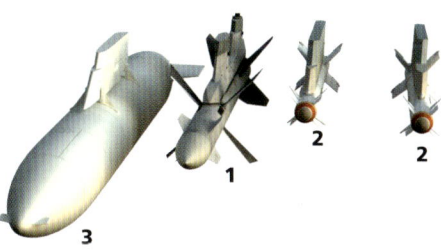

LOAD 3
SEAD

1 4x Kh–31
2 1x 1900l (502gal) fuel tank

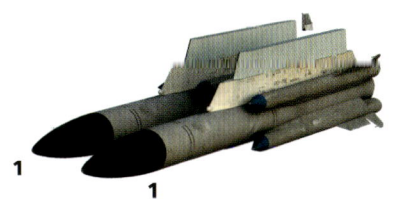
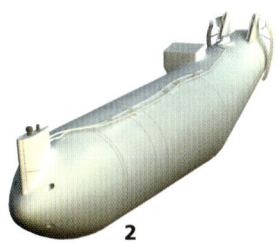
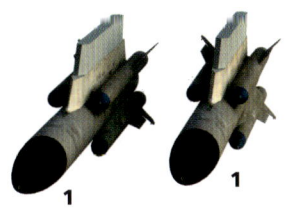

MODERN AIR-LAUNCHED WEAPONS

Above: A Polish MiG-29 deploys its braking chute. The Polish Air Force inherited Soviet-era aircraft but has replaced them with Western designs starting with the F-16 and eventually including F-35 Lightnings.

The MiG-29 was developed in the 1970s in response to the new generation of Western fighters then taking shape, including the F-15 and F-16. This necessitated significant advances in both performance and electronics systems over the MiG-25, which was built as an interceptor rather than an air-superiority fighter. Where the MiG-25 was designed for high speed in a relatively straight line, so that it could intercept high-flying bombers, the Fulcrum was expected to meet the best Western fighters on equal terms at any range.

The Fulcrum is a very agile aircraft capable of pulling 9gs in subsonic manoeuvring and attaining a top speed of Mach 2.25 at altitude. Its turn rate was greatly improved compared to previous Russian fighters, and both resistance to and recovery from a spin or other control loss are good.

Capable of operating from very rudimentary forward bases, the MiG-29 has dual-mode air intakes for the engines to protect them from foreign-object damage. While on the ground, the main intakes are closed and air is drawn in through louvres in the top of the wing. Once airborne and away from the threat of loose objects, the intakes are opened and operate normally.

The Fulcrum has been built in a wide range of variants for various specialist purposes and foreign customers, in addition to a programme of upgrades, which also spawned a great many variants. NATO reporting name taxonomy recognizes a number of broad types, while different designations are used by the manufacturer to delineate specific upgrade packages or variant capabilities. It is usually sufficient for observers to identify MiG-29s by their general type using the Western reporting names rather than as precise models, which can often be difficult to tell apart.

The Original Fulcrum

To Western analysts, Fulcrum-A is the original air-to-air model, with its associated two-seat trainer being named Fulcrum-B. The model named Fulcrum-C by NATO is slightly enlarged and has significant upgrades. It corresponds to a number of models including those designated MiG-29S and MiG-29SM by the designers. The Fulcrum-C was given a distinct dorsal hump to carry an ECM system, and has improved flight electronics and better controls. The SM version can use guided weapons including missiles and laser-guided bombs.

Fulcrum-D is the NATO reporting name for the carrier-capable version, which is designated MiG-29K by its manufacturers. A series of upgraded and export variants of this model also exist. The Western designation

Air Campaign 1: Counter-Air and SEAD Phase

The first stages of the air campaign are aimed at enemy air defences, especially radar installations. Those that are not destroyed are forced to remain off the air much of the time to avoid being attacked with radar-homing weapons. As the campaign develops, more of the enemy's missile and radar sites are identified and attacked, gradually wearing down defensive capabilities and opening the way for other missions.

Meanwhile, airfields are targeted with strikes intended to crater the runway and destroy parked aircraft, while operations are disrupted by strikes with cluster bombs and other anti-personnel weapons. If possible, enemy fighters are drawn out and ambushed by superior forces as they attempt to intercept real or feigned strikes.

Counter-air and SEAD operations carry on as the campaign develops, but gradually resources can be shifted to other missions as the threat diminishes.

Fighters like the MiG-29 can contribute to the counter-air and SEAD campaign in the same mission, attacking radar sites, and then ambushing any response force with air-to-air missiles. If they are successful enough the fighters can all but put themselves out of a job.

MODERN AIR-LAUNCHED WEAPONS

Above: The MiG-29 is one of the world's most widely exported fighter aircraft. However, many export buyers lack the technical expertise to enable them to get the most from their Fulcrum fleet.

Fulcrum-E was assigned to a variant not put into production, and the Fulcrum-F is otherwise known as the MiG-29M OVT or MiG-35, which incorporates a thrust-vectoring system for improved manoeuvrability.

MiG-29 Variants and Upgrades

Other MiG-29 variants include the multi-role MiG-29M and MiG-29UBM, its two-seat trainer version. The M models are sometimes referred to as MiG-33 instead. Further variants and sub-variants have also appeared, such as upgrades to earlier land- and carrier-capable versions, each with their own factory designation. The MiG-29SMT, for example, is not a new model but represents older Fulcrums that have received an upgrade package to extend their service lives and increase capability. The naval equivalent is designated MiG-29SMTK.

The Fulcrum carries a 30mm cannon and has seven hardpoints. In the air-superiority role it can accommodate short-range dogfight missiles as well as beyond-visual-range weapons. Unguided bombs, napalm canisters, cluster munitions and rockets can be deployed by all variants, which gives the Fulcrum a limited close-support or strike capability. Some variants can make use of laser-guided weapons for precision-strike missions, including bunker-busting penetrator bombs. Nuclear bombs can also be delivered by some aircraft.

MIG-29/35

The MiG-29 closely resembles a smaller Su-27. This is hardly surprising. Both aircraft arose out of the same design project, which was split when it became apparent that too much was being asked of a single design.

LOAD 4 — Ground Attack

1 2x AA–11 (R-73)
2 6x S–8 rocket pod
3 1x 1900l (502gal) fuel tank

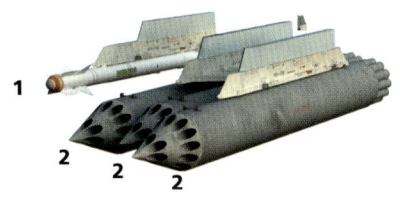
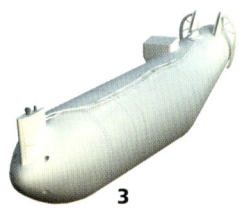

Land-based Fulcrums have been purchased by many air forces, including Cuba, Eritrea, Malaysia, Romania, Sudan and Yemen. India operates land-based Fulcrums and has purchased the carrier-based version for its naval aviation forces. Many export MiGs are configured to be compatible with Western weapons, as well as Russian ones, which is attractive to many potential buyers.

A changing world political situation has resulted in many air forces operating both Russian and Western aircraft and weapon systems, necessitating modifications to improve interoperability and reduce the chances of friendly-fire incidents. Thus in 2004 the Slovak airforce upgraded its Fulcrums with Russian cockpit systems and Western communications equipment systems including IFF (Identification-Friend-or-Foe). A joint project between Russian and Western firms was also initiated to convert Romanian MiGs, while those in Polish service required updating to ensure compatibility with Poland's new NATO allies.

MiG-29s have seen active service with several air forces, not all of which had the capabilities to make best use of them, so the aircraft's performance has not always lived up to its potential. During the conflicts arising from the break-up of Yugoslavia, Yugoslav MiGs served in the air-to-ground role, for which they were not very well suited. None were lost to ground fire and no air-to-air combat occurred.

As the Balkans conflict continued, Yugoslav MiG-29s engaged the Western fighters they were designed to counter, albeit in a biased contest. Yugoslavia was at the time under an embargo and no spares were available to maintain the Fulcrum force, which was kept flying by cannibalizing some aircraft to support others. Four of these poorly maintained MiG-29s were downed by F-15s, while two more shot down by F-16s in U.S. and Dutch service. Others were destroyed on the ground as part of the Allied counter-air campaign.

Fulcrums flown by Iraqi forces fared little better in the 1991 Gulf War.

MODERN AIR-LAUNCHED WEAPONS

Of those that ventured up to engage Coalition air units, five were shot down by F-15 Eagles, for no loss. Other MiG-29 pilots defected to Iran rather than face the Coalition in the air. Iran kept the aircraft and bought more from Russia.

There are reports that MiG-29s in Eritrean service were engaged by Ethiopian Su-27 Flankers during the 1999 conflict between these nations. The Flankers were crewed by Russian pilots and emerged victorious, though the Eritrean Fulcrums are credited with victories over Ethiopian jets of previous generations, namely MiG-21s and MiG-23s. Reportedly, Sudanese MiG-29s have operated in a ground-attack role against insurgents.

Those air forces that can train pilots adequately and provide suitable support facilities have had better results with the Fulcrum. The Indian air force was sufficiently pleased with its MiG-29s to enter into an extensive upgrade programme. In addition to good results on routine operations, the Indian air force deployed Fulcrums to protect ground-attack aircraft during the short conflict with Pakistan known as the Kargil War. No air-to-air combat took place, but Indian Fulcrums locked Beyond-Visual-Range missiles on Pakistani F-16s operating on their side of the border.

Evaluation of MiG-29s gained by Germany at the reunification of East and West Germany indicated that a well-flown Fulcrum might be superior to an F-15 in a dogfight. The use of off-boresight missile aiming, which was implemented by the U.S. Air Force some years later, was found to be devastatingly effective and, in addition, the MiG-29's slow-speed agility was found to be somewhat better than that of the Eagle. Thus the poor performance of the MiG-29 may not be due to deficiencies in the aircraft itself.

Below: Germany inherited a Fulcrum force at reunification, which was adapted to meet NATO standards. In 2003 the German MiGs were transferred to Poland, which has the largest Fulcrum fleet in NATO.

LOAD 5

Precision Strike (MiG 35)

1 2x AA–11 (R-73)
2 6x KH–29
3 1x 1900l (502gal) fuel tank

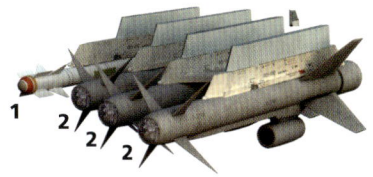
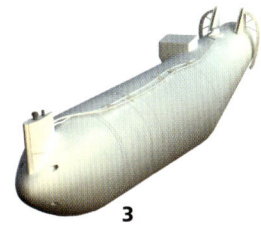

LOAD 6

Iron Bomb

1 2x AA–11(R-73)
2 8x KAB500KR bomb
3 1x 1900l (502gal) fuel tank

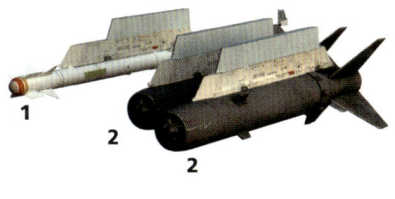
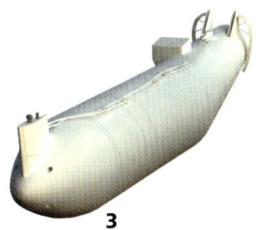
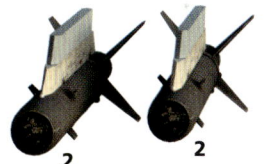

The Fulcrum remains in front-line service with a large number of air forces, and continues to spawn new variants. Older aircraft are being upgraded by both Russian and foreign firms, ensuring that they will remain in service for many years to come. This is despite concerns over the original lifetime estimate of 2500 flight hours. However, it has since been discovered that, with proper maintenance, a MiG-29 can expect a lifetime in the region of 4000 flight hours.

Continued Upgrades

The standard upgrade package on offer to existing users or purchasers of older Fulcrums brings the aircraft up to a level of capability designated MiG-29SMT by the designers. This incorporates upgraded radar and an infrared search-and-track system. New flight systems include digital fly-by-wire and better cockpit electronics. Continued upgrades will ensure the Fulcrum remains attractive to export customers for some years, and competitive in the combat environment.

In Russian service, MiG-29 fleet suffered from a lack of correct maintenance for many years, causing a proportion of the force to be retired prematurely. The remainder were earmarked to receive upgrades, and new aircraft were ordered, though not enough to replace the lost units. Nevertheless, the MiG-29 will probably remain in Russian service into the 2020s. Even when it is outdated, the Fulcrum lineage may continue with the MiG-35, which was derived from it.

MODERN AIR-LAUNCHED WEAPONS

MiG-31 Foxhound

The MiG-31, given the NATO reporting name of Foxhound, is a two-seat all-weather interceptor developed to replace the MiG-25 Foxbat. Initially flying in 1975, it was the first Soviet fighter aircraft to feature look-down, shoot-down radar capability, and the first to carry a passive electronically scanned array radar.

Fuselage recesses
The Foxhound carries up to four long-range radar-guided missiles in fuselage recesses. These stations reduce drag, which is critical for a high-speed interceptor expected to reach Mach 2.8 when necessary. Fuselage recesses cannot carry other weapons or fuel tanks.

Cannon bay
A six-barrel 23mm cannon is carried in a fuselage mount, but it was never intended that the Foxhound engage with guns if at all possible. The gun is prone to malfunction, occasionally seriously enough to detonate its ammunition and destroy the aircraft, so most Foxhounds fly without ammunition to save weight.

Wing pylons
The MiG-31 has four wing stations for ordnance. The outer pylons can carry pairs of short-range air-to-air missiles, while the inner pylons are equipped for medium-range air-to-air missile or, in some cases, anti-radiation missiles for the SEAD mission. External fuel tanks can sometimes be carried.

MIG-31 FOXHOUND

LOAD 1
Interceptor

1 2x AA–6 (R40T)
2 4x AA–9 (R–33)

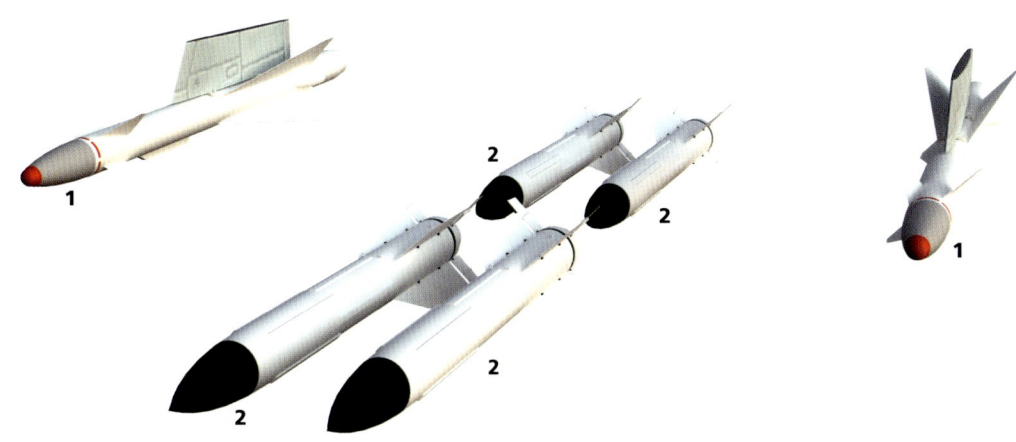

LOAD 2
Air to Air

1 2x AA–11 (R–73)
2 2x AA–6 (R40T)

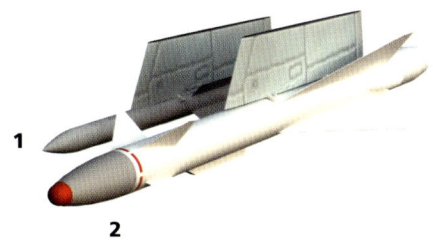  

LOAD 3
Air-to-Air II

1 4x AA–12 (R–77) Missiles
2 2x AA–6 (R40T) Missiles

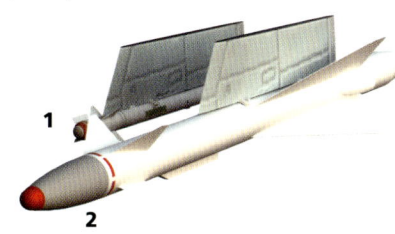 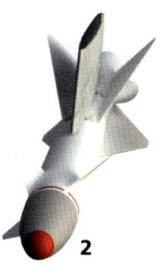 

165

MODERN AIR-LAUNCHED WEAPONS

Above: The MiG-31's interceptor role is apparent from its design features. It devotes a significant fraction of its takeoff weight to fuel for the sustained use of afterburners when racing to intercept intruders.

The Foxhound's predecessor, the MiG-25, caused some alarm in the West when it first appeared, but this apprehension was eventually found to be misplaced. The Foxbat turned out to be an interceptor rather than an air-superiority fighter, and its capabilities were not as great as they had at first seemed. Dogfighting was never its forte – the Foxbat was not designed to be an agile combatant. Indeed, as an interceptor its main assets were speed and climb rate.

However, the MiG-25's engines were inefficient, hampering low-altitude operations and shortening its combat range. High speeds quickly destroyed the engines, making the Foxbat much less capable. Rather than the deadly air-superiority aircraft it was first thought to be, the Foxbat turned out to be a merely adequate interceptor and no real threat to the F-15s that were expected to have to fight it.

Overcoming Deficiencies

Experience with the Foxbat showed that these deficiencies could be overcome. The MiG-31 Foxhound was thus intended from the outset to be able to operate at low altitudes, flying at subsonic speeds. It was also given far more efficient engines, which greatly extended its combat range, an important asset in an interceptor.

Top speed at altitude is 3,000km/h (1,850mph), corresponding to Mach 2.83. The Foxhound can reportedly exceed Mach 3, but only at the cost of damage to the airframe and/or engines. At sea level it can attain Mach 1.25, and has an operating range of 1200km (650nm) with a full payload. Although there is a multi-role variant, the Foxhound is very much a missile platform, and not a dogfighter. In a turning fight, the Foxbat would be outmanoeuvred very quickly. While it is capable of pulling a maximum of 5gs, most air-superiority fighters can achieve nearly twice that.

However, this is not the environment that the Foxhound was designed to function in. Interceptors, by definition, operate in or close to

MIG-31 FOXHOUND

Defeating Enemy Missiles

Ideally, enemy air forces and defences are suppressed and rendered unable to interfere in a mission, but this cannot be relied upon, so a combat aircraft must be capable of defending itself against enemy missiles. One method is to evade the missile by turning and diving or climbing in such a way that the weapon cannot follow. 'Turn towards the missile' was the basic concept behind evading early surface-to-air missiles, which were not manoeuvrable enough to deal with a close target.

Evasion is still valuable but modern missiles cope with most manoeuvres, so more countermeasures are required. Radar-guided weapons can be jammed by emitting a powerful signal that swamps the weapon's receiver, effectively blinding it. But some missiles can automatically switch to a home-on-jam mode to counter this effect. In response, many aircraft carry electronic countermeasures pods, while specialist Electronic Warfare aircraft accompany large strikes, protecting several other planes with their considerable capabilities.

Decoys attempt to seduce the missile into locking on to a more attractive target than the aircraft they are protecting, or at least confusing the missile as to which is the real target. Combined with evasive manoeuvres, decoys can be highly effective if they are launched at the right time.

Heat-seeking missiles can be countered by flares that offer a stronger heat source for the seeker to lock on to, while radar-guided missiles are distracted by bundles of chaff, such as aluminium-coated glass fibres launched in a cartridge and scattered by a small amount of propellant. Early missiles were extremely susceptible to decoys but modern seekers are much more selective, necessitating the deployment of increasingly sophisticated decoy systems.

An F-15E Strike Eagle executes a hard break as it deploys thermal decoy flares. A combination of manoeuvring and countermeasures can defeat most missiles, but advances in missile-seeker technology force decoy manufacturers to constantly update their systems.

MODERN AIR-LAUNCHED WEAPONS

Above: A MiG-31 without its nose cone. Many fighter aircraft carry their radar systems in the nose, where they can be easily accessed, and to keep them away from other systems that may cause interference.

friendly airspace where enemy fighters are uncommon. The MiG-31 is designed to quickly reach a firing position and launch missiles at hostile aircraft from a safe distance. It can engage targets flying as low as 50m (165ft) from the ground, using a lookdown, shoot-down radar that is not confused by the cluttered returns received from the ground. This enables the Foxhound to remain at a high altitude while it attacks. It can engage targets in the forward or rear arc, tracking some while scanning for others.

Space Tourism Applications

After entering service in 1982, variants of the MiG-31 began to appear. Not all of these are combat aircraft, because the MiG-31S is also used to train cosmonauts and to launch a suborbital glider for 'space tourism' applications. The MiG-31D variant, on the other hand, was to be able to launch anti-satellite missiles. However, this version has never entered service.

Advanced versions of the standard Foxbat have gradually emerged during its career. The MiG-31E carries a long-range phased-array radar that can track up to 10 targets simultaneously. This variant also carries an infrared scanning system. The MiG-31M model was given improved cockpit systems and the capacity to carry additional missiles.

MIG-31 FOXHOUND

The Foxhound has much in common with its predecessor, the MiG-25 Foxbat, but it is an altogether more cogent aircraft. Despite being the world's heaviest interceptor its rate of climb and top speed are very impressive.

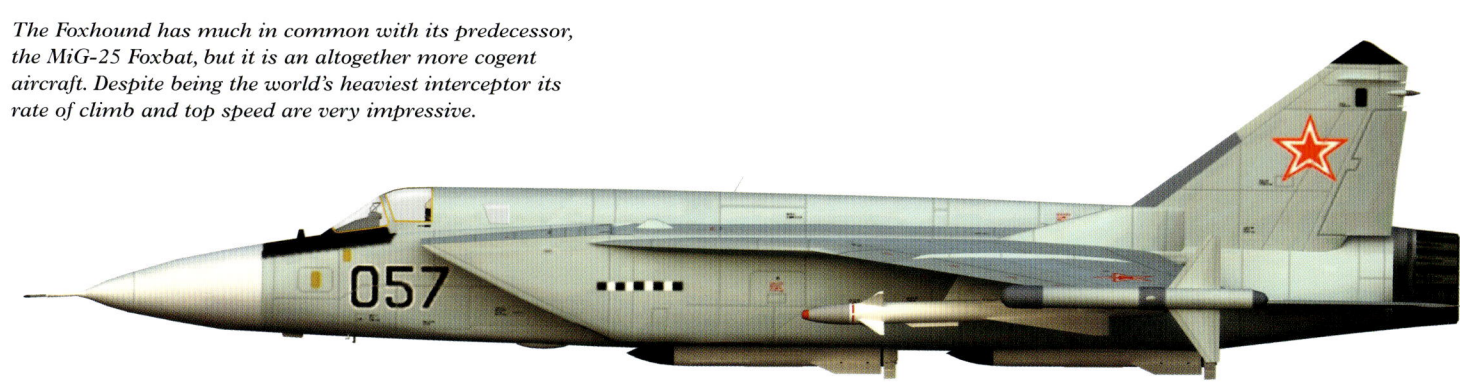

LOAD Precision Strike

1 2x AA–6 Acrid (R40T)
2 4x KH–31P

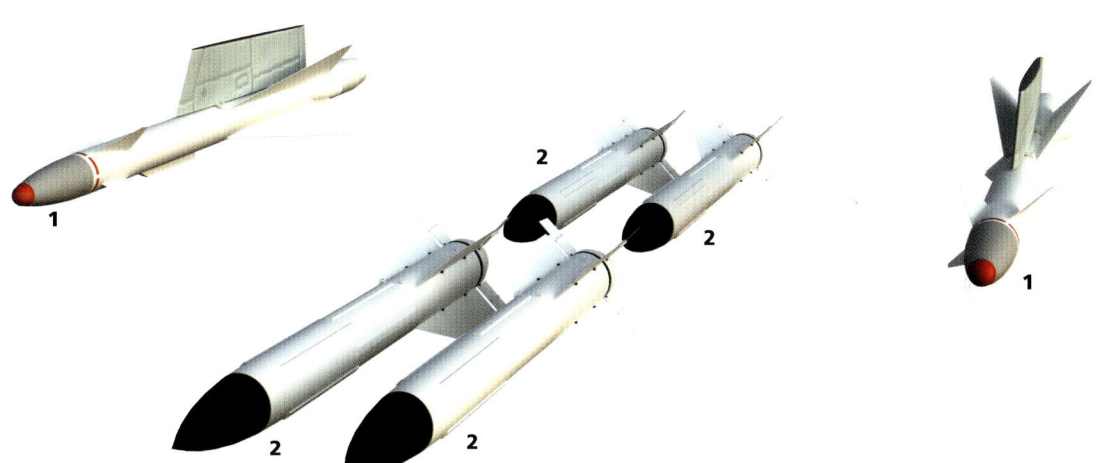

The MiG-31BM variant marks a departure from the high-altitude interceptor role. It has advanced controls and electronic systems, and can employ both air-to-air and air-to-ground weapons. However, this model, along with other advanced variants, has suffered from a lack of funding and may never enter service.

The Foxhound has a crew of two; pilot and weapon systems officer (WSO). The WSO has a restricted field of view as his canopy blends into the fuselage. Thus although the back-seater has a set of flight controls it would be difficult to fly the Foxhound from this position. The WSO is not responsible for flight operations however. He handles radar and missiles and leaves manoeuvring to the pilot. In an air-superiority fighter it might be advantageous for the WSO to have a better field of view to enable him to watch for threats. However, the WSO has an advanced radar and other instruments that are far more capable than his eyes and besides, an interceptor – at least in theory – should not be in a situation where visual-range threats are likely.

For the interceptor role, four R-33E 'Amos' long-range missiles can be carried. These use inertial navigation to reach the target vicinity, with semi-active radar for midcourse guidance. Terminal homing is by means of active radar, which can function even in an environment of heavy jamming. The Foxhound is the only aircraft that can use this missile, which has a range of 160km (100 miles) and a top speed of Mach 4.5.

MODERN AIR-LAUNCHED WEAPONS

Above: The Foxhound is not an aerobatic aircraft but is impressive enough at air shows. By the time a warplane begins to appear in public like this, its capabilities are usually familiar to foreign militaries.

Medium- and short-range missiles are also carried, along with a 30mm Vulcan cannon. In addition, the multi-role MiG-31BM version can utilize a range of air-to-ground missiles including anti-radiation weapons for the SEAD role and laser-guided bombs and missiles for precision strikes. Unguided weapons can also be used, but the Foxhound is not especially well suited to this role.

The Foxhound has had a difficult career. The collapse of the Soviet Union resulted in a desperate lack of funding for development and even maintenance. A high proportion of Foxhounds in service had to be grounded for lack of support, and by the time funding was once again available some of these aircraft were in a poor condition. However, the majority were returned to service and a small proportion upgraded to the standard of later models.

Overseas Sales

Most existing MiG-31s are in service with the Russian air force, though a small number went to Kazakhstan at the break-up of the Soviet Union. Only a handful of these aircraft, if any, are likely to remain operational. Syria has expressed an interest in purchasing MiG-31s, but this sale has run into difficulty. Some sources cite a lack of funds as the cause of the problem, others suggest that the Syrian purchase is a front for a transfer to Iran, which is under an embargo.

It is possible, though not very likely, that the Foxhound will achieve future overseas sales. Specialist aircraft are not currently popular in the international marketplace, and few potential operators are likely to perceive a need for an advanced interceptor instead of an air-superiority, ground-attack or multi-role platform. The Foxhound's multi-role variant might find some favour, but there are cheaper alternatives that will do the same job.

Thus the likely future of the MiG-31 is in Russian service. It is probable that funding will become available to update the existing fleet to the standards of later models, or possibly to create a further upgraded version. The cost of developing a new interceptor is likely to make it attractive to simply upgrade and extend the service lives of the existing fleet, so the Foxhound can probably look forward to a lengthy career.

MIG-31 FOXHOUND

LOAD 5 — Precision Strike

1 2x AA–6 Acrid (R40T)
2 4x Kh–29T

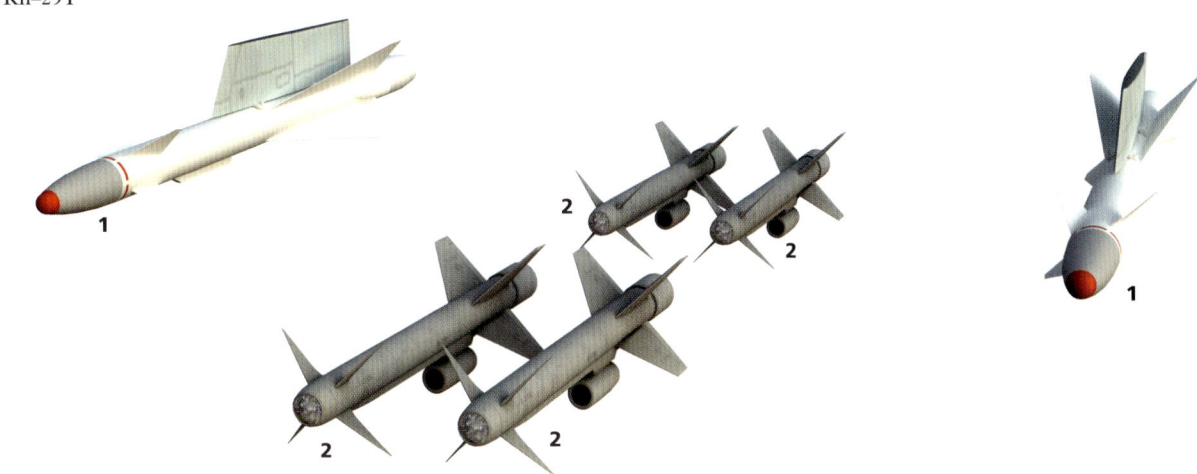

Above: Air shows are to some extent the equivalent of naval 'flag-showing' port visits. They exhibit a nation's air power to the wider world, which benefits national prestige as well as possibly generating export sales.

MODERN AIR-LAUNCHED WEAPONS

Su-25

The Su-25 is a single-seat, twin-engine close support and strike aircraft with extremely good rough-field performance. Despite the fact that it carries armour protection for the pilot and vital systems, its performance is good enough for a demilitarized version to be used in aerobatic displays. The Su-25 is nicknamed 'Grach' (Rook) by Russian personnel, though in the West it is known by NATO reporting name 'Frogfoot'.

Armoured fuselage
The Su-25 is designed to operate at low level and no great speed in an environment where it will receive ground fire. The pilot is well protected by a 'bathtub' of armour, though this reduces both cockpit space and pilot vision in the rearwards arc. A periscope partially compensates for this shortfall. The aircraft's 30mm cannon is mounted under the cockpit.

Centre wing pylon
The central pylon on each wing can carry a large external fuel tank, improving operational radius. This pylon can also carry the same range of weapons as the other four underwing pylons. The appearance of a fully loaded Su-25 seen from underneath gives the aircraft its unofficial nickname of 'The Comb'.

Wing pylons
Five pylons on each wing can carry a range of air-to-ground weaponry including missiles, guided and unguided bombs, napalm tanks, rocket pods, cluster munitions and gun packs containing 23mm cannon for strafing attacks on 'soft' targets. Short-range air-to-air missiles can also be carried if the mission environment merits it.

SU-25

LOAD 1

Hardened Target Strike

1 2x R–60 (AA-8)
2 4x KH–29

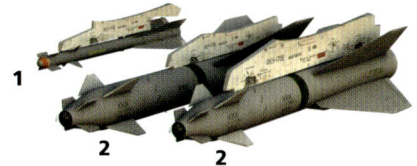
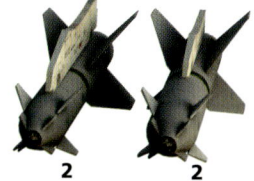

LOAD 2

Ground Attack

1 2x R–60 (AA-8)
2 2x PTB–1150 1150l (304gal) fuel tank
3 4x RBK–250 cluster bomb
4 2x FAB-500 unguided bomb

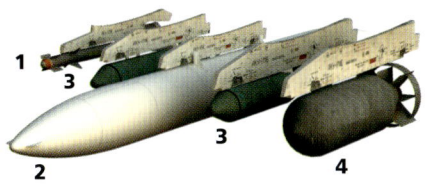
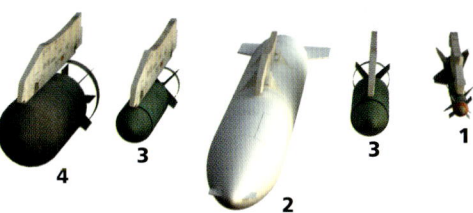

LOAD 3

Iron Bomb

1 2x R–60 (AA-8)
2 6x FAB–500 bomb

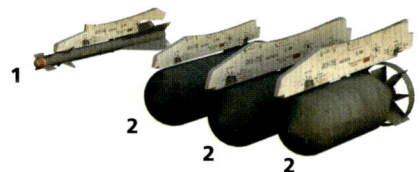

MODERN AIR-LAUNCHED WEAPONS

Above: An Su-25 loaded for close support work. The rocket pods on the outer pylons can be effective weapons when they are fired from a relatively slow-moving aircraft or a helicopter.

The Su-25 has at times been presented as the Russian equivalent to the A-10 Thunderbolt. While not unreasonable, given the similarities in role, the Frogfoot is actually a very different aircraft. Most notably, it was not built around a huge tank-killing cannon. The Su-25 does have a gun armament but this is a fairly conventional twin-barrel 30mm weapon of little use in the anti-armour role. The Frogfoot is also smaller and significantly faster than the A-10, but carries a smaller warload and is less resistant to damage. It is not so much an equivalent aircraft as an alternative approach to meeting the same mission requirements.

The Su-25 first flew in 1975 and entered service three years later. It was designed from the outset for low-level strike and support missions, often in the face of enemy fire. Although not fast, the Frogfoot's small size and good low-level manoeuvrability make it an elusive target. Its airframe and cockpit are armoured, and the engines are positioned as far apart as possible to reduce the effects of a hit. As a result, the Su-25 is an extremely survivable aircraft. One is known to have taken hits from two Sidewinder missiles and still managed to return to base.

The Frogfoot's wings are configured to provide maximum lift at fairly low speed, and have five hardpoints for stores under each. This gives the Su-25 its alternative nickname of 'the Comb', because it somewhat resembles one when seen from underneath with weapons on all positions. The engines are not fitted with afterburners because the Frogfoot is not a high-performance aircraft. Nevertheless, combat radius without external fuel tanks is fairly limited at 275km (170 miles). Maximum speed is 950km/h (590mph), at low level. This equates to Mach 0.82.

As with many other Russian aircraft, the Su-25 has been the basis for a large number of variants. NATO reporting names for these aircraft group them by broad type. The original production model was

Air Campaign 2: Decapitation/Infrastructure Strike and Rear-Area Interdiction

Strikes against enemy command posts and government centres are carried out using standoff weapons or guided bombs, with penetrator warheads deployed against deeply buried bunkers. If key enemy personnel can be killed or injured, the disruption to the overall war effort may be extensive. Attacks on communications installations can prevent these personnel from receiving reports and issuing orders even if they survive the 'decapitation' strikes.

Meanwhile enemy infrastructure is attacked, disrupting the movement of troops and supplies and possibly forcing a negotiated end to hostilities in order to avoid crippling economic damage. Where possible, targets are selected to cause maximum disruption to the enemy for the effort expended by the attacker, while avoiding unnecessary civilian casualties. Power stations are destroyed, depriving industry of electricity, while ports, bridges and railways are targeted to impede logistical and industrial movement. Standoff missiles or guided bombs may be used for these strikes, possibly with specialist warheads designed to attack specific targets such as power substations.

Enemy forces are also targeted during this phase of operations, with the intent of disrupting their movements and wearing down their capabilities. These strikes use the full range of weaponry available, from rockets and cluster bombs for 'soft' targets to large bombs and missiles for armoured units. It may be more effective to attack a combat formation's support base rather than the unit itself; planners only have so many sorties to work with and must consider the overall effects on the campaign of any given strike.

Once the threat from enemy air defences and fighters is diminished, aircraft like the Su-25 can roam the enemy's rear area smashing up the logistics train and attacking targets of opportunity, weakening the enemy's front-line combat forces.

MODERN AIR-LAUNCHED WEAPONS

The lack of rear visibility from the SU-25's cockpit is obvious from this angle. It is prone to being ambushed from behind and would be severely restricted in a dogfight. However, if protected by other assets it is an impressive ground-attack platform.

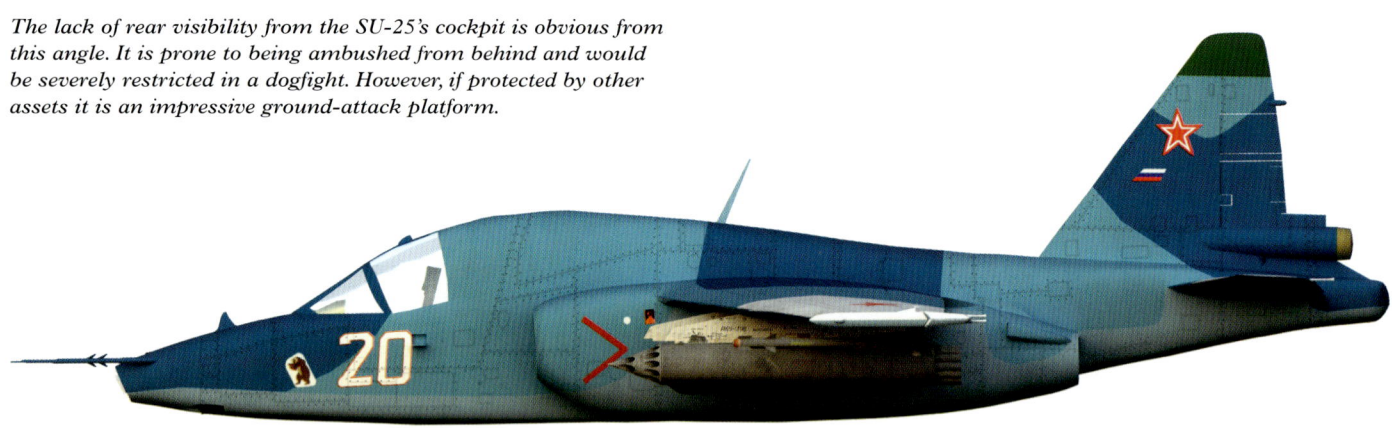

LOAD

Anti-Personnel

1 2x 2x R–60 (AA-8)
2 2x Z–500 napalm tank
3 2x S–8 rocket pod

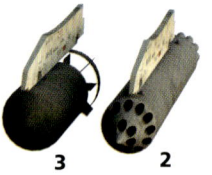

designated Frogfoot-A in the West. Variants included the Su-25K, which had downgraded electronics for the export market. The Su-25UB (and UBK export version), known to NATO as Frogfoot-B, was developed as a trainer but remained fully combat capable. A naval version, designated Su-25UTG, varied from the land-based variants mainly in that its drogue parachute, designed to slow it after landing, was replaced by an arrester hook.

Later Su-25 models received upgraded electronics, enabling them to function in all weather and at night. The Su-25TM, also designated Su-39, was primarily an anti-armour close-support platform but can conduct maritime strike missions as well, and was followed by the Su-25SM. Upgraded older SU-25s are designated Su-25SM, with upgraded Su-25UB models designated Su-25UBM. An upgrade programme was implemented in the early 2000s to bring all Russian Su-25s up to this standard. A new member of the Frogfoot family is the Su-25KM, which has the nickname 'Scorpion'. It has colour multi-function displays, a new HUD and an optional helmet-mounted display.

The Su-25 is very much a ground-attack aircraft, but it can engage airborne targets with its gun or with short-range air-to-air missiles carried on the outer pylons. More commonly, it deploys a range of unguided weapons including rocket pods, cluster munitions, freefall bombs and gun pods containing twin 23mm cannon. Upgraded models can use laser-guided bombs and short-range missiles.

The Su-25 saw action in Afghanistan from 1981–89, serving as the backbone of Soviet close support and strike operations. Approximately 60,000 sorties were generated, for a loss of 21 aircraft. Several of these losses occurred soon after the Stinger missile was supplied to Mujahadeen fighters. Investigation showed that a hit on either engine caused the fuel

SU-25

tank, located above them, to catch fire, which would ultimately cripple both engines and cause a crash. The insertion of light armour between the engines and the fuel tank remedied this deficiency; the loss of one engine proved to be survivable.

The Frogfoot showed itself to be a useful counter-insurgency aircraft in Afghanistan, attacking groups of enemy personnel that were often located in inaccessible areas. Similar tactics were successfully used by the Macedonian air force against Albanian fighters. The aircraft also performed convincingly as a strike platform against hostiles that lacked good anti-air capability; Su-25s flew around 900 sorties during the Iran-Iraq war with only one combat loss.

However, the Frogfoot has not fared as well against an enemy that could field its own air assets. During the 1991 Gulf War the Iraqi Su-25 fleet was rendered powerless in the face of overwhelming Coalition air superiority. Several pilots fled with their planes to Iran, where some joined the Iranian forces. Two were shot down, along with two MiG-21s, probably also trying to escape to Iran.

Most recently, the SU-25 has seen action on both sides of the South Ossetia War between Russia and Georgia. Both combatants lost aircraft to ground fire. Ironically, Su-25s in Russian service were used to attack the aircraft plant at Tblisi where the Frogfoot is manufactured.

The Frogfoot is intended to operate from the most primitive of forward airbases. It can reportedly taxi

Right: *The SU-25 is a 'bomb truck', able to carry a significant warload for a small aircraft. Up to 4,400kg (9700lb) of its 20,500kg (45,200lb) maximum takeoff weight can be made up of external stores.*

MODERN AIR-LAUNCHED WEAPONS

LOAD 5
Close Air Support

1 2x R–60 (AA–8)
2 2x FAB–500 unguided bomb
3 2x S–8 rocket pod

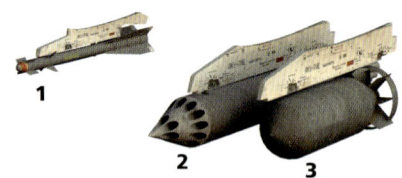
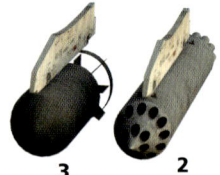

LOAD 6
Extended-Range Strike

1 4x KAB–500KR
2 4x PTB–1150 1150l (304gal) fuel tank

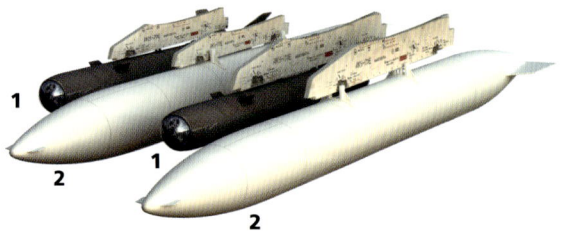
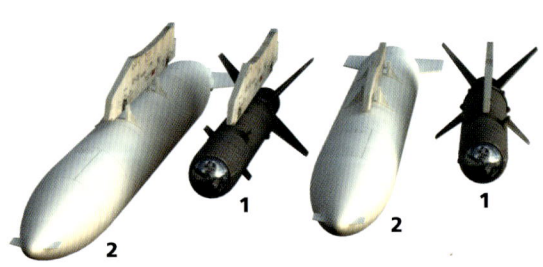

LOAD 7
Extended-Range Hardened-Target Strike

1 2x KH–29
2 4x PTB–1150 1150l (304gal) fuel tank

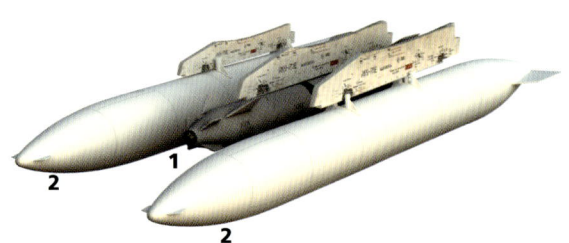
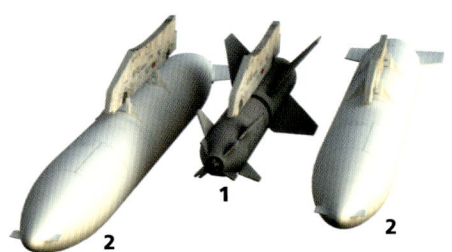

through mud that could stop all-wheel-drive vehicles, and can run its engines on diesel, though this causes damage very quickly. Experience in Afghanistan demonstrated that the Su-25 can be kept in service for long periods. By the end of the conflict the Frogfoot force had accrued an average of 2600 flight hours per aircraft.

Although a mooted project to create pods for the transport of ground crews came to nothing, the Su-25 can carry small quantities of spares in underwing containers, which may be of benefit when redeploying forward in support of a ground advance. The capability to operate without complex maintenance and support facilities is attractive to many potential users. As a result, the Frogfoot has been bought by several nations seeking a simple, robust strike platform.

The major operators of the Frogfoot are Russia and other nations that inherited a force of Su-25s as part of the break-up of the Soviet Union, and former Warsaw Pact countries. These include Belarus, Bulgaria, Georgia, Kazakhstan and the Ukraine. Among the export customers for the Frogfoot are Angola, Chad, The Republic of the Congo, Equatorial Guinea, Eritrea, Ethiopia, Gambia, Iran, North Korea, Peru and Sudan. A number of other nations have operated Su-25s in the past but no longer do so.

The Su-25 family has good prospects for future export sales to developing nations. Its relative simplicity and sturdiness make it a good choice for air forces on a very limited budget. For similar reasons it may well remain in service with more advanced air forces; if air superiority can be established by more expensive aircraft then the Frogfoot can go about the business of close support and rear-area strike in a cost-efficient manner.

Below: The Su-25 is designed to operate from the most basic of forward bases. It can carry spares to a new base in underwing pods, though a plan to enable the transport of ground crews the same way failed to come to fruition.

MODERN AIR-LAUNCHED WEAPONS

Post-Soviet Bombers
Tu-22M, Tu-160 and Tu-95

The Tu-22M, Tu-160 and Tu-95 are large bombers designed by the Soviet Union and currently in service with the Russian air force. All were designed to deliver conventional and nuclear weapons over a long distance, with a secondary maritime reconnaissance and anti-ship strike capability.

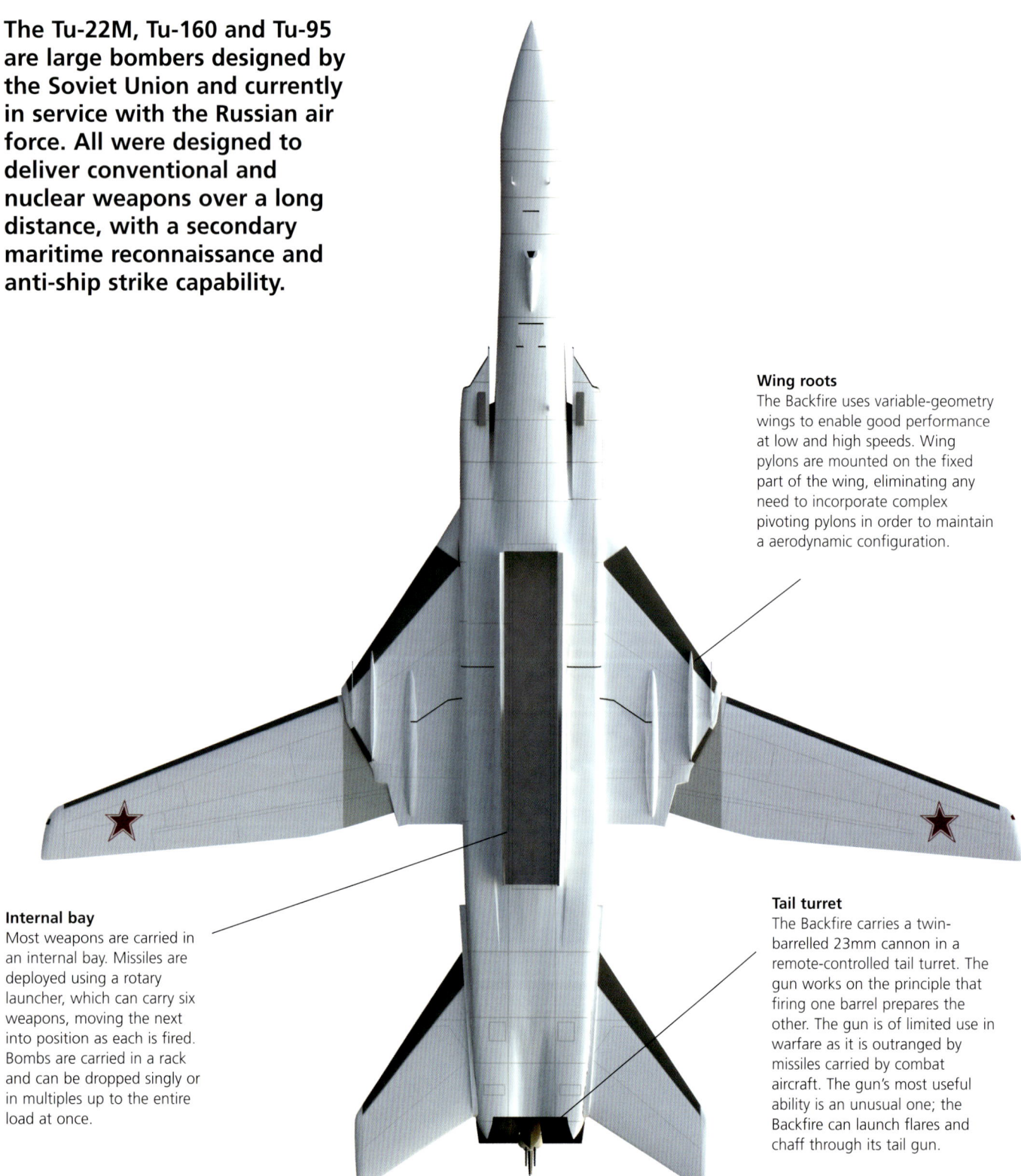

Wing roots
The Backfire uses variable-geometry wings to enable good performance at low and high speeds. Wing pylons are mounted on the fixed part of the wing, eliminating any need to incorporate complex pivoting pylons in order to maintain a aerodynamic configuration.

Internal bay
Most weapons are carried in an internal bay. Missiles are deployed using a rotary launcher, which can carry six weapons, moving the next into position as each is fired. Bombs are carried in a rack and can be dropped singly or in multiples up to the entire load at once.

Tail turret
The Backfire carries a twin-barrelled 23mm cannon in a remote-controlled tail turret. The gun works on the principle that firing one barrel prepares the other. The gun is of limited use in warfare as it is outranged by missiles carried by combat aircraft. The gun's most useful ability is an unusual one; the Backfire can launch flares and chaff through its tail gun.

POST SOVIET BOMBERS: TU-22M, TU-160 AND TU-95

LOAD 1
Tu-22M: Maritime Strike

1 10x KH–15

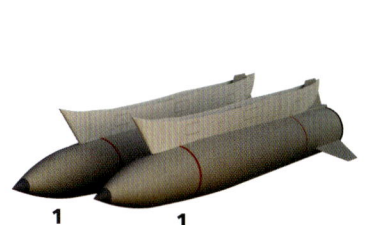
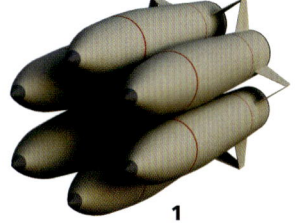
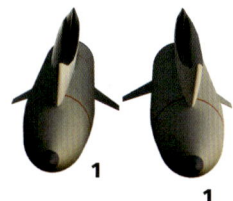

LOAD 2
Tu-22M: Iron Bomb

1 60x FAB–69 unguided bomb

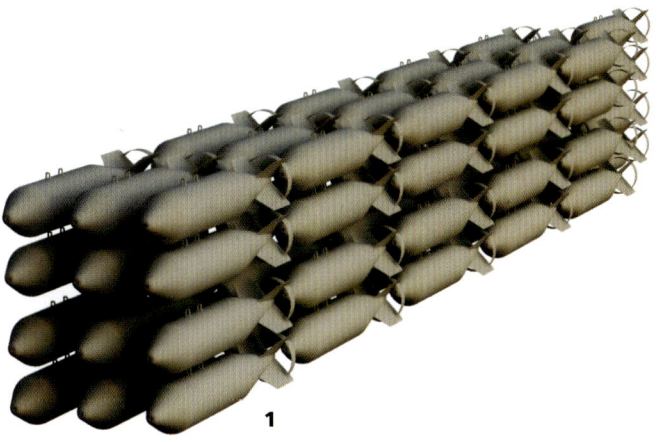

Tu-22M 'Backfire'

The Tu-22M, designated 'Backfire' by NATO, entered service in 1972. The initial production model, designated Tu-22M2 (Backfire-B to Western observers) was followed in 1983 by the upgraded Tu-22M3 (Backfire-C), which featured a greater payload and a more aerodynamic tail turret assembly. A model with upgraded equipment and avionics, designated Tu-22ME, has since emerged. This is not a newly built variant but an upgrade package retrofitted to existing Backfires.

The Backfire was designed for supersonic speed and low-level penetration, greatly increasing its survivability compared to earlier bombers. In order to enhance both economical cruising and supersonic 'dash' performance, the Tu-22M was built with variable-geometry wings. Cruising speed is subsonic, and the Backfire cannot attain supersonic speeds at low altitude. Its best sea-level performance is Mach 0.88. At altitude it can reach Mach 1.88, though this reduces combat range considerably.

With a maximum range of 2400km (1490 miles) with 10,430kg (23,000lb) of ordnance aboard, flying high to the target area and descending to low altitude for penetration of enemy air defences, the Backfire has, at times, been designated an intercontinental bomber, but this label was disputed as it had implications for strategic arms limitation negotiations. A long operating range made the Tu-22M ideal for use as a maritime reconnaissance and strike platform, carrying cruise missiles far out over the ocean to attack enemy shipping.

MODERN AIR-LAUNCHED WEAPONS

Above: The Tu-22M's wings are swept forward to generate maximum lift during takeoff and landing, shortening takeoff distance and reducing fuel consumption during the climb to cruise altitude.

The Backfire can carry three large Kh-22 cruise missiles, or a payload of up to 24,040kg (53,000lb) including conventional or nuclear bombs, missiles or mines. It carries two 23mm cannon in a tail turret for self-defence, but primarily relies on its speed to avoid interception. It served through the Cold War as a strategic bomber, standing ready to carry out nuclear strikes, and as a maritime reconnaissance/strike platform. It did not see action during these years.

From 1987–89, Backfires operated over Afghanistan in support of Soviet troops there, and in 1995 Russian Backfires were active against Chechen forces. In these 'small wars' the Backfire acted as a conventional strike platform, delivering large payloads of unguided ordnance. One Tu-22M was lost to Georgian air defences in 2008.

The Tu-22M was not exported while the Soviet Union was in existence, but various post-Soviet states inherited examples. Belarus retained a significant number, but without any real need for strategic bombers they were not well maintained and are probably no longer serviceable. Ukraine also inherited a force of Backfires, but began destroying them as the Ukrainian government divested itself of nuclear-capable platforms. Fewer than 100 Backfires are in service with the Russian air force and naval aviation squadrons. An equivalent number of aircraft are held in reserve and could be brought into service at need.

Tu-160 'Blackjack'

The Tu-160, designated 'Blackjack' by NATO observers, in many ways resembles the U.S. B-1B Lancer, but it is somewhat larger. Small numbers were in service before the collapse of the Soviet Union and a shortage of funds prevented any more from being built for some time. Recently, construction of the Blackjack has resumed, albeit in small numbers.

The Blackjack's flight electronics are relatively simple by today's standards, using conventional electro-

182

POST SOVIET BOMBERS: TU-22M, TU-160 AND TU-95

The Tu-22M 'Backfire' has similar lines to the Tu-160 Blackjack. The easiest way to distinguish them is to look at the engines. Those of the Backfire are in the fuselage with exhausts under the tail; the Blackjack has two engines in each wing root.

LOAD 3

Tu–160: Cruise Missile Delivery

1 12x Kh–55

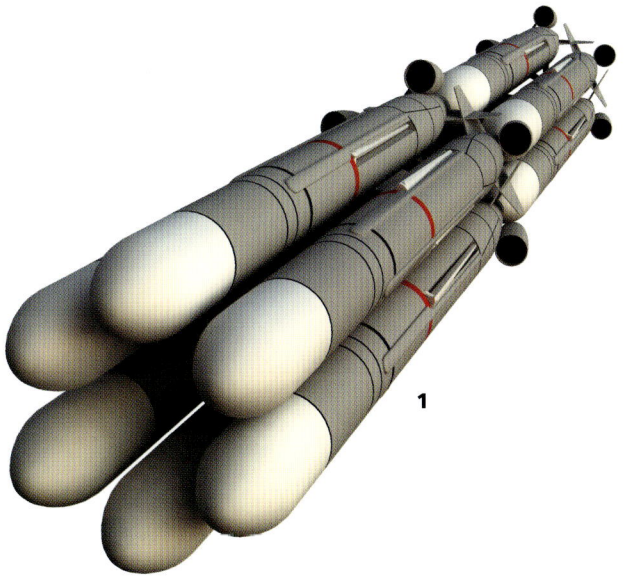

LOAD 4

Tu–160: Standoff Strike Against Strong Air Defences

1 12x Kh–101

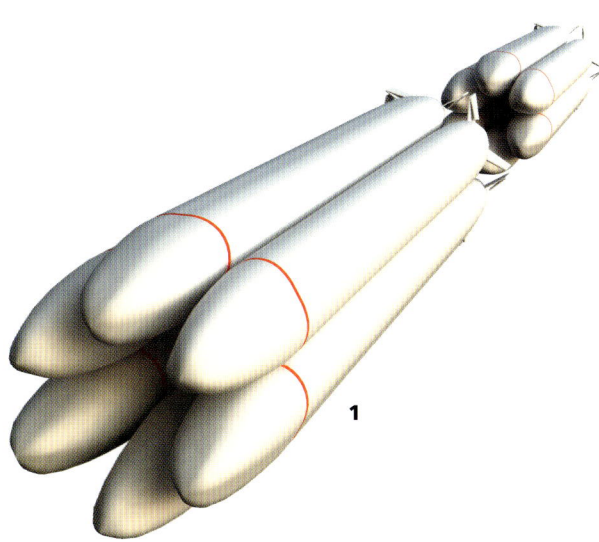

MODERN AIR-LAUNCHED WEAPONS

Above: A Tu-160 Blackjack. Another key difference between the Blackjack and the Backfire is the tailplane. The Blackjack carries its high on the fin while the Backfire's is low, close to the engine exhausts.

mechanical indicators rather than modern head-up displays or multi-function display units. The pilot's controls resemble those of a fighter more than a bomber, with a stick instead of a yoke. Internally, individual Blackjacks tend to vary from one to the next. Development was still ongoing when most production models were being delivered. Each example received the latest equipment fit and layout as it was completed.

The Blackjack is capable of in-flight refuelling. Even without it, a 15-hour flight is possible at a cruising speed of Mach 0.77. Some low-observable technology was incorporated into the design, but the Tu-160 was never meant to be a stealth platform. Instead, it was designed to fly to a release point and deliver a cruise missile strike, relying on its speed to avoid interception. Using afterburners, it can reach Mach 2.05 at altitude.

The Tu-160 can deliver cruise missiles or shorter-range ordnance, including nuclear and conventional weapons. It can carry as many as 12 Kh-55Ms nuclear cruise missiles, with a maximum range of 3,000km (1865 miles). Weapons are carried in two internal bays, and can be configured for conventional ordnance or with a rotary launcher for missiles. Additional missiles can be carried externally, though this increases drag.

Sole Operator

Russia is the only operator of Blackjacks. Ukraine inherited a force at the break-up of the Soviet Union but sold some back to Russia, destroying the rest. The Tu-160 fleet suffered from a lack of funding in the 1990s, with some aircraft becoming unserviceable, but it has now returned to front-line service. Strategic patrol flights across the Atlantic, a feature of the Cold War, have been restarted and newly built Blackjacks are currently entering service. Modernization of older aircraft has also begun, adding advanced flight controls and avionics, the capacity to employ laser-guided

POST SOVIET BOMBERS: TU-22M, TU-160 AND TU-95

LOAD 5   **Tu-95M: Cruise Missile Strike**

1 6x KH–55

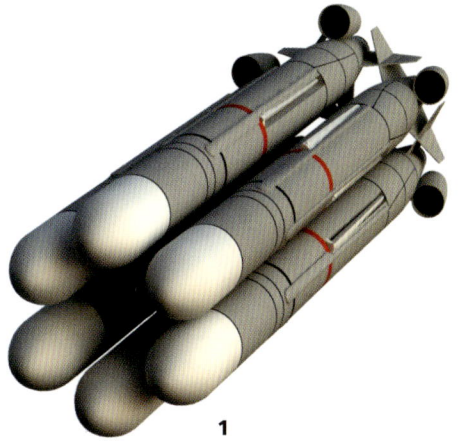

LOAD 6   **Tu-95M: Maritime Strike**

1 16x Kh–55

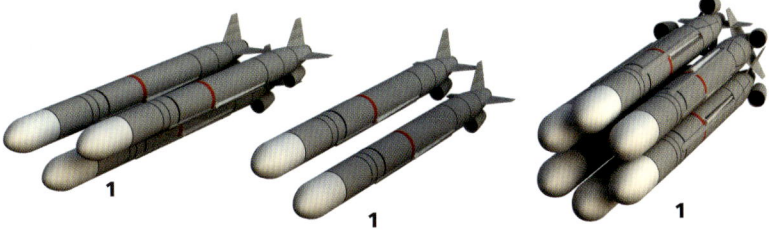  

Above: The huge wingspan of the Blackjack is seen here. Enormous quantities of lift and engine thrust are required to get this aircraft, which can lift off with 160 tonnes (176 tons) of fuel aboard, off the ground.

MODERN AIR-LAUNCHED WEAPONS

Above: The Tu-95 Bear is the world's only turboprop-powered strategic bomber. Turboprops were used on this aircraft because the jet engines of the day lacked the necessary performance.

bombs, and compatibility with GLONASS, the Russian version of GPS. Radar-absorbent coatings are also to be added. This will have the effect of reducing detectability by radar, though it will not turn the Tu-160 into a stealth aircraft.

Although Russia's period of economic instability is largely over and funding is once more available for military aviation, there is only so much money to go around. International sales are unlikely; few nations can afford, or even see the need for, a long-range strategic bomber. Exports would help ease the cost of modernization or replacement of the Russian bomber fleet, but without such a source of income it may be some time before new bomber development gets underway. It is likely that the ageing Backfire fleet will soldier on for years to come, with small numbers of Blackjacks gradually augmenting them. When Russia does design a new strategic bomber, it may well be a developed version of the Blackjack.

The Venerable Bear

The Tu-95 Bear is a Turboprop-powered strategic bomber dating from 1952. It has performed well enough to be adapted to various roles, including a maritime version designated Tu-142. Originally designed to employ free-fall nuclear or conventional ordnance, the Bear has the distinction of being the aircraft that dropped the world's most powerful nuclear device. This was the 100-megaton 'Tsar Bomba', which was downgraded to 50MT for the test.

Today, the Bear is mainly a missile platform. Its relatively low speed makes it vulnerable to interception, but this is offset by the ability to deliver long-range cruise missiles. Ideally, it can cruise to the attack area and perhaps loiter there for some time before launching a strike from outside interception range. The Bear's warload is some 15,000kg (33,000lb) of missiles carried in an internal bay and on wing pylons, plus a tail turret mounting one or two 23mm cannon.

The Tu-95 was a symbol of Russian power during the Cold War, making patrols as far as the Eastern seaboard of the USA and probing at airspace around Europe as well as U.S. carrier groups in the Atlantic Ocean. After several years of relative dormancy, the Bear has returned to this role. It has also joined other long-range aircraft on exercises. Although it seems highly unlikely that any more will be built, the Tu-95 is versatile enough to remain in service for some time to come.

POST SOVIET BOMBERS: TU-22M, TU-160 AND TU-95

Air Campaign 3: Close Support and Ground Attack

Enemy formations are 'softened up' by air attack before an offensive, and those involved in combat are harassed by close air support aircraft. Enemy forces attempting to retreat from the battle zone are also attacked to prevent them from regrouping.

Weapons used in this phase depend very much on the target. Cluster bombs and GPS-guided 225, 450 or 910kg (500, 1000 or 2000lb) bombs are effective against 'area' targets, such as a large formation on the move, while guided missiles and laser-guided bombs are employed against such smaller targets as individual armoured vehicles. Close air support aircraft make use of rockets and guns in addition to bombs and missiles.

The closer a mission is carried out to the battle front, the greater the precision required to avoid friendly casualties. Attacks against enemy forces further back can be fairly general, i.e. aimed at a unit rather than specific components of it. Wearing down a formation's capabilities is an effective means of assisting friendly forces. However, once the enemy is in close contact then attacks on specific enemy units or vehicles may be required in order to assist friendly troops who are under severe pressure or undertaking a difficult assault.

Rocket pods and small- to medium-sized bombs are ideal weapons for close support, enabling an aircraft to engage several targets in the course of one mission. Such a target might be an artillery battery or infantry position, or simply an individual tank. Even relatively light weapons are capable of dealing with such targets.

DIRECTORY OF MODERN AIR-LAUNCHED WEAPONS

Weapons and supporting systems carried by aircraft fall into several distinct categories, notably powered missiles and rockets, bombs, munitions dispensers and a range of mission- or survivability-enhancing pods. The following directory contains many of the air-launched weapon systems in service today, but it is not exhaustive.

Local variants of many weapon systems, built under license or copied from examples obtained by various means, are in use with some air forces, while others use specialist versions of weapons listed here. Bombs and munitions dispensers lend themselves most readily to this sort of conversion; a dispenser designed to deliver cluster bombs can also be used for anything from propaganda leaflets to specialist munitions constructed for a single mission.

Many of the weapons presented here show a family resemblance, often as the result of evolutionary development. Several distinct versions of a given weapon, with upgraded seekers, propulsion systems and/or warheads, may appear over the course of its service life. Alternatively, the weapon's casing and propulsion unit may be used as the basis for an entirely different weapon which nevertheless resembles the original.

The fact that stores must fit the pylons and bays of aircraft currently in service forces new weapon systems to retain the general dimensions of their predecessors. Aerodynamic factors further constrain weapon designers with the result that two weapons designed for the same task will tend to look fairly similar. Key differences tend to be imposed by the shape of seeker equipment and guidance fins.

Selecting the right weapon for a given mission is a matter of balancing a number of factors. The mobility, size and composition of the target, risk to the attacking aircraft from short-range air defence systems in the area, and the proximity of non-combatants all guide the mission planners in their choice of weapon systems. Cost-effectiveness is also a key factor; most targets can be destroyed by standoff missiles but this would quickly become prohibitively expensive. Thus, for all the vast array of stores available, the composition of a mission loadout is often surprisingly obvious.

AS-30L Air-to-ground missile

MODERN AIR-LAUNCHED WEAPONS

AIR-TO-AIR MISSILES

AA-6 ACRID (R-40T)

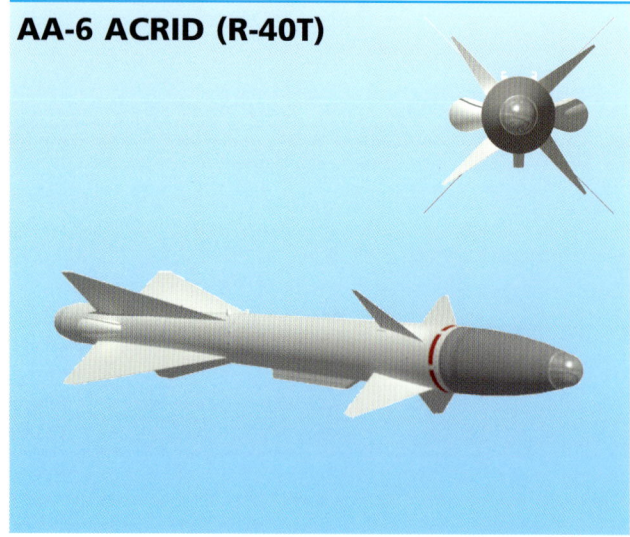
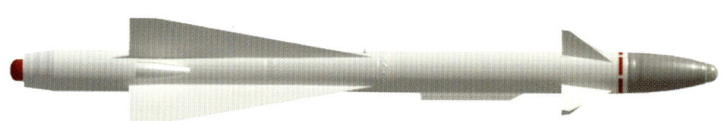

Description: The Vympel R-40T (NATO reporting name AA-6 Acrid) is a development of the original R-40 long-range air-to-air missile that armed the MiG-25 Foxhound. Production of the weapon ended in 1991, but it remains in limited use with various states of the former Soviet Union. It was used in action during the Gulf War of 1991.

Country of origin: Russia
Weight: 990lb (450kg)
Diameter: 12.2in (310mm)
Length: 19ft 7.5in (5.98m)
Warhead: 154lb (70kg) blast fragmentation
Wingspan: 4 ft 9in (1.45m)
Range: 19-37 miles (30-60km)
Guidance System: infrared homing

AA-8 APHID-B (R-60M)

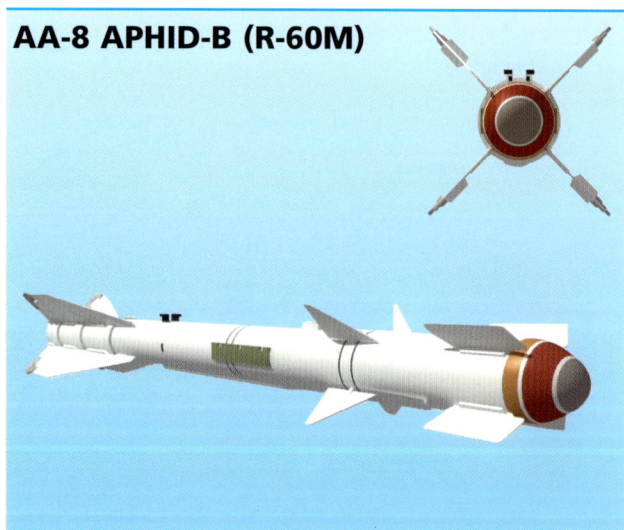

Description: Given the NATO reporting name AA-8 Aphid-B, the Vympel R-60 is a lightweight short-range air-to-air missile. The R-60M is an improved version with a sensitive nitrogen-cooled seeker, but has only limited all-aspect capability. The missile's main attribute is that is very agile, with a very short minimum range of only 984ft (300m).

Country of origin: Russia
Weight: 96lb (43.5kg)
Diameter: 4.75in (120mm)
Length: 6ft 10in (2090mm)
Warhead: 6.6lb (3kg) high explosive
Wingspan: 15.25in (390mm)
Range: 5 miles (8km)
Guidance System: infrared homing

AA-9 AMOS (R-33E)

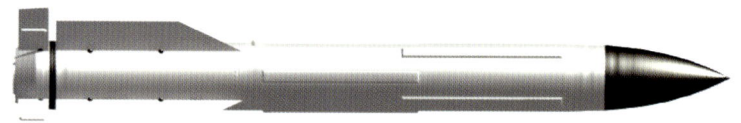

Description: The Vympel R-33 (NATO reporting name AA-9 Amos) is a long-range air-to-air missile developed specifically for use by the MiG-31 Foxhound interceptor. It was originally designed to intercept US supersonic bombers at very long range and subsequently underwent modifications to give it a capability against low-flying cruise missiles.

Country of origin: Russia
Weight: 1080lb (490kg)
Diameter: 15in (380mm)
Length: 13ft 7in (4.15m)
Warhead: 104lb (47.5kg)
Wingspan: 3ft 8in (1.16m)
Range: 80.7 miles (130km)
Guidance System: inertial and semi-active radar homing

DIRECTORY

AA-10 ALAMO-A (R27R) RADAR-GUIDED MISSILE

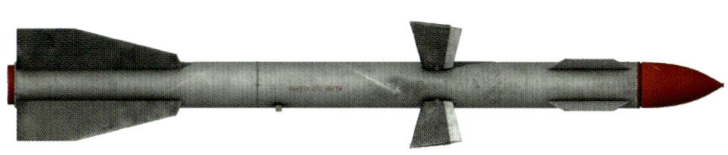

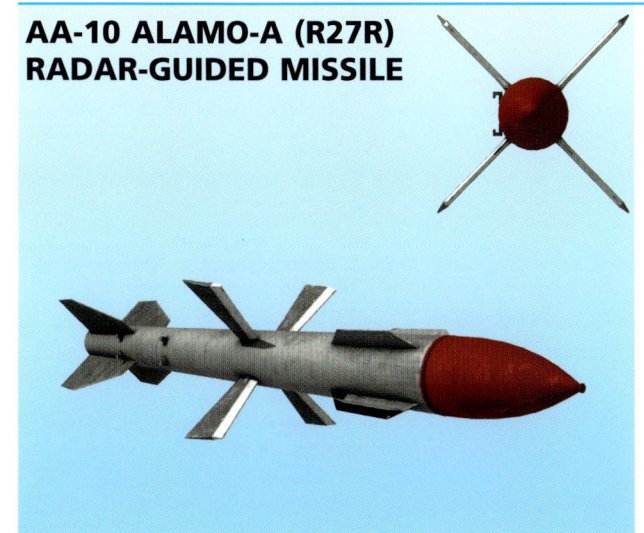

Description: The Vympel R-27R, which carries the NATO reporting name AA-10 Alamo-A is a semi-active radar homing version of this family of Russian air-to-air missiles and is carried by the MiG-29 Fulcrum and Su-25 Flanker. The weapon is license produced in the People's Republic of China, which developed its own seeker.

Country of origin: Russia
Weight: 141lb (253kg)
Diameter: 9in (230mm)
Length: 9.3ft (4.08m)
Warhead: 64lb (39kg) blast fragmentation
Wingspan: 30in (772mm)
Range: 656ft-50 miles (200m-80km)
Guidance System: semi-active radar homing

AA-11 (R73E) IR MISSILE

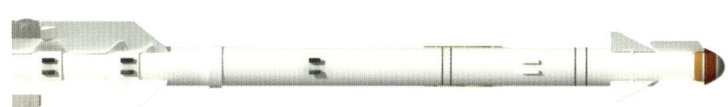

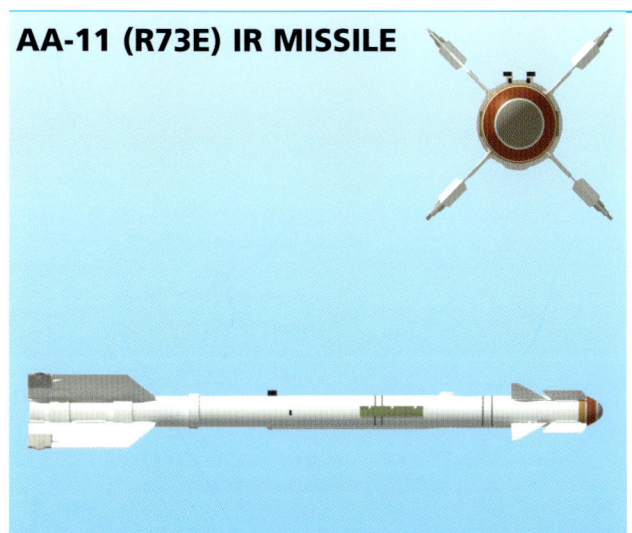

Description: The Vympel R-73E (NATO reporting name AA-11 Archer) is a highly manoeuvrable shot-range air-to-air missile, first deployed by the former Soviet Air Force in 1982. It can be targeted by a helmet-mounted sight. A longer-range version, the R-73M, entered service in 1997. The R-37 is used by all types of Russian fighter aircraft.

Country of origin: Russia
Weight: 231lb (105kg)
Diameter: 6.7in (170mm)
Length: 9ft 6in (2.90m)
Warhead: 16.3lb (7.4kg) blast fragmentation
Wingspan: 20in (510mm)
Range: 12 miles (20km)
Guidance System: all-aspect infrared homing

AA-12 ADDER (R-77)

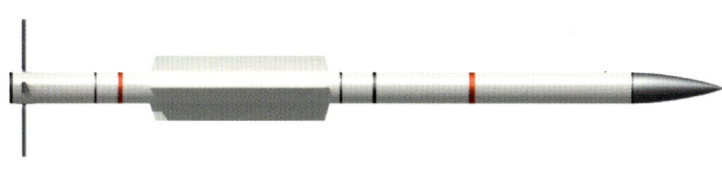

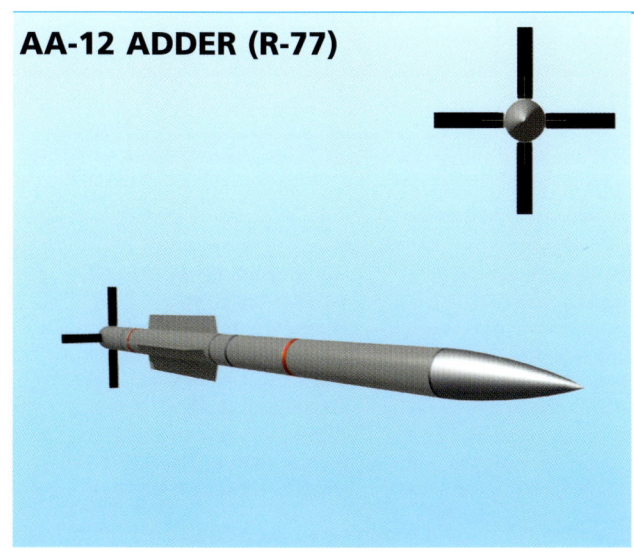

Description: The Vympel R-77 (NATO reporting name AA-12 Adder) is the Russian counterpart of the American AIM-120, and is a fire-and-forget weapon that can be used against a wide range of aircraft targets from fast low-level attack aircraft to hovering helicopters, as well as cruise missiles and SAMs such as Patriot.

Country of origin: Russia
Weight: 385lb (175kg)
Diameter: 7.85in (200mm)
Length: 11ft 9in (3.6m)
Warhead: 48.5lb (22kg) fragmenting
Wingspan: 13.75 in (350mm)
Range: 55.92 miles (90km)
Guidance System: inertial, terminal active radar homing

MODERN AIR-LAUNCHED WEAPONS

AA-13 ARROW (R-37)

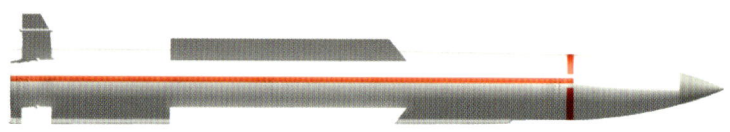
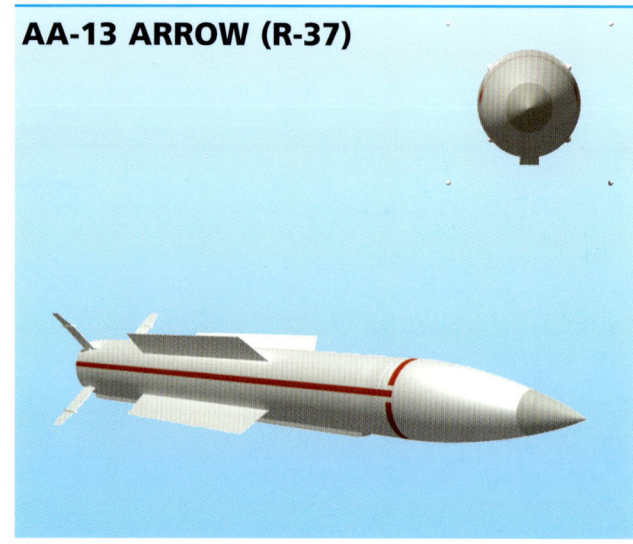

Description: The Vympel R-37 (NATO reporting name AA-13 Arrow) is an extremely long-range air-to-air missile. Testing continued throughout the 1990s and the weapon is intended as primary armament for a future generation of Russian fighters as well as the current MiG-31BM Foxhound and Sukhoi Su-35BM. There are two variants, the R-37 and R-37M.

Country of origin: Russia
Weight: 1320lb (600kg)
Diameter: 15in (380mm)
Length: 13ft 9in (4.20m)
Warhead: high explosive fragmentation
Wingspan: 2ft 4in (0.7m)
Range: 80-215nm (150-298km)
Guidance System: inertial, semi-active and active radar homing

AIM-7F SPARROW

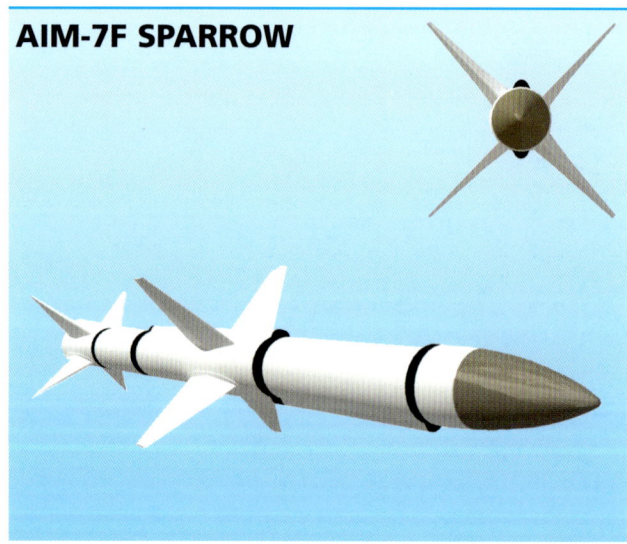

Description: Developed by Raytheon and General Dynamics, the AIM-7 Sparrow is a long-range dogfight-capable weapon which has seen widespread service with the air forces of NATO. The AIM-7F variant has a dual-stage rocket motor to provide greater range, solid-state electronics and a larger warhead than the earlier models.

Country of origin: USA
Weight: 510lb (230kg)
Diameter: 8in (200mm)
Length: 12ft (3.7m)
Warhead: 88lb (40kg) high explosive blast fragmentation
Wingspan: 2ft 8in (810mm)
Range: 31 miles (50km)
Guidance System: semi-active radar

AIM-9J SIDEWINDER

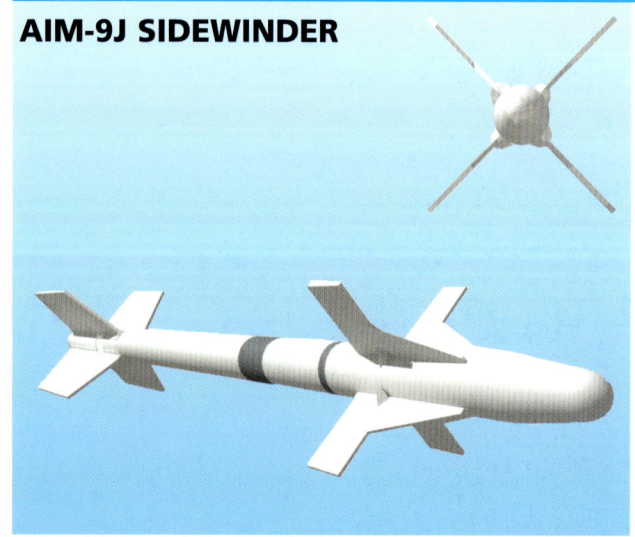

Description: For many years, NATO's standard short-range air-to-air missile has been the AIM-9 Sidewinder. Even after five decades, the missile remains in widespread use with many air forces around the world. The first true dogfight version was the AIM-9J, which was rushed into service to counter the MiG-21 during the Vietnam war.

Country of origin: USA
Weight: 190lb (91kg)
Diameter: 5in (127mm)
Length: 9ft 4.2in (2.85m)
Warhead: 20.8lb (9.4kg) annular blast fragmentation
Wingspan: 24.8in (630mm)
Range: 0.6-11.3 miles (1-18km)
Guidance System: infrared homing

DIRECTORY

AIM-9L SIDEWINDER

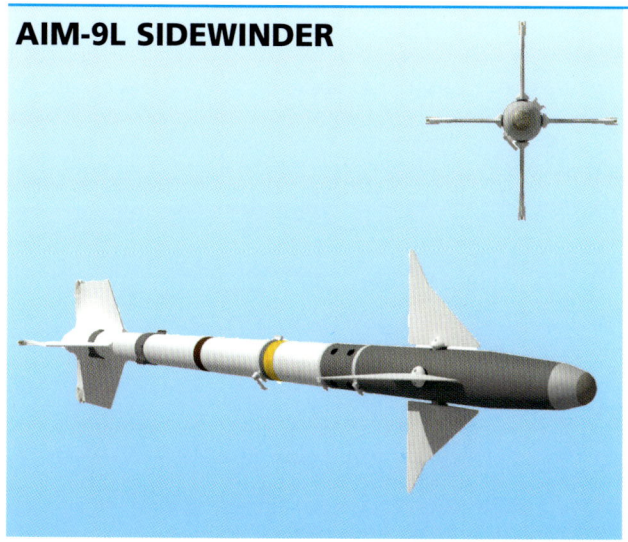

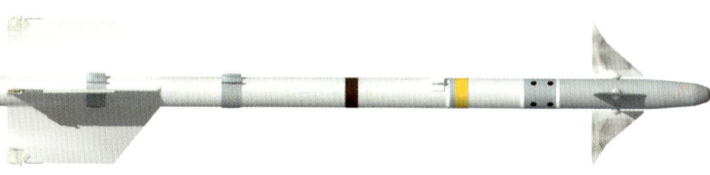

Description: The AIM-9L Sidewinder was the first 'all-aspect' version, with the ability to attack from all directions, including head-on. This capability made a dramatic difference to the weapon's use in close combat, and was employed to good effect by the Royal Navy's Sea Harriers during the Falklands War of 1982.

Country of origin: USA
Weight: 190lb (91kg)
Diameter: 5in (127mm)
Length: 9ft 4.2in (2.85m)
Warhead: 20.8lb (9.4kg) annular blast fragmentation
Wingspan: 24.8in (630mm)
Range: 0.6-11.3 miles (1-18km)
Guidance System: infrared homing

AIM-9M SIDEWINDER

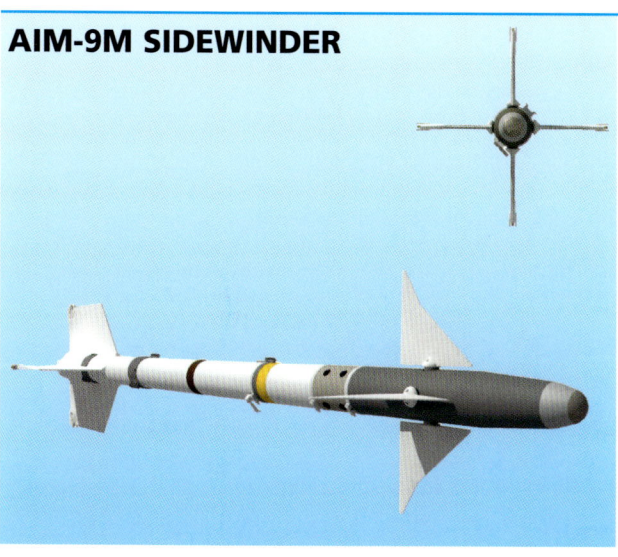

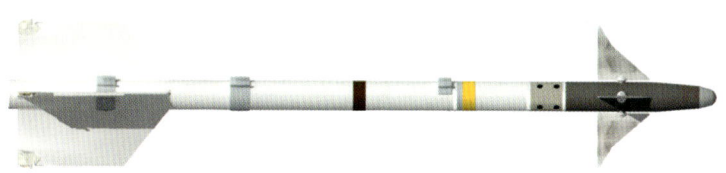

Description: The AIM-9M had all the attributes of the AIM-9L, including an all-aspect attack capability, but also featured all-round higher performance. Other enhancements included a better resistance to infrared counter-measures and a reduced-smoke rocket motor. The AIM-9M was subjected to further modifications during its operational life to counter specific threats.

Country of origin: USA
Weight: 190lb (91kg)
Diameter: 5in (127mm)
Length: 9ft 4.2in (2.85m)
Warhead: 20.8lb (9.4kg) annular blast fragmentation
Wingspan: 24.8in (630mm)
Range: 0.6-11.3 miles (1-18km)
Guidance System: infrared homing

AIM-9P SIDEWINDER

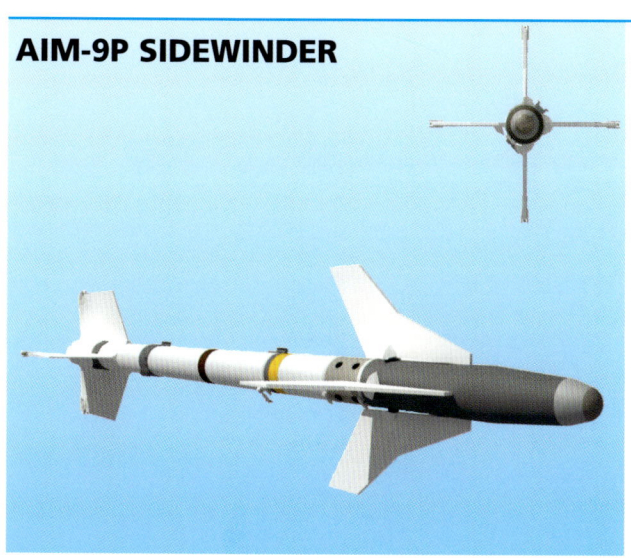

Description: The AIM-9J Sidewinder evolved into the AIM-9P series, with five versions being produced. The AIM-9P incorporated the all-aspect capability of the AIM-9L, as well as improvements such as new fuzes. A German company developed a conversion kit for upgrading the AIM-9J guidance and control system to -9P standard.

Country of origin: USA
Weight: 190lb (91kg)
Diameter: 5in (127mm)
Length: 9ft 4.2in (2.85m)
Warhead: 20.8lb (9.4kg) annular blast fragmentation
Wingspan: 24.8in (630mm)
Range: 0.6-11.3 miles (1-18km)
Guidance System: infrared homing

MODERN AIR-LAUNCHED WEAPONS

AIM-9X SIDEWINDER

Description: The AIM-9X Sidewinder was developed as a counter to the Russian AA-11 Archer air-to-air missile and new infrared countermeasures. The missile entered service with the USAF and US Navy in r 2003 and is used by the F-15C and F/A-18 Hornet. The weapon uses a new three-dimensional thrust-vectoring control.

Country of origin: USA
Weight: 190lb (91kg)
Diameter: 5in (127mm)
Length: 9ft 4.2in (2.85m)
Warhead: 20.8lb (9.4kg) annular blast fragmentation
Wingspan: 24.8in (630mm)
Range: 0.6-11.3 miles (1-18km)
Guidance System: infrared homing

AIM-120 AMRAAM

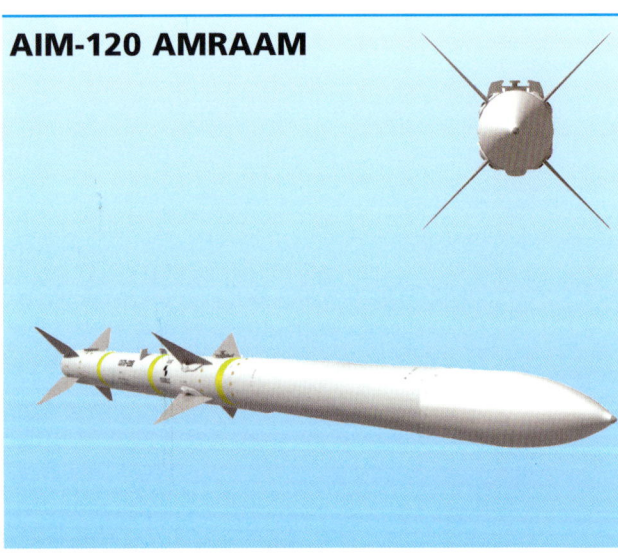

Description: The AIM-120 Advanced Medium-Range Air-to-Air Missile (AMRAAM) is a modern beyond-visual-range weapon capable of all-weather, day and night performance. It is gradually replacing the AIM-7 Sparrow in NATO and other western air forces. Faster, smaller and lighter than the AIM-7, it has improved capability against low-flying targets.

Country of origin: USA
Weight: 335lb (152kg)
Diameter: 7in (178mm)
Length: 12ft (3.66m)
Warhead: high explosive blast fragmentation
Wingspan: 20.7in (526mm)
Range: 30 miles (48km)
Guidance System: inertial navigation system, active radar

AIM-132 ASRAAM

Description: The AIM-132 ASRAAM (Advanced Short-Range Air-to-Air Missile) was developed by the United Kingdom to replace the Sidewinder in Royal Air Force service. It features conventional aerodynamic surfaces in the form of four delta wings at the extreme rear of the missile, rather than a thrust-vectoring system. It is also in service with the RAAF.

Country of origin: UK
Weight: 220.5 lb (100kg)
Diameter: 6.6in (168mm)
Length: 8ft 11.5in (2.73m)
Warhead: 22.05lb (10kg) blast fragmentation
Wingspan: 17.7in (45cm)
Range: 984ft-9.3 miles (300m-15km)
Guidance System: imaging infrared, strapdown inertial

DIRECTORY

DARTER

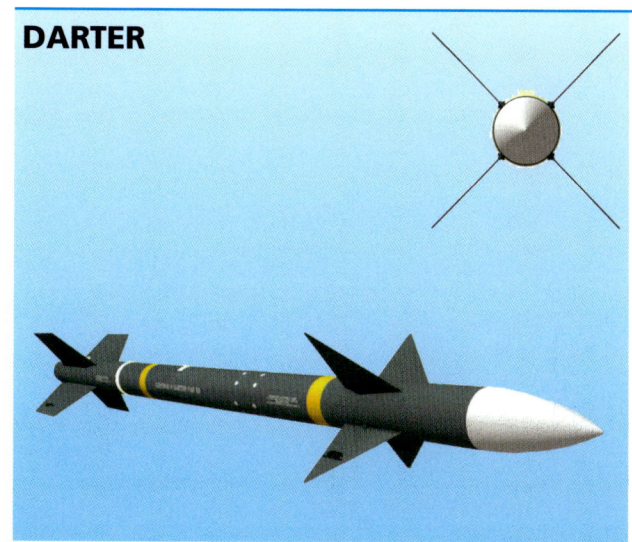

Description: The Darter is a short-range air-to-air missile developed by Denel Aerospace Systems of South Africa and Brazilian Mectron for the Brazilian Air Force. The original missile design is known as A-Darter to distinguish it from a radar-guided BVR version known as R-Darter. The missile has been offered to the South African and Pakistan Air Forces.

Country of origin: SA/Brazil
Weight: 196lb (89kg)
Diameter: 6,47in (166mm)
Length: 9.77ft (2.980m)
Warhead: high explosive fragmentation
Wingspan: 19.17in (488mm)
Range: Not available
Guidance System: infrared homing

IRIS-T

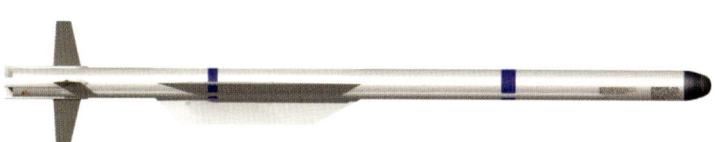
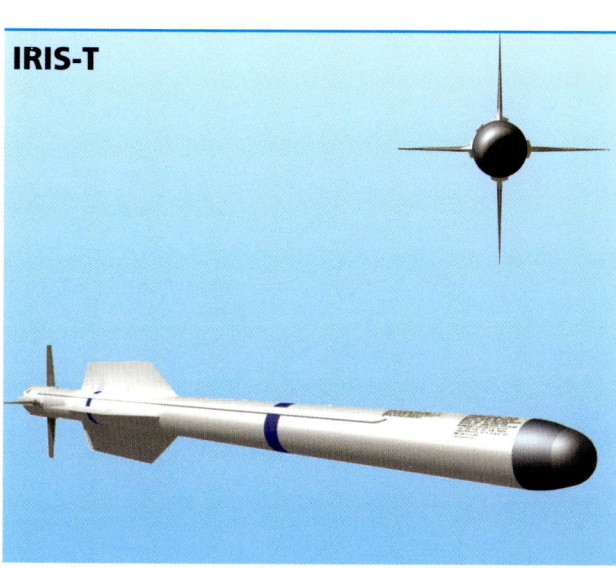

Description: IRIS-T (Infra Red Imaging System Tail/Thrust Vector-Controlled) is a German-led programme to develop a short-range air-to-air missile to replace the AIM-9 Sidewinder. It was started when Britain and Germany failed to reach agreement on the joint development of the AIM-132 ASRAAM, mainly because the latter lacked a thrust-vectoring system.

Country of origin: German-led international program
Weight: 192.6lb (87.4kg)
Diameter: 5in (127mm)
Length: 9.6ft (2.936m)
Warhead: high explosive fragmentation
Wingspan: 17.5in (447mm)
Range: 15.5 miles (25km)
Guidance System: Infrared homing

MATRA R550 MAGIC

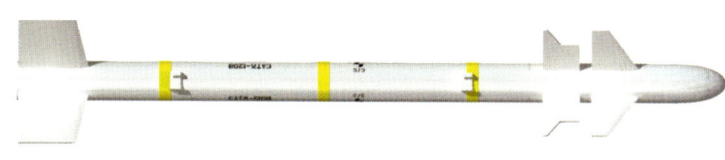

Description: Designed in the late 1960s, the Matra R550 Magic short-range air-to-air missile was deployed in 1976. The missile is still carried by the Super Etendard, Mirage 2000 and Rafale and was supplied to the many air forces within the French sphere of influence. It is gradually being replaced by the MBDA MICA.

Country of origin: France
Weight: 196lb (89kg)
Diameter: 6.1in (157mm)
Length: 8.92ft (2.72m)
Warhead: 28.5lb (13kg) fragmentation
Wingspan: not available
Range: 984ft–9.3 miles (300m–15km)

MODERN AIR-LAUNCHED WEAPONS

METEOR

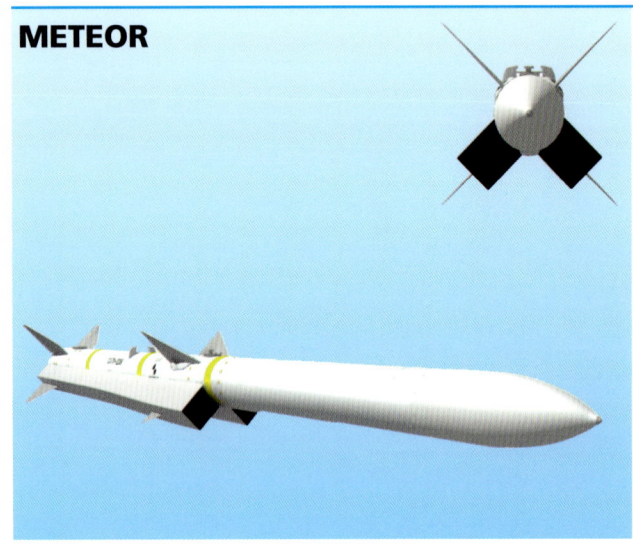

Description: Meteor is an active radar-guided beyond-visual-range (BVR) air-to-air missile being developed by MBDAS (Matra BAE Dynamics Alenia) for the Eurofighter Typhoon and other modern combat types. It is designed to give its operators a multi-shot capability against agile targets manoeuvring in a heavy ECM environment and has a novel form of ramjet propulsion.

Country of origin: UK/France/Germany/Italy
Weight: 407lb (185kg)
Diameter: 7.00in (0.178m)
Length: 12.00ft (3.65m)
Warhead: high explosive blast fragmentation
Wingspan: Not known
Range: 60+miles (100+km)
Guidance System: inertial mid-course with datalink updates, active radar

MICA RF

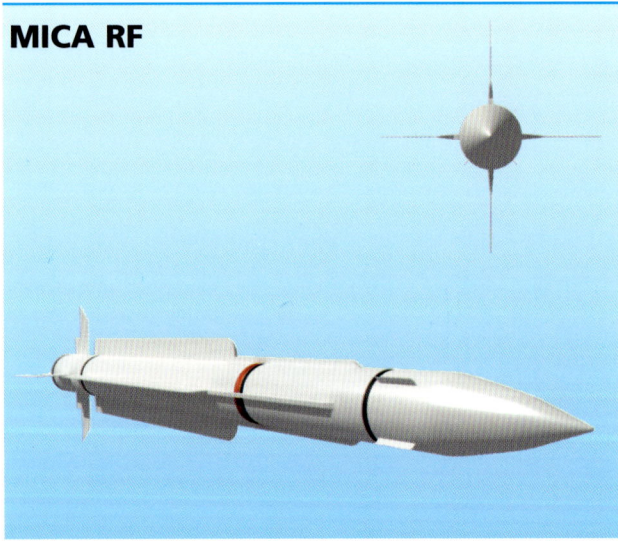
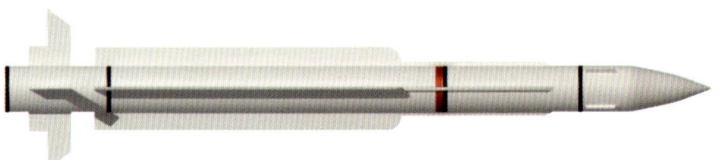

Description: The MBDA Mica (Missile d'interception et de combat aerien) is a multi-target fire-and-forget short and medium-range AAM system. It was developed from 1982 to arm France's Mirage 2000 and Rafale fighters. The MICA RF has an active radar homing seeker and is also known as the MICA EM.

Country of origin: UK/France/Germany/Italy
Weight: 246.8lb (112kg)
Diameter: 6.24in (160mm)
Length: 10.16ft (3.1m)
Warhead: 26.5lb (12kg) focused splinters high explosive
Wingspan: 21.9in (560mm)
Range: 1640ft-37 miles (500m-60km)
Guidance System: Inertial guidance active radar homing

MICA IR

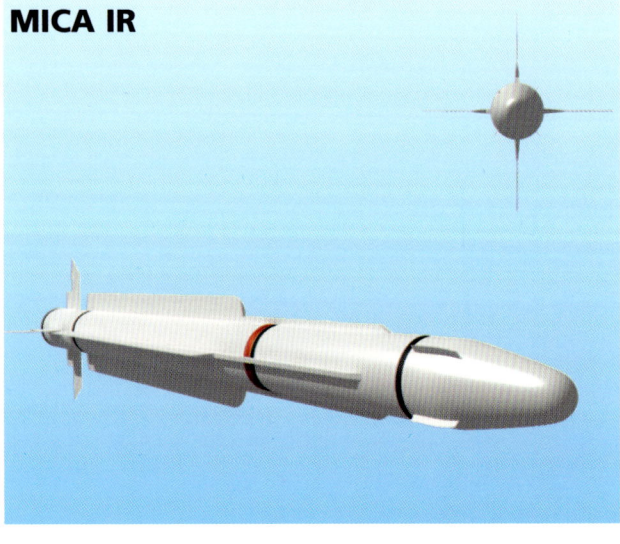
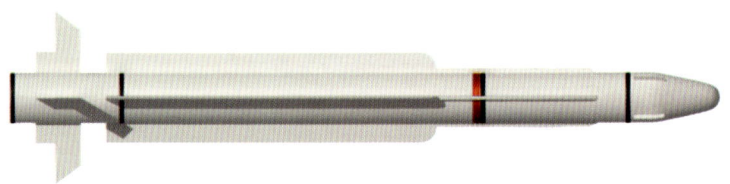

Description: MICA IR is the designation of the infrared homing version of the MICA missile. MICA, which can also be launched from ground platforms, is designed to lock-on after launch, which means it can be launched at a specific threat before its seeker head has acquired the target.

Country of origin: UK/France/Germany/Italy
Weight: 246.8lb (112kg)
Diameter: 6.24in (160mm)
Length: 10.16ft (3.1m)
Warhead: 26.5lb (12kg) focused splinters high explosive
Wingspan: 21.9in (560mm)
Range: 1640ft–37 miles (500m–60km)
Guidance System: Infrared homing

DIRECTORY

MISTRAL

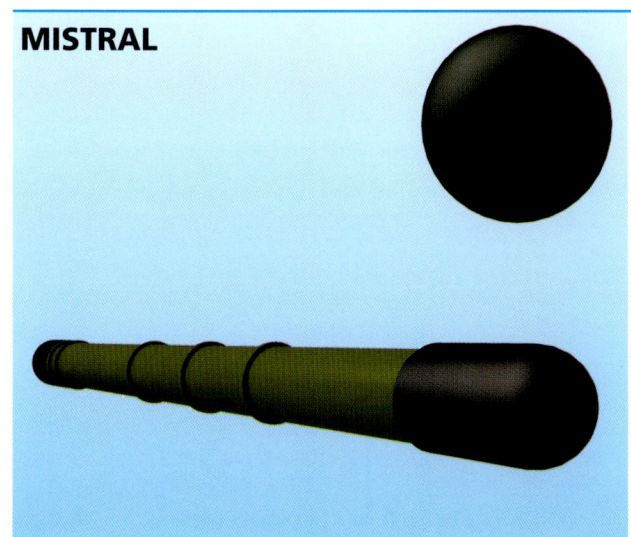

Description: Developed by the European multinational company MBDA, Mistral was designed as a short-range man-portable air defence missile. However, specialized launch units also allow it to be fired from armoured vehicles, ships or helicopters such as the Eurocopter Tiger, Denel Rooivalk and Aerospatiale Gazelle. Airborne launchers usually hold six missiles.

Country of origin: UK/France/Germany/Italy
Weight (warhead): 6.5lb (2.95kg)
Diameter: 3.5in (90mm)
Length: 6.1ft (1.86m)
Warhead: high explosive
Wingspan: n/a
Range: 3.3 miles (5.3km)
Guidance System: infrared homing

PYTHON

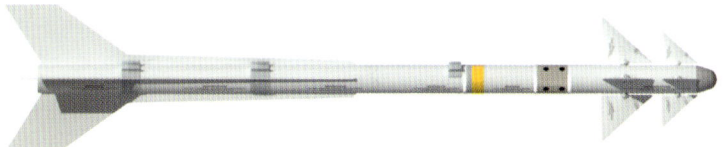

Description: Originally known as Shafrir, Python is a family of air-to-air missiles developed by Israel's RAFAEL Armament Development Authority. The Shafrir-2 variant was in widespread use during the Yom Kippur war of 1973, shooting down 89 enemy aircraft, and the 1982 Lebanon war, destroying 35 aircraft. It is license-built in the People's Republic of China.

Country of origin: Israel
Weight: 228lb (103.6kg)
Diameter: 6.24in (160mm)
Length: 10.16ft (3.1m)
Warhead: 24lb (11kg)
Wingspan: 25in (640mm)
Range: 12.4 miles (20km)
Guidance System: dual waveband electro-optical imaging seeker

AIR-TO-GROUND WEAPONS

AASM

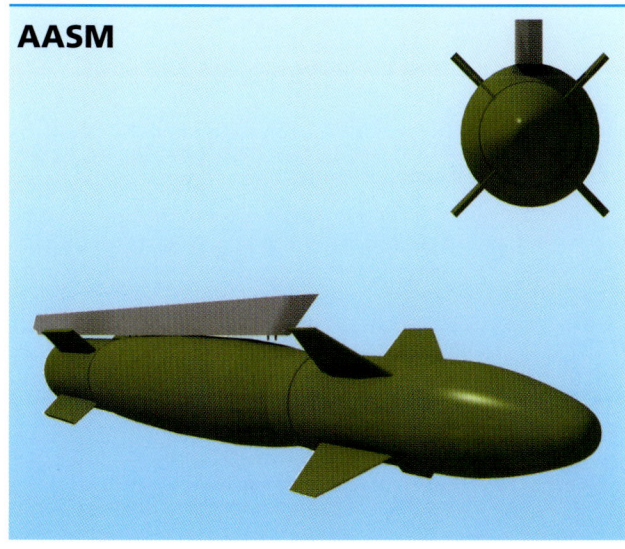

Description: The AASM (Armement Air-Sol Modulaire) is a French air-to-surface modular weapon which became operational in 2006. A precision guided weapon, it is designed to penetrate hardened targets and buried bunkers and gains altitude during the final stages of its attack profile in order to gain more kinetic energy during its terminal dive.

Country of origin: France
Weight: 750lb (340kg)
Diameter: Not known
Length: 10ft (3.10m)
Warhead: 550lb (250kg) standard or penetration bomb
Wingspan: n/a
Range: 9-37 miles (15-60km) depending on launch altitude
Guidance System: Hybrid GPS/INS

MODERN AIR-LAUNCHED WEAPONS

AGM-65 MAVERICK

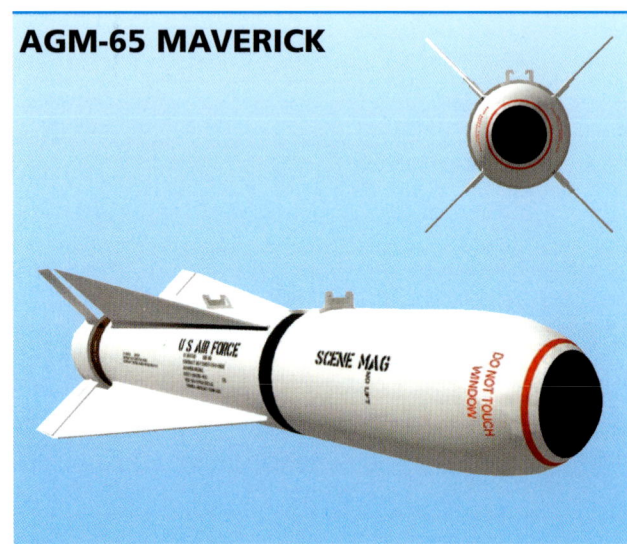

Description: Although essentially a battlefield missile, the AGM-65 Maverick can also be used on interdiction missions. It is compatible with a wide variety of aircraft weapons systems and comes in several versions, including TV-guided, imaging infrared and laser-guided. Once the missile is launched, it locks on to its target automatically.

Country of origin: USA
Weight: 466-670lb (211-304kg)
Diameter: 12in (300mm)
Length: 8ft 2in (2.49m)
Warhead: 125lb (57kg) hollow charge or 300lb (140kg) high explosive
Wingspan: 2ft 4in (710mm)
Range: 17 miles (28km)
Guidance System: electro-optical, infrared imaging or laser-guided

AGM-78 STANDARD ARM

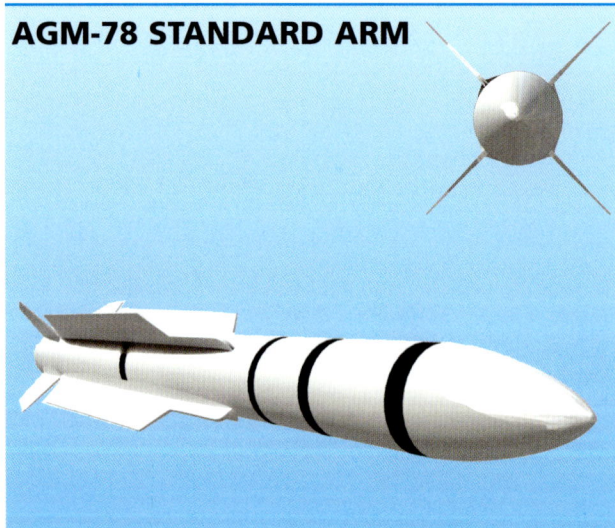
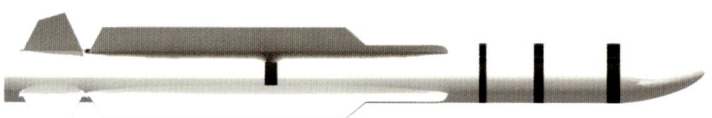

Description: As its name implies, the AGM-78 Standard ARM was an anti-radar missile, and was developed by General Dynamics from the RIM-66 surface-to-air missile to replace the AGM-45 Shrike, which was less than adequate for its task in some respects. The AGM-78 was the primary anti-radar weapon of the USAF's 'Wild Weasel' defence suppression aircraft.

Country of origin: USA
Weight: 780lb (355kg)
Diameter: 10in (254mm)
Length: 13ft (4.1m)
Warhead: high explosive direct fragmentation
Wingspan: 3.6ft (1,1m)
Range: 66 miles (106km)
Guidance System: passive radar homing

AGM-86C

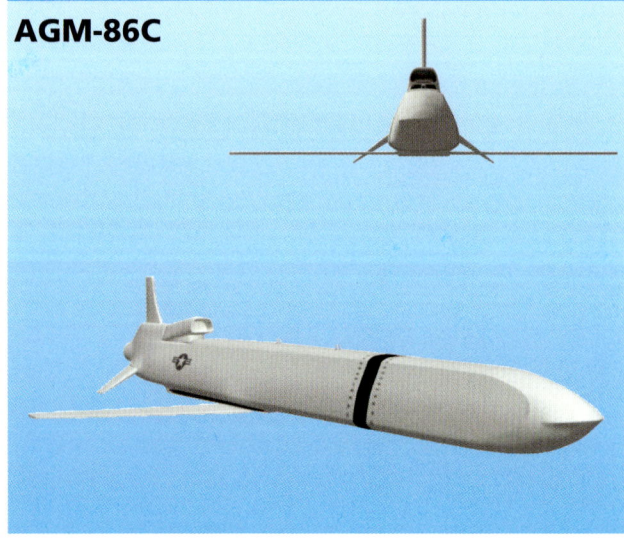
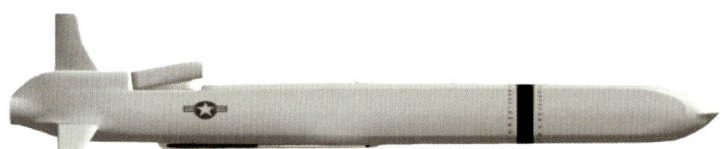

Description: The AGM-86B/C air-launched versions of the cruise missile were developed to enhance the survivability of the USAF's ageing fleet of B-52 bombers. The B-52H could carry six missiles on each of two underwing pylons, and eight internally on a rotary launcher, giving the aircraft a total capacity of twenty missiles.

Country of origin: USA
Weight: 3200lb (1429kg)
Diameter: 2.0ft (0.62m)
Length: 20ft 10in (6.35m)
Warhead: Nuclear (AGM-86B); 3000lb (1400kg) conventional (AGM-86C)
Wingspan: 12ft 0in (3.65m)
Range: 680 miles (1100km) (AGM-86C)
Guidance System: INS-GPS

DIRECTORY

AGM-88 HARM

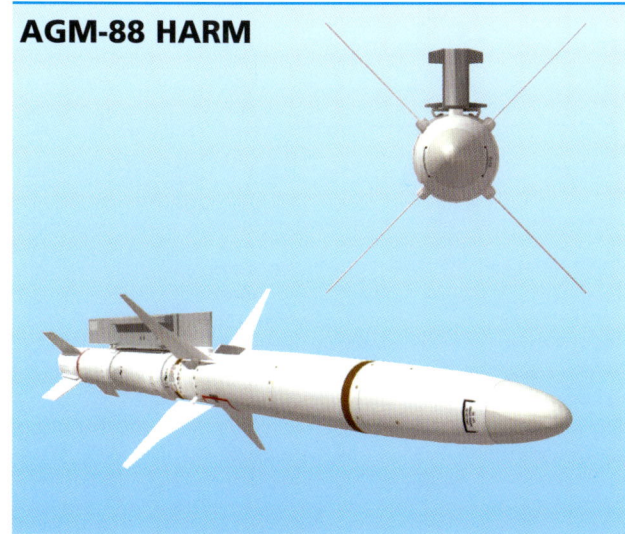

Description: The AGM-88 HARM high-speed anti-radar missile was developed to replace the AGM-45 Shrike and AGM-78. Its smokeless, solid propellant, dual-thrust rocket motor gives it a speed of over Mach 2. The latest upgrade is the AGM-88E Advanced Anti Radiation Guided Missile (AARGM), a joint American-Italian venture.

Country of origin: USA
Weight: 780lb (355kg)
Diameter: 10in (254mm)
Length: 13ft (4.1m)
Warhead: high explosive direct fragmentation
Wingspan: 3.6ft (1,1m)
Range: 66 miles (106km)
Guidance System: passive radar homing

AGM-114 HELLFIRE

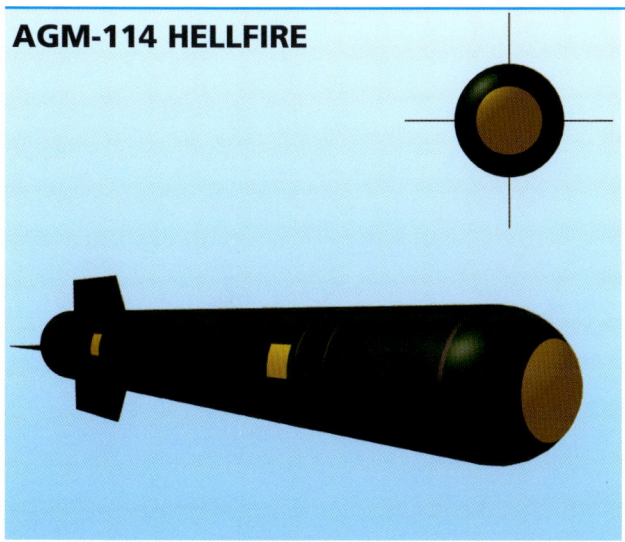

Description: The AGM-114 Hellfire is a very comprehensive weapons system. It was designed primarily for use by attack helicopters, but can also be deployed from fixed-wing aircraft as well as from naval and land-based launch systems. Hellfire II is an upgraded version, developed in the early 1990s, is a modular missile system.

Country of origin: USA
Weight: 100-108lb (45.4-49kg)
Diameter: 7in (178mm)
Length: 64in (1.63m)
Warhead: high explosive anti-tank; blast fragmentation
Wingspan: 13in (33cm)
Range: 1638ft-5 miles (500m-8km)
Guidance System: semi-active laser homing; millimetre wave radar seeker

AGM-130

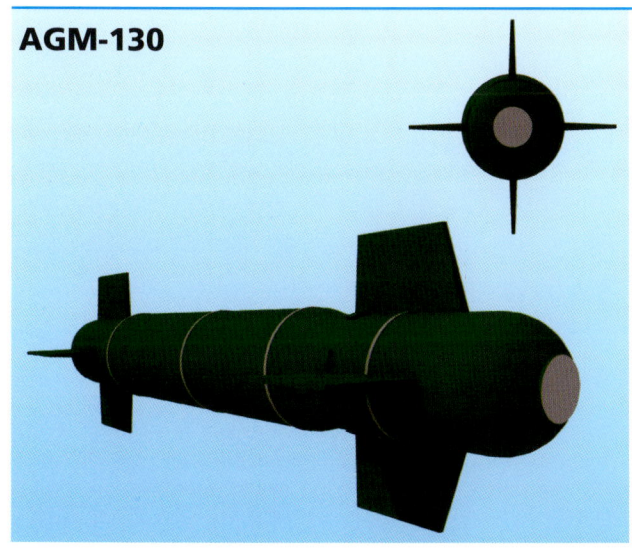
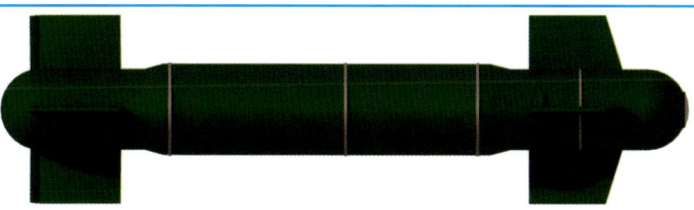

Description: Essentially a rocket-powered version of the GBU-15 bomb, the Boeing AGM-130A, which became operational in 1998, uses inertial navigation aided by the Global Positioning System (GPS) and can be re-targeted in flight. Two AGM-130As can be carried by the F-15E Strike Eagle and a lighter version, the AGM-130LW, is designed to be carried by the F-16C/D.

Country of origin: USA
Weight: 2917lb (1323kg)
Diameter: 15-18in (380-460mm)
Length: 12ft 10.5in (3.92m)
Warhead: 530lb or 950lb (240kg or 430kg) BLU-109 or Mk 84
Wingspan: 59in (1.50m)
Range: over 40 miles (60km)
Guidance System: inertial, GPS

MODERN AIR-LAUNCHED WEAPONS

AGM-154 JSOW

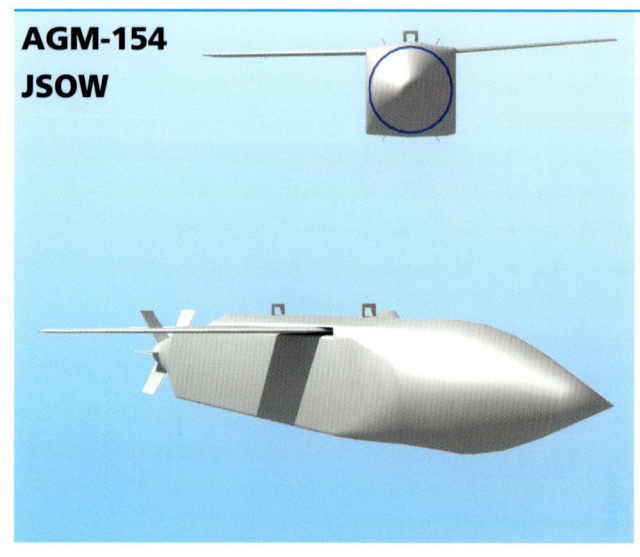
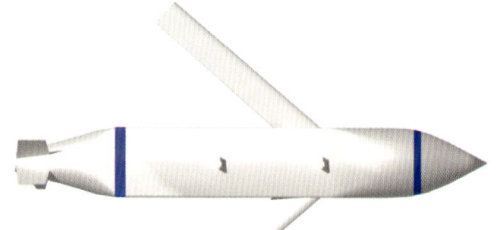

Description: The AGM-154 Joint Standoff Weapon was developed to provide the US Navy and USAF with a common high-precision missile for use over medium ranges against defended targets. Full-scale production began in December 1999 and the weapon has been used operationally in Iraq, the Balkans and Afghanistan.

Country of origin: USA
Weight: 1065-1095lb (483-497kg)
Diameter: 13in (330mm)
Length: 13.3ft (4.1m)
Warhead: combined effects bomblets
Wingspan: 8.8ft (2.70m)
Range: 14-81 miles (22-130km) depending on launch altitude
Guidance System: INS/GPS

AGM-158 JASSM

Description: The turbojet-powered AGM-158 JASSM (Joint Air-to-Surface Standoff Missile is a 'stealthy' standoff missile developed for use by a wide range of US combat aircraft, including the B-2 Spirit bomber Production of JASSM began in December 2001, but the programme was delayed as a result of failures during the evaluation phase.

Country of origin: USA
Weight: 2150lb (975kg)
Diameter: Not known
Length: 14ft (4.27m)
Warhead: 1000lb (450kg) penetrator
Wingspan: 7ft 11in (2.4m)
Range: 230+ miles (370+km)
Guidance System: INS/GPS

ALARM

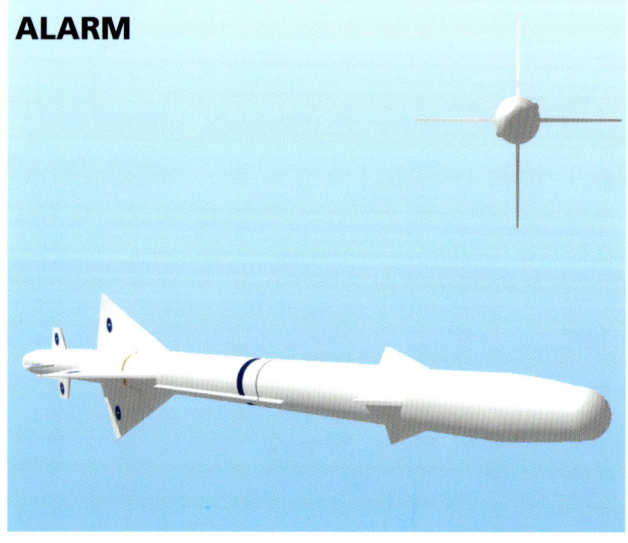
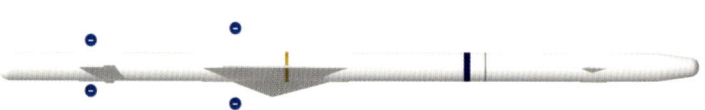

Description: Developed by British Aerospace Dynamics, ALARM (Air Launched Anti-Radiation Missile) is a defence suppression weapon, designed to destroy enemy radars. It is a fire-and-forget system with a loiter capability. If the target radar shuts down, it climbs to 8 miles (13km) and then loiters under a parachute until the radar illuminates again.

Country of origin: UK
Weight: 590lb (268kg)
Diameter: 9.1in (230mm)
Length: 13.9ft (4.24m)
Warhead: proximity fuzed high explosive
Wingspan: 2.4ft (0.73m)
Range: 58 miles (93km)
Guidance System: pre-programmed passive radar seeker

DIRECTORY

AS-30L

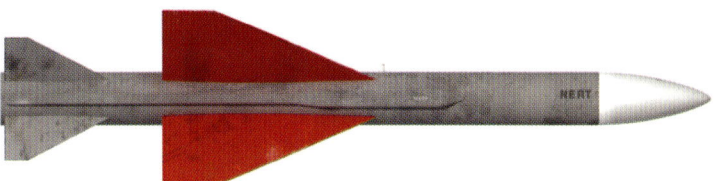
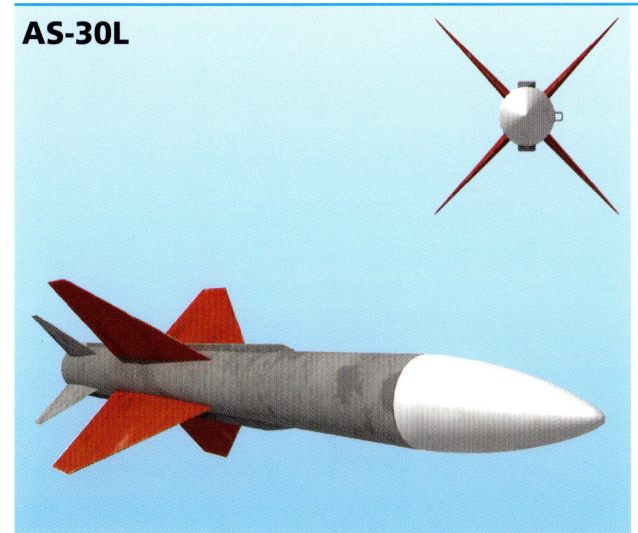

Description: Developed from the original well-tried Aérospatiale AS-30, the AS-30L is a French short-to-medium range air-to-ground standoff laser-guided attack missile. It was used operationally by French SEPECAT Jaguar strike aircraft in the 1991 Gulf War and in NATO operations over Bosnia. The weapon is also used by the Israeli and Indian Air Forces.

Country of origin: France
Weight: 1146lb (520kg)
Diameter: 13in (340mm)
Length: 12ft 1in (3.7m)
Warhead: 529lb (240kg) semi-armour-piercing high explosive
Wingspan: 3.2ft (1m)
Range: 1.8-6.8 miles (3-11km)
Guidance System: semi-active laser homing

BRAHMOS

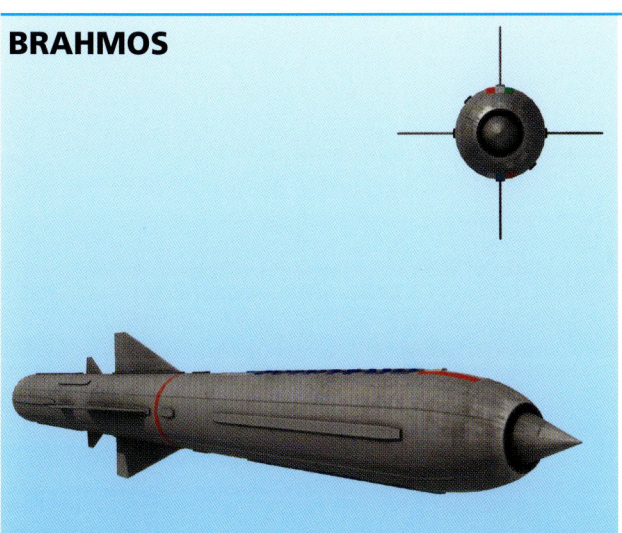

Description: BrahMos is a supersonic cruise missile and is a joint Indian-Russian venture; its name derives from the Brahmaputra river of India and Russia's Moskva. It is designed to be launched from land, ships or aircraft and, with a top speed of Mach 2.8, is the world's fastest cruise missile.

Country of origin: India/Russia
Weight: 6612lb (3000kg)
Diameter: 2ft (0.6m)
Length: 27.5ft (8.4m)
Warhead: 661lb (300kg) conventional semi-armour-piercing
Wingspan: not known
Range: 180 miles (290km)
Guidance System: INS/GPS

BRIMSTONE

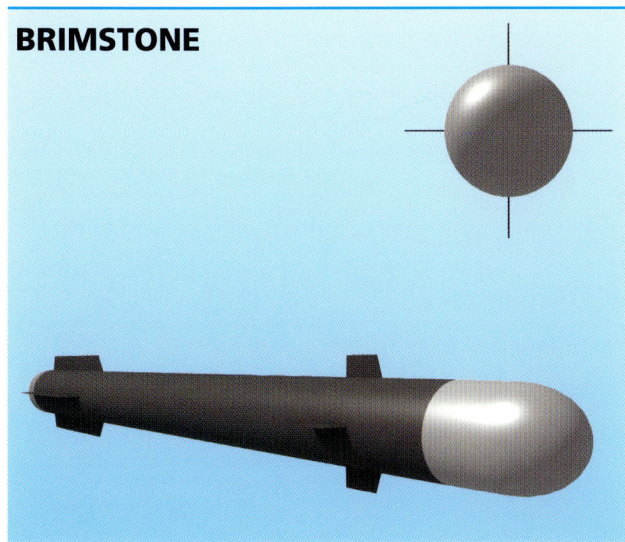

Description: Brimstone was designed to meet an RAF requirement for a long-range anti-armour weapon to replace the BL755 cluster bomb, enabling strike aircraft to attack tanks and armoured vehicles at stand-off range. It is a fire-and-forget weapon, its computer being loaded with target data by the Weapon Systems Officer (WSO) prior to launch.

Country of origin: UK/France/Germany/Italy
Weight: 107lb (48.5kg)
Diameter: 7in (178mm)
Length: 6ft (1.8m)
Warhead: high explosive anti-tank
Wingspan: n/a
Range: 7.5 miles (12km)
Guidance System: radar and INS autopilot

MODERN AIR-LAUNCHED WEAPONS

KH-15 (AS-6) KICKBACK

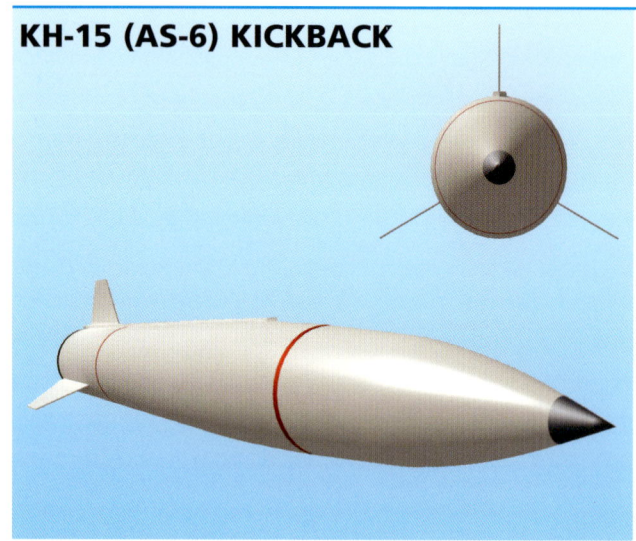
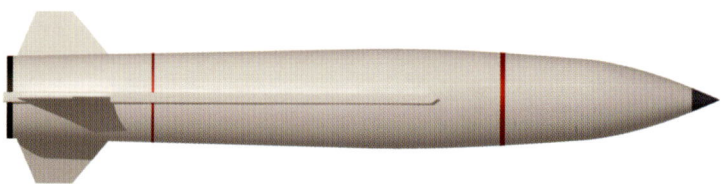

Description: Originally developed as a standoff nuclear weapon, the Raduga Kh-15 (NATO reporting name AS-16 Kickback) was intended primarily as an anti-shipping weapon, to be carried by the Tupolev Tu-22M Backfire bomber. The Tu-22M3 can carry ten missiles, six in its rotary bomb bay and four on underwing pylons.

Country of origin: Russia
Weight: 2650lb (1200kg)
Diameter: 17.9in (455mm)
Length: 15ft 8in (4.78m)
Warhead: conventional, various
Wingspan: 36.2in (92cm)
Range: 160nm (300km)
Guidance System: inertial, active radar

KH-25L (AS-10) KAREN

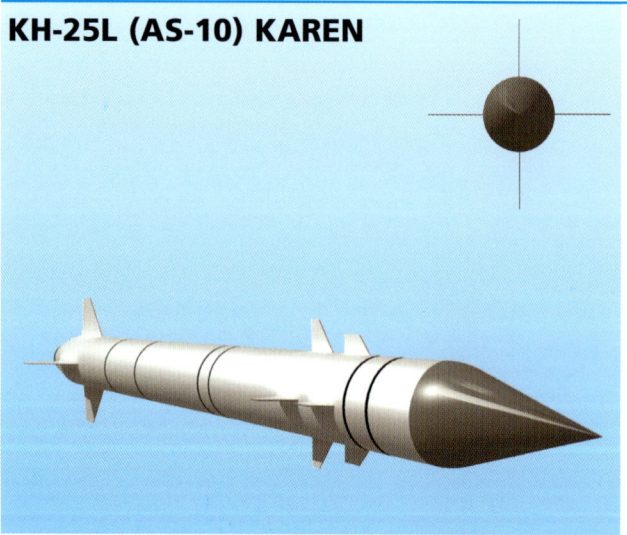

Description: The Kh-25 (NATO reporting name AS-10 Karen) is a family of Russian lightweight air-to-ground missiles, which includes an anti-radar variant, the Kh-25MP. The missile is derived from the beam-riding Kh-66, which was the Soviet Union's first tactical air-to-ground missile. Another variant, the Kh-25L, has a semi-active laser seeker.

Country of origin: Russia
Weight: 659lb (299kg)
Diameter: 10.8in (275mm)
Length: 12ft 2in (3.75m)
Warhead: high explosive
Wingspan: 29.7in (75.5cm)
Range: 5.4nm (10km)
Guidance System: laser, passive radar

KH-29L (AS-14) KEDGE

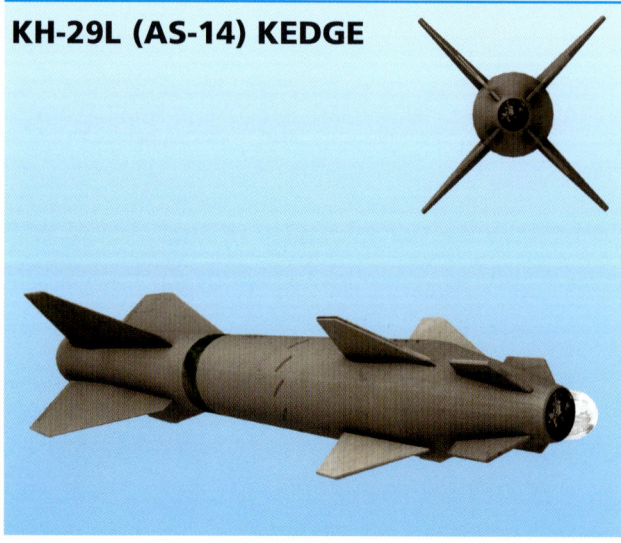

Description: The Kh-29 (NATO reporting name AS-14 Kedge) is a Russian air-to-surface missile with a large warhead, either laser or TV guidance, and is carried by tactical aircraft such as the Su-25 Fencer. It is intended for use mainly against larger battlefield targets, hardened aircraft shelters, depots, bridges and ships.

Country of origin: Russia
Weight: 1460lb (660kg)
Diameter: 15in (380mm)
Length: 12ft 10in (3.9m)
Warhead: high explosive penetrator
Wingspan: 43in (110cm)
Range: 5.4nm (10km)
Guidance System: semi-active laser

DIRECTORY

KH-29T

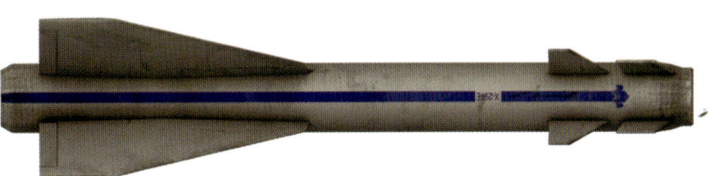

Description: The Kh-29T is a TV-guided version of the basic Kh-29 design which is equipped with automatic optical homing to a distinguishable object identified by the pilot. The Kh-29TE is a long-range development of the Kh-29T. The Kh-29 has been in service in its various forms since 1980.

Country of origin: Russia
Weight: 1510lb (690kg)
Diameter: 15in (380mm)
Length: 12ft 10in (3.9m)
Warhead: high explosive penetrator
Wingspan: 43in (110cm)
Range: 6.5nm (12km)
Guidance System: passive TV

KH-31A (AS-17) KRYPTON

Description: The Kh-31 (NATO reporting name AS-17 Krypton) is a Russian air-to-surface missile carried by the MiG-29 Fulcrum and Su-27 Flanker. It is a sea-skimming cruise missile with a speed of Mach 3.5, and is the first supersonic cruise missile capable of being launched by tactical aircraft. The Kh-31A is an anti-shipping variant.

Country of origin: Russia
Weight: 1340lb (610kg)
Diameter: 14in (360mm)
Length: 15.5ft (4.7m)
Warhead: high explosive shaped charge
Wingspan: 3.7ft (1.15m)
Range: 15.5-31 miles (25-50km)
Guidance System: inertial, active radar

KH-31P

Description: The Kh-31P is the anti-radar version of this missile, and is fitted with a passive seeker head. It remains at high altitude throughout its flight, permitting a higher speed and longer range. The seeker has three interchangeable modules to cover different frequency bands, but these can only be pre-set in the factory.

Country of origin: Russia
Weight: 1320lb (600kg)
Diameter: 14in (360mm)
Length: 15.5ft (4.7m)
Warhead: high explosive shaped charge
Wingspan: 3.7ft (1.15m)
Range: 70 miles (110km)
Guidance System: inertial with passive radar

MODERN AIR-LAUNCHED WEAPONS

KH-55 (AS-15) KENT

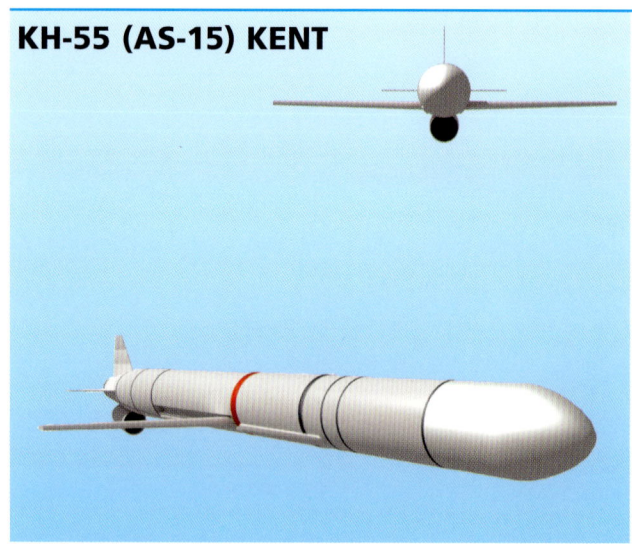
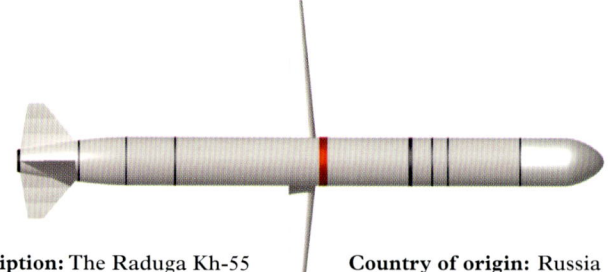

Description: The Raduga Kh-55 (NATO reporting name AS-15 Kent) is an air-launched cruise missile that can be armed with either nuclear or conventional warheads. The missile's folding wings, tail surfaces and turbofan engine pod deploy after launch. The Kh-55 was introduced into service in 1984 and several variants have been produced.

Country of origin: Russia
Weight: 4900-5300lb (2200-2400kg)
Diameter: 20.2 in (514mm)
Length: 24ft 5in (7.45m)
Warhead: nuclear or conventional
Wingspan: 10.16ft (3.1m)
Range: 1600nm (3000km)
Guidance System: inertial with Doppler/TERCOM updates

KH-59 (AS-13) KINGBOLT

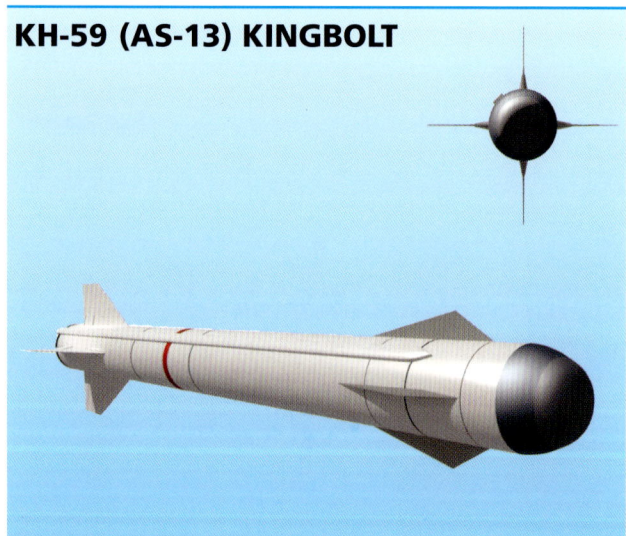
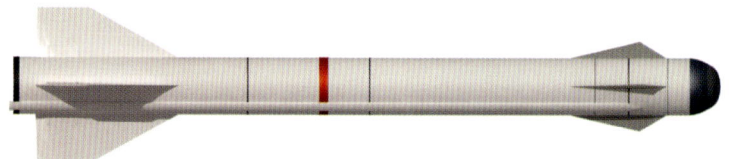

Description: The Raduga Kh-59, known to the Russians as Ovod (Gadfly) and to NATO as the AS-13 Kingbolt, is a TV-guided cruise missile with a two-stage solid fuel propulsion system. It is mainly a land attack weapon, but one version, the Kh-59MK, targets shipping. The design is based on that of the Kh-58 (AS-11 Kilter).

Country of origin: Russia
Weight: 2050lb (930kg)
Diameter: 15in (380mm)
Length: 18.3ft (5.7m)
Warhead: 705lb (320kg) cluster or shaped-charge fragmentation
Wingspan: 51.2in (1.3m)
Range: 110nm (200km)
Guidance System: inertial, then TV guidance

KH-59M (AS-18) KAZOO

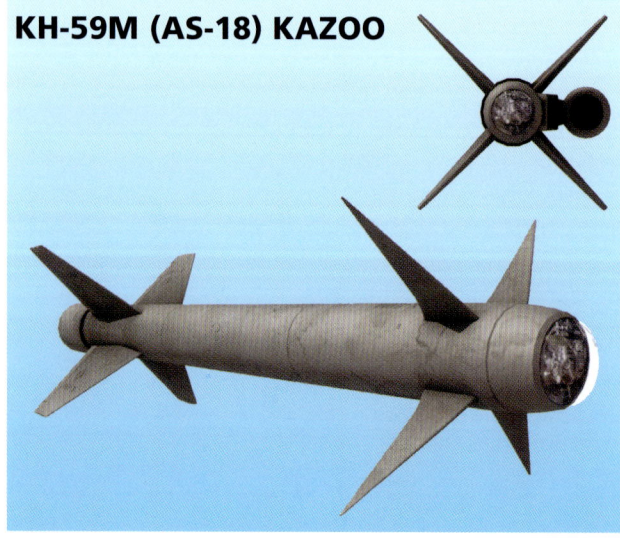
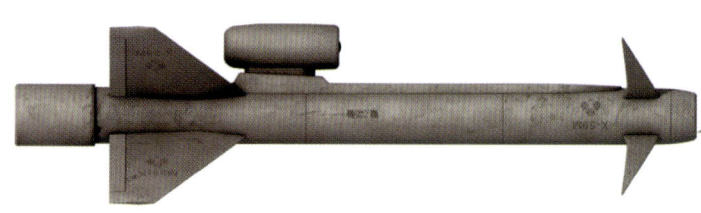

Description: In 1999 the Russians revealed that an export version of the Kh-59 had been developed. This was the Kh-59M, which was given the NATO reporting name AS-18 Kazoo. Target co-ordinates are fed into the missile before launch, and the initial flight phase is conducted under inertial guidance.

Country of origin: Russia
Weight: 2050lb (930kg)
Diameter: 15in (380mm)
Length: 18ft 3in (5.7m)
Warhead: 705lb (320kg) cluster or shaped-charge fragmentation
Wingspan: 51.2in (1.3m)
Range: 62nm (115km)
Guidance System: inertial, then TV guidance

DIRECTORY

KH-101

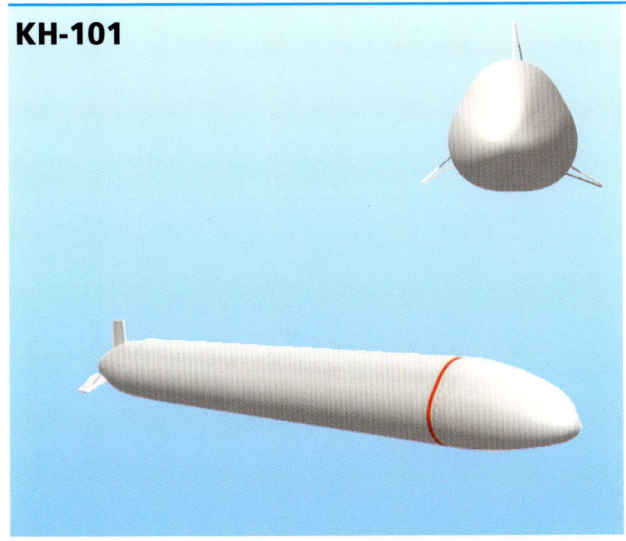

Description: Developed in the 1990s, the Kh-101 is a cruise missile with a conventional warhead, intended to be carried by the Tupolev Tu-95MS Bear-H, which would be armed with up to eight of the missiles, and possibly the Tu-160 Blackjack variable-geometry bomber, which could carry twelve. The status of the missile was unclear in 2010.

Country of origin: Russia
Weight: 5289lb (2400kg)
Diameter: not known
Length: not known
Warhead: 2204lb (1000kg) high explosive
Wingspan: not known
Range: up to 3100 miles (5000km)

LAU-68

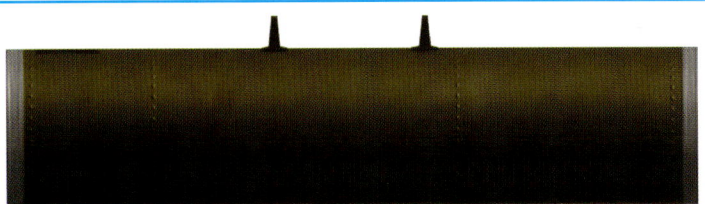
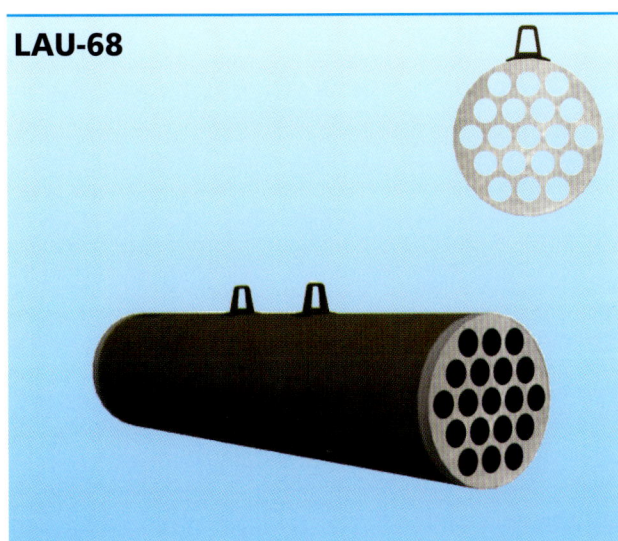

Description: The LAU-68 is a seven-tube rocket launcher originally designed to fire the American 2.75in (70mm) Folding-Fin Aircraft Rocket (FFAR) as an air interception weapon. During the Korean War it was deployed on aircraft such as the Lockheed F-94C Starfire, the pods being mounted on the wingtips. It later evolved into an air-to-ground weapon.

Country of origin: USA
Dimensions apply to rocket:
Weight: 18.5lb (8.4kg) (empty)
Length: 4ft (1.2m)
Warhead: 6lb (2.7kg)
Wingspan: n/a
Range: 11,000ft (3400m)
Guidance System: none

LAU-131

Description: While the US Army and Marine Corps use the LAU-68 rocket pod, the Air Force employs the LAU-131. The rocket launchers can discharge their missiles in single-shot or ripple-fire mode. They are cheap enough to be disposable, yet durable enough to be re-used up to 32 times. The launch tubes are held together with metal ribs and covered with an aluminium skin.

Country of origin: USA
Dimensions apply to rocket:
Weight: 18.5lb (8.4kg) (empty)
Length: 4ft (1.2m)
Warhead: 6lb (2.7kg)
Wingspan: n/a
Range: 11,000ft (3400m)
Guidance System: none

MODERN AIR-LAUNCHED WEAPONS

S-8 POD

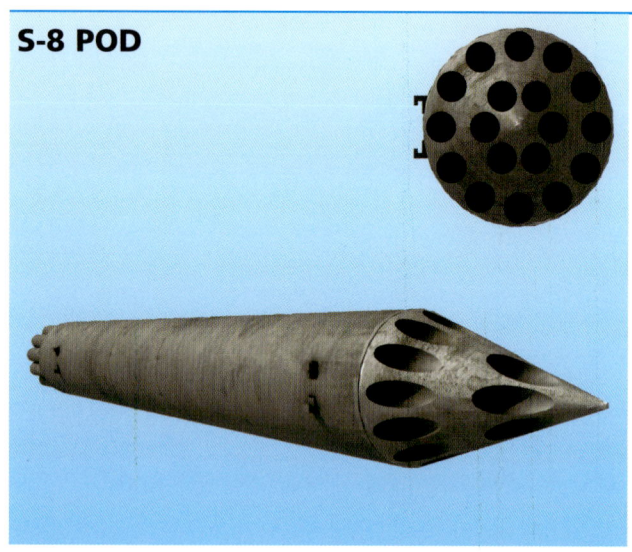

Description: Developed in the 1970s, the S-8 air-to-ground rocket is widely used by the fighter-bombers of the Russian Air Force and various export customers. Up to 20 can be carried in one pod, shown here. The weapon is produced in many subtypes, each with a different warhead for use against different targets.

Country of origin: Russia
Dimensions apply to rocket:
Weight: 25lb (11.3kg)
Diameter: 3.1in (80mm)
Length: 5.2ft (1.57m)
Warhead: high explosive anti-tank
Wingspan: n/a
Range: up to 2.5 miles (4km)
Guidance System: none

S-8BM

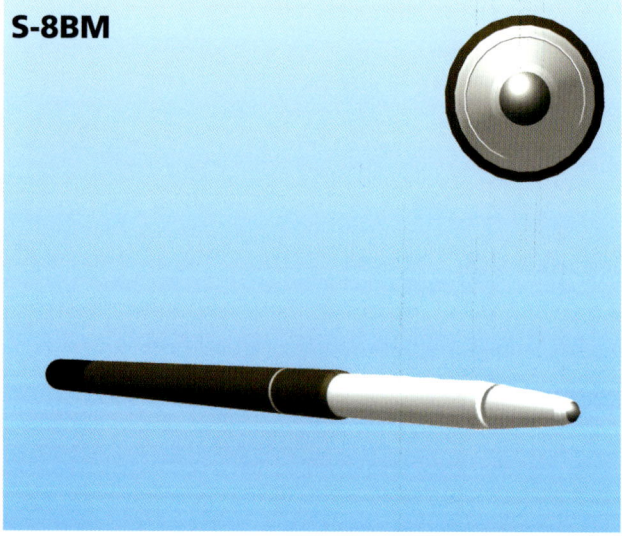

Description: The S-8BM is a runway-cratering version of the basic S-8. The munition has a velocity of 1476ft/sec (450 m/sec) and can penetrate 32 in (800mm) of reinforced concrete. It was developed from the slightly less powerful S-8B. The weapon can be used by either tactical aircraft or battlefield helicopters.

Country of origin: Russia
Weight: 33.5lb (15.2kg)
Diameter: 3.1in (80mm)
Length: 5.0 ft (1.54m)
Warhead: 16lb (7.41kg) penetrating
Wingspan: n/a
Range: up to 1.4 miles (2.2km)

S-8OM

Description: The S-8OM version of the Russian S-8 unguided rocket is an illuminator, deploying a flare warhead that burns for 30 seconds. It is intended primarily for use by battlefield helicopters such as the Mi-24 Hind, operating in the forward battle area close to concentrations of enemy armour.

Weight: 27lb (12.1kg)
Diameter: 3.1in (80mm)
Length: 5.4ft (1.63m)
Warhead: illuminating
Wingspan: n/a
Range: 2.8 miles (4.5km)
Guidance System: none

DIRECTORY

S-13OF

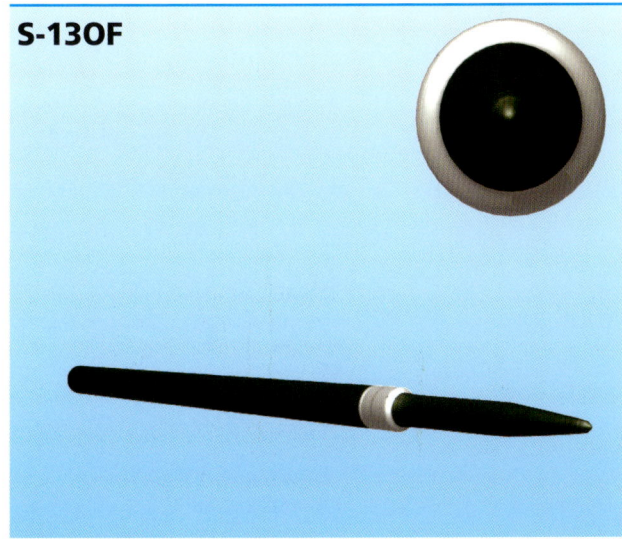

Description: First deployed with the then Soviet Air Force in the mid-1980s, the S-13 aircraft rocket pod system was designed to destroy a variety of front-line targets, including runways, command and control centres and command vehicles. The S-13OF has a high explosive warhead with 450 precut fragments.

Country of origin: Russia
Weight: 152lb (69kg)
Diameter: 4.79in (122mm)
Length: 9.80 ft (2.99m)
Warhead: high explosive, fragmentation
Wingspan: n/a
Range: 2 miles (3.2km)
Guidance System: none

S-13T

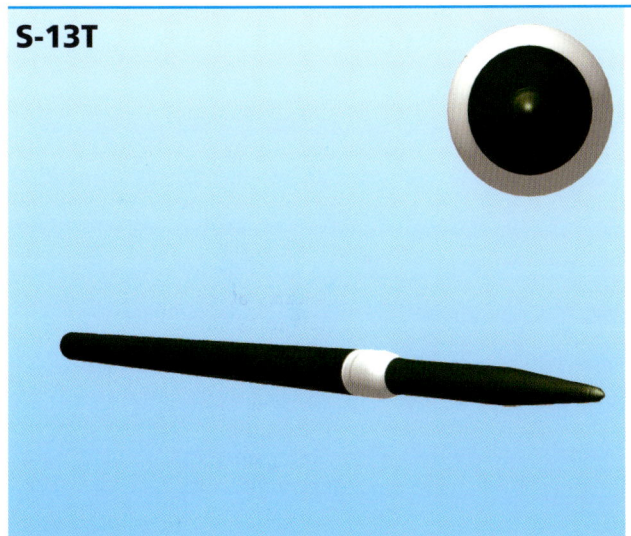

Description: The S-13T is a tandem-warhead version of the Russian S-13 unguided air-launched rocket, which was developed in the 1970s to meet a Soviet Air Force requirement for a weapon capable of penetrating hardened aircraft shelters and pillboxes and cratering runways. Its combined warhead can penetrate 20ft (6m) of earth and 3.28ft (1m) of concrete.

Country of origin: Russia
Weight: 165lb (75kg)
Diameter: 5in (130mm)
Length: 9.80 ft (2.99m)
Warhead: combined penetrator, high explosive
Wingspan: n/a
Range: 2 miles (3.2km)
Guidance System: none

S-24B

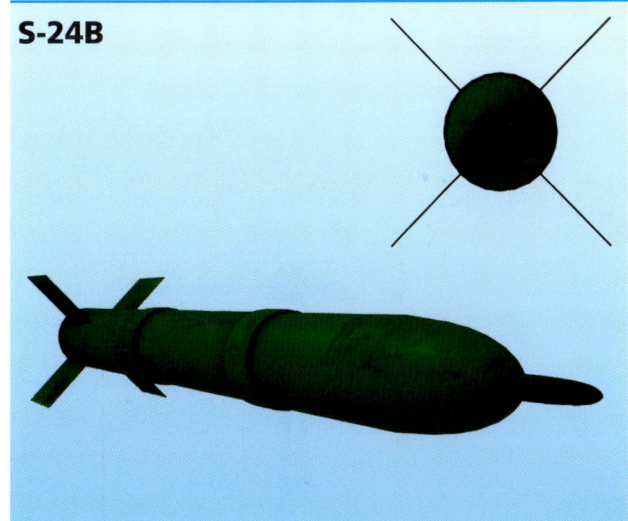

Description: The S-24B is a long-serving air-to-ground missile that remains a viable weapon in today's Russian Air Force. It is large and powerful, and is carried on underwing pods by tactical aircraft like the Sukhoi Su-25 Frogfoot. The Russians were pioneers in the development of air-launched rocket weapons.

Country of origin: Russia
Weight: 518lb (235kg)
Diameter: 9.5in (240mm)
Length: 7ft 8in (2.33m)
Warhead: 271lb (123kg) blast fragmentation
Wingspan: n/a
Range: 1.3 miles (2km)
Guidance System: none

MODERN AIR-LAUNCHED WEAPONS

S-25LD

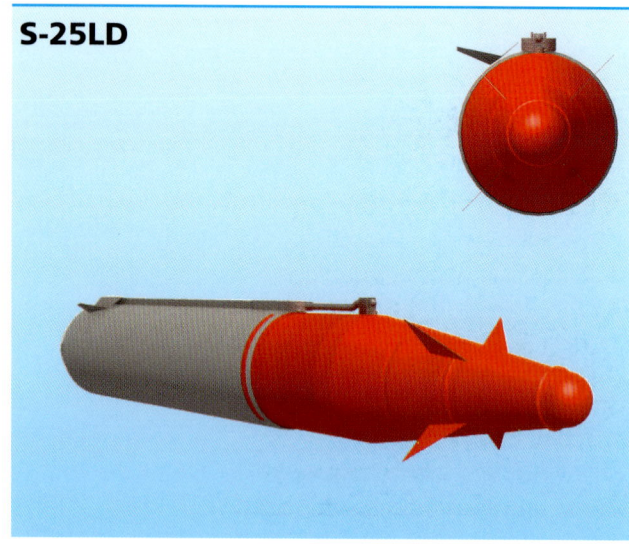

Description: The S-25LD is a laser-guided variant of the Russian S-25 air-to-ground rocket, the basic version of which is unguided. The principal carrier is the Sukhoi Su-25 Frogfoot. The S-25LD is roughly the equivalent of the US AGM-65 Maverick and is intended for use mainly as an anti-armour weapon.

Country of origin: Russia
Weight: 1058lb (480kg)
Diameter: 13.4in (340mm)
Length: 10.8ft (3.31m)
Warhead: 419lb (190kg) high explosive
Wingspan: not known
Range: 1.9 miles (3km)
Guidance System: laser designator

STORM SHADOW

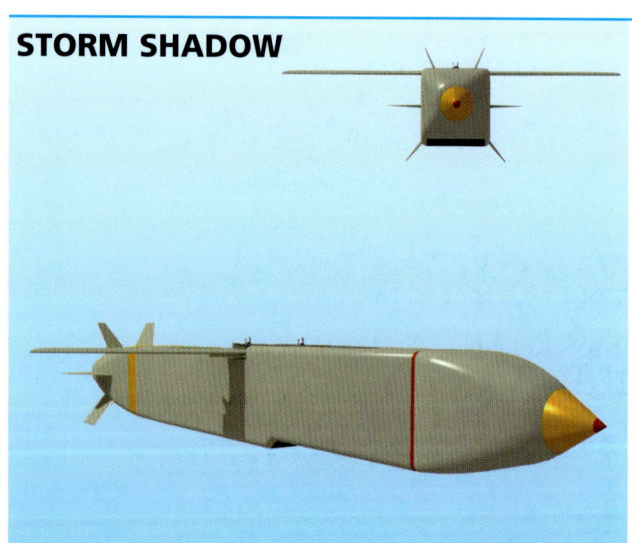

Description: Storm Shadow is a 'stealthy' air-launched cruise missile developed by the European MBDA consortium. It can be carried by the Panavia Tornado GR4 (UK), Tornado IDS (Italy), Saab Gripen (Sweden), Eurofighter Typhoon, Dassault Mirage 2000 and Rafale. It is a fire-and-forget weapon, pre-programmed before launch, and has a penetrator warhead.

Country of origin: UK/France/Germany/Italy
Weight: 2710lb (1230kg)
Diameter: 5.5ft (1660mm)
Length: 16.7ft (5.1m)
Warhead: 992lb (450kg) BROACH (Bomb Royal Ordnance Augmented Charge)
Wingspan: 9.3ft (2.84m)
Range: 155 miles (250km) plus
Guidance System: Inertial, GPS, TERPROM

TAURUS KEPD350

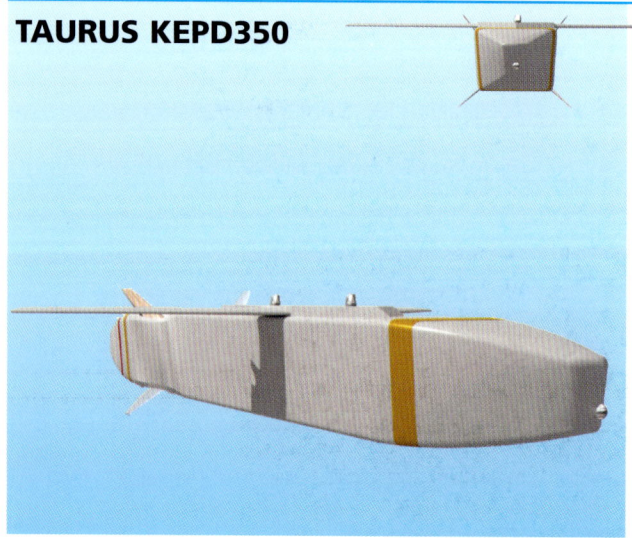

Description: The Taurus KEPD 350 is a long-range air-launched cruise missile manufactured jointly by Germany and Spain. It has a number of stealth features a dual-charge penetrator warhead called Mephisto, one charge being detonated to blast a path into a bunker and the second to detonate inside. It climbs to altitude and then dives on its target.

Country of origin: Germany/Spain
Weight: 3086lb (1400kg)
Diameter: 3.5ft (1080mm)
Length: 16.7ft (5.1m)
Warhead: 1100lb (499kg) Mephisto (Multi-Effect Penetrator, High Sophisticated Target Optimised)
Wingspan: 8.5ft (2.6m)
Range: 310 miles (500km) plus
Guidance System: Image based navigation, TERPROM, GPS

DIRECTORY

ZAB-500 NAPALM TANK

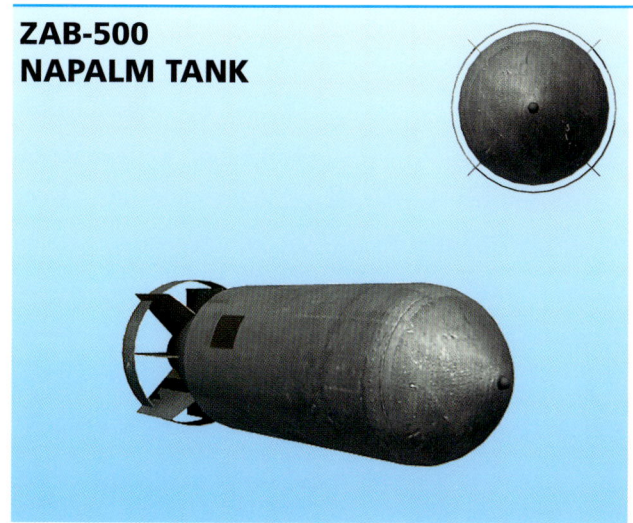

Description: The ZAB-500 is a Russian napalm bomb that has been in widespread use for many years. It can be carried by all types of Russian tactical aircraft. It can be released from any altitude between 160 and 4900ft (950 and 1500m) at a speed of up to 930mph (1500km/h).

Country of origin: Russia
Weight: 943lb (428kg)
Diameter: 22.5in (570mm)
Length: 6.4ft (1.95m)
Warhead: napalm
Wingspan: n/a
Range: n/a
Guidance System: n/a

ANTI-SHIP MISSILES

AGM-84 HARPOON

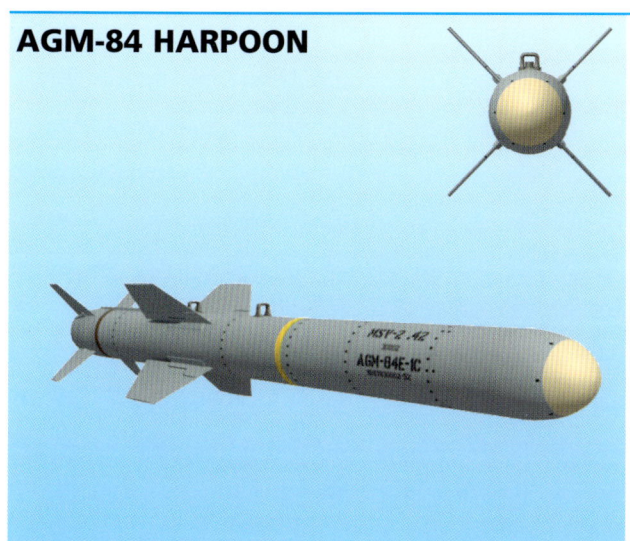
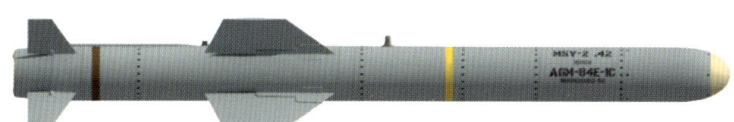

Description: The AGM-84 Harpoon is an all-weather, over-the-horizon anti-ship missile that was first introduced in 1977. Originally developed as an air-launched missile for the Lockheed P-3 Orion maritime patrol aircraft, it was later adapted for use on the Boeing B-52H, which could carry from eight to twelve missiles.

Country of origin: USA
Weight: 1144-1385lb (519-628kg) depending on launch platform
Diameter: 1.1ft (0.34m)
Length: 15.4ft (4.7m)
Warhead: 487lb (221kg) high explosive
Wingspan: 3.0ft (0.91m)
Range: 58-196 miles (93-315km) depending on launch platform
Guidance System: active radar

AGM-84H SLAM-ER

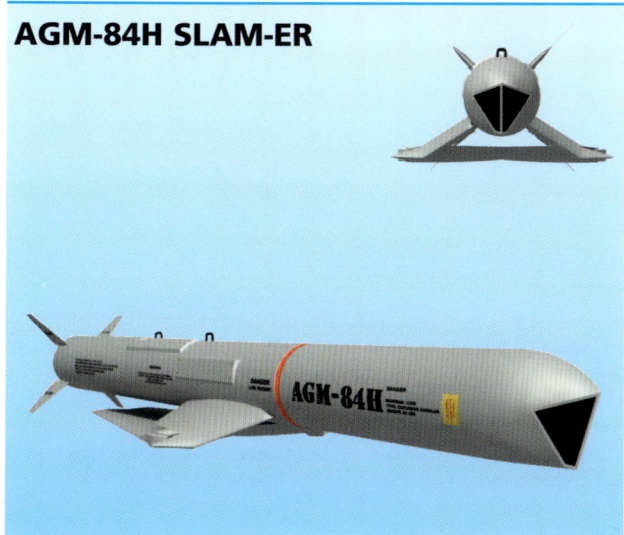
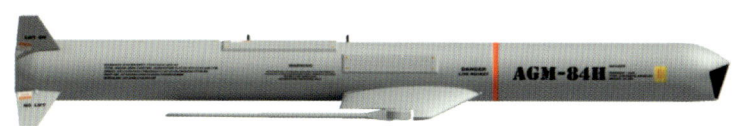

Description: SLAM-ER (Standoff Land Attack Missile – Extended Response) is a supersonic upgrade of the original subsonic SLAM, which was itself a development of the AGM-84 Harpoon. It is capable of attacking land and sea targets automatically, at long range, and thanks to its General Electric Automatic Target Recognition Unit (ATRU) it is a true 'fire-and-forget' weapon.

Country of origin: USA
Weight: 1400lb (635kg)
Diameter: 13.5in (343mm)
Length: 14.3ft (4.36m)
Warhead: high explosive
Wingspan: 7.15ft (2.18m)
Range: more than 150 miles (240km)
Guidance System: ring laser gyro, imaging infrared

MODERN AIR-LAUNCHED WEAPONS

EXOCET

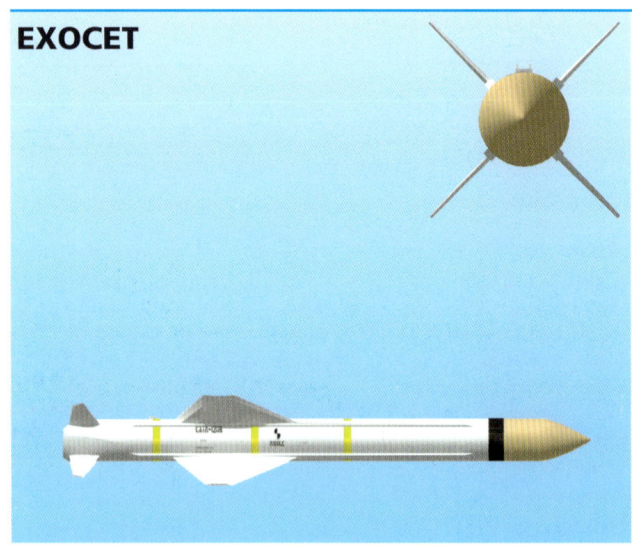
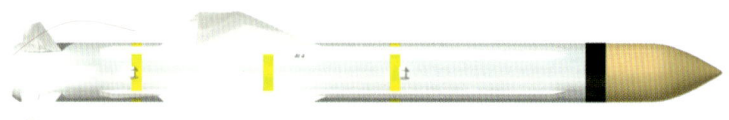

Description: In its original form, known as the MM38, the MBDA Exocet was a ship-launched missile. The air-launched version was developed in 1974 and was deployed with the French Navy five years later. During the 1982 Falklands War, Exocets launched by Argentinian Navy Super Etendards sank the destroyer HMS *Sheffield* and the container ship *Atlantic Conveyor*.

Country of origin: France
Weight: 1500lb (670kg)
Diameter: 1ft 1.7in (348mm)
Length: 15ft 5in (4.7m)
Warhead: 360lb (165kg) high explosive
Wingspan: 3ft 7in (1.1m)
Range: 43-110 miles (70-180km)
Guidance System: inertial, active radar homing

KORMORAN

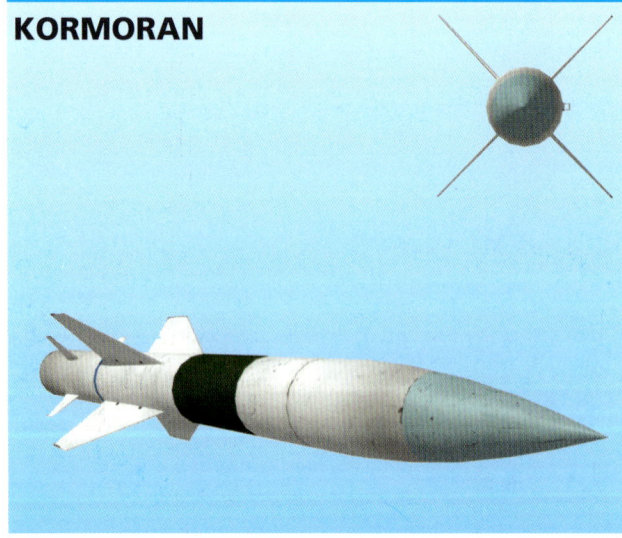
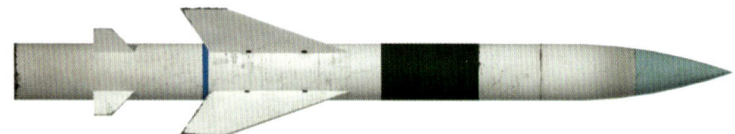

Description: The MBB (EADS) Kormoran air-launched anti-ship missile was based on a Nord-Aviation missile project, the AS-34. Development of the Kormoran 1 began in 1962 and the missile was carried by the Federal German Navy's F-104G Starfighters. A more advanced version, the Kormoran 2, is carried by the Tornado IDS.

Country of origin: Germany
Weight: 1388lb (630kg)
Diameter: 13.5in ((344mm)
Length: 14.4ft (4.40m)
Warhead: 485lb (220kg) high explosive
Wingspan: 4ft (1.22m)
Range: 22miles (35km)
Guidance System: INS, active radar homing

PENGUIN

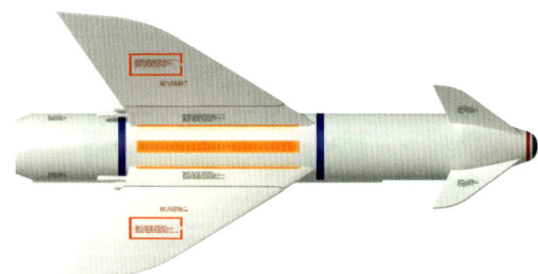

Description: Norway's Penguin anti-ship missile, developed by the Kongsberg Vapenfabrikk, comes in two variants: the Mk II ship-launched passive homing missile, deployed mainly on fast attack boats, and the Mk III air-launched version, which is carried by the F-16. The weapon is used by nine navies and is designated AGM-119 in US service.

Country of origin: Norway
Weight: 815lb (370kg)
Diameter: 11in (280mm)
Length: 10ft 6in (3.20m)
Warhead: 286lb (130kg) high explosive
Wingspan: 3.28ft (1.0m)
Range: over 34 miles (55km)
Guidance System: passive infrared, radar altimeter

DIRECTORY

RBS-15F ANTI-SHIP MISSILE

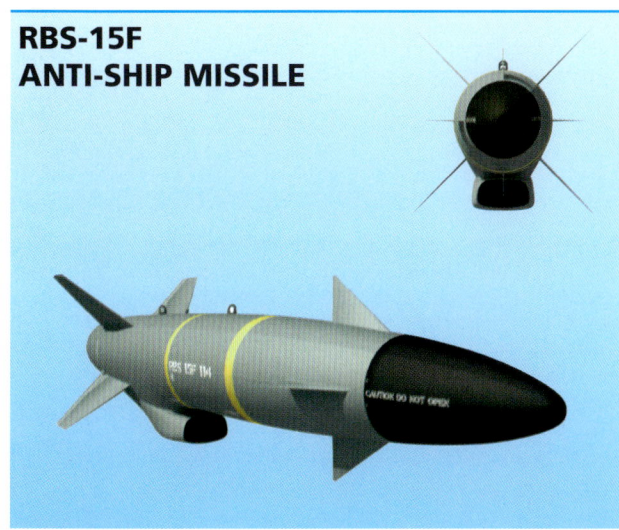

Description: Sweden's RBS-15 (Robotsystem 15) is a long-range, fire-and-forget surface-to-surface and air-launched missile, the latter being deployed with the Swedish Air Force in 1987. Several variants have been developed, with a very long range version, the Mk IV, under development in 2010. The weapon is carried by the JAS-39 Gripen.

Country of origin: Sweden
Weight: 1763lb (800kg)
Diameter: 19.65in (500mm)
Length: 14.2ft (4.33m)
Warhead: 440lb (200kg) high explosive
Wingspan: 4.6ft (1.4m)
Range: 155 miles (250km)
Guidance System: inertial, active radar

BOMBS

BETAB

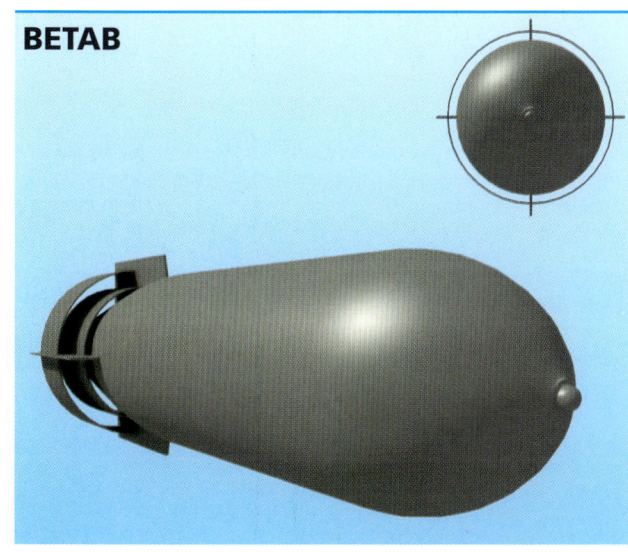

Description: The acronym BETAB stands for *Betonoboynaya Aviabomb* (Anti-concrete Aviation Bomb), which describes this weapon's purpose precisely. Two variants were eventually developed: the BETAB-500, which was a free-fall weapon, and the BETAB-500ShP, which was fitted with a rocket motor to enhance its penetration capability.

Country of origin: Russia
Weight: 1051lb (477kg)
Diameter: 9in (230mm)
Length: 7.2ft (2.2m)
Warhead: 500lb (226kg) high explosive
Wingspan: n/a
Range: n/a
Guidance System: none

BLG1000

Description: Developed by the MATRA company, the BLG1000 Arcole is a French laser-guided bomb carried by the Dassault Mirage 2000 strike aircraft. It usually forms part of an ordnance mix that also includes the BLG-66 Beluga cluster bomb, giving the aircraft the ability to attack different targets on the same mission of required.

Country of origin: France
Weight: 2138lb (970kg)
Diameter: 3ft (900mm)
Length: 14.3ft (4.37m)
Warhead: 500lb (226kg) high explosive
Range: 4–8 miles (7–13km)
Guidance System: laser designator

MODERN AIR-LAUNCHED WEAPONS

CBU-87 COMBINED EFFECTS MUNITION

Description: Developed by Aerojet General/Honeywell and first deployed in 1986, the CBU-87 Combined Effects Munition is a cluster bomb widely used by the US Air Force. During Operation Desert Storm in 1991, the USAF dropped 10,035 of these weapons in operations against the Iraqi armed forces. The bomb can be dropped from any altitude and at any air speed.

Country of origin: USA
Weight: 950lb (430kg)
Diameter: 15.6in (390mm)
Length: 7.6ft (2.3m)
Warhead: 202 armour-piercing bomblets
Wingspan: n/a
Range: n/a
Guidance System: none

FAB-250

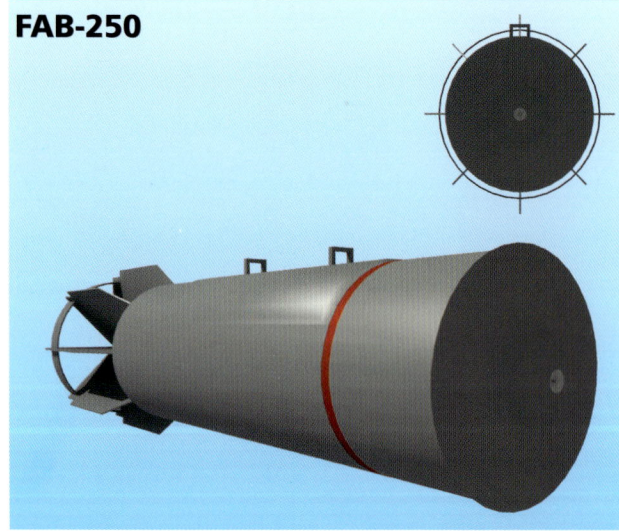
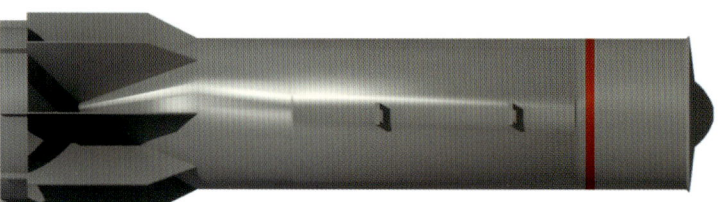

Description: The Russian FAB-250 is a general-purpose bomb designed to be carried by tactical aircraft. FAB is an abbreviation of Fugasnaya Aviatsionnaya Bomba, the Russian term for this type of weapon. Its development history goes back to 1946, the ballistic qualities of successive designs having been improved over the years.

Country of origin: Russia
Weight: 550lb (250kg)
Diameter: 381mm (15in)
Length: not known
Warhead: high explosive
Wingspan: n/a
Range: n/a
Guidance System: none

FAB-500

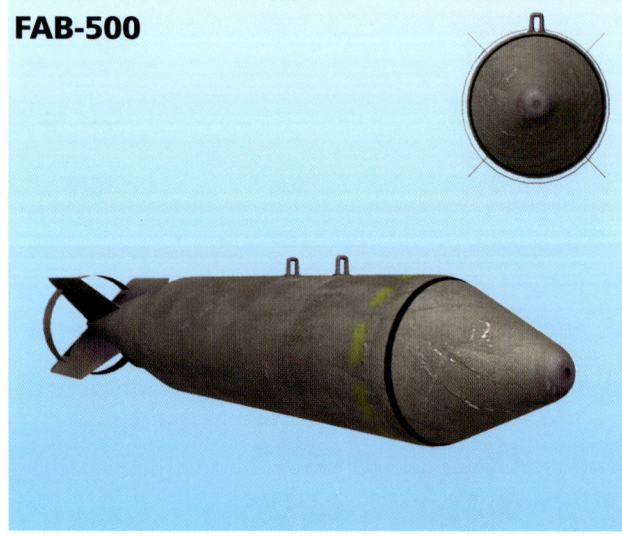

Description: In 1946 the Soviet Union developed a series of freefall bombs in four sizes, but all sharing a single nose and a single tail fuze. The bombs could be dropped from all altitudes up to 40,000ft (12,000m) and speeds of up to 625mph (1000km/h). As its designation implies, the FAB-500 was the 1100lb (500kg) version.

Country of origin: Russia
Weight: 1100lb (500kg)
Diameter: 18in (457mm)
Length: not known
Warhead: high explosive
Wingspan: n/a
Range: n/a
Guidance System: none

DIRECTORY

FAB-1500

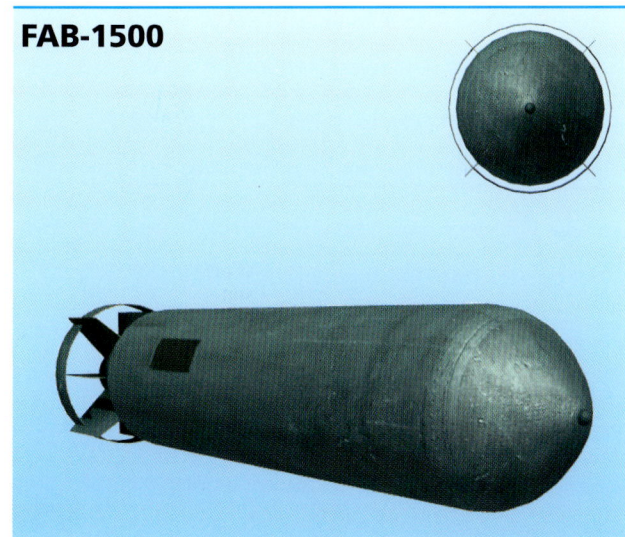

Description: In common with other bombs in the FAB series, the FAB-1500 had poor ballistic characteristics when falling at supersonic speed, and their construction was fragile. From 1954, until a new design could be implemented, the bombs were built with thicker walls and no nose fuze. Construction of the thick-walled versions ended in 1956.

Country of origin: Russia
Weight: 3300lb (1500kg)
Diameter: 24in (609mm)
Length: not known
Warhead: high explosive
Wingspan: n/a
Range: n/a
Guidance System: n/a

GBU-10

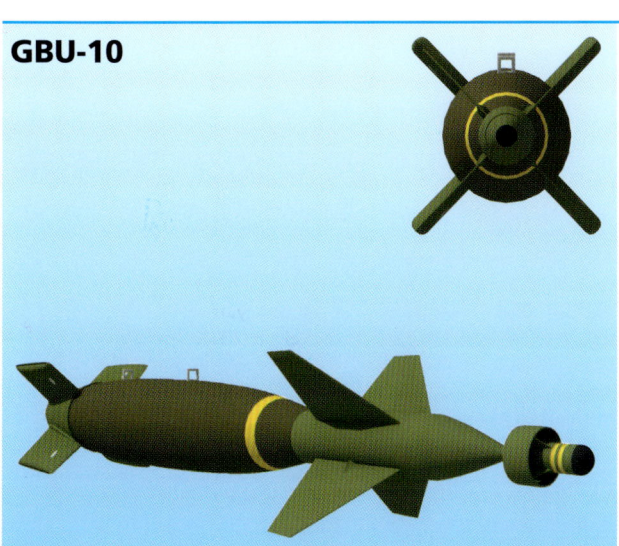

Description: The GBU-10 Paveway II laser-guided bomb is based on the Mk 84 general-purpose bomb and has been produced in several variants, with different wing and fuze combinations. Lockheed Martin and Raytheon, who produce the bombs, have developed GPS-guided versions of the weapon, which is in widespread use with the US armed forces and NATO.

Country of origin: USA
Weight: 2000lb (906kg)
Diameter: 18in (460mm)
Length: 14ft 4in (3.84m)
Warhead: high explosive penetrator
Wingspan: 4ft 11in (1.49m)
Range: over 8nm (14.8km)
Guidance System: laser seeker

GBU-12

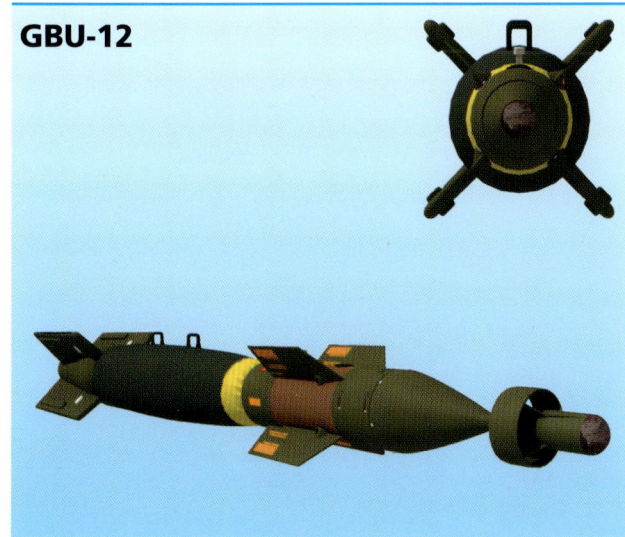

Description: The GBU-12 Paveway II laser-guided bomb is based on the 500lb (227kg) Mk 82 bomb, with the addition of guidance fins and a laser seeker. Paveway II entered service in 1976 and has been widely used in various conflicts ever since. The same guidance unit is fitted to the Mk 83 bomb.

Country of origin: USA
Weight: 500lb (227kg)
Diameter: 11in (273mm)
Length: 10ft 9in (3.27m)
Warhead: high explosive penetrator
Wingspan: 4ft 11in (1.49m)
Range: over 8nm (14.8km)
Guidance System: laser seeker

MODERN AIR-LAUNCHED WEAPONS

GBU-13

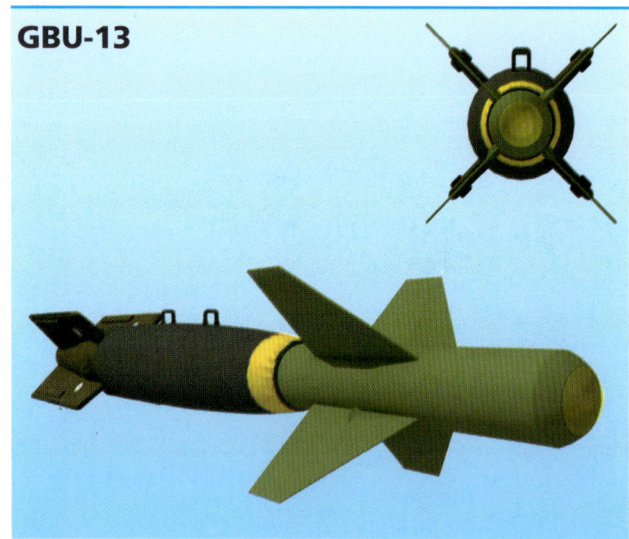

Description: Although there is no official GBU-13 designation for this weapon in the Paveway series, it is unofficially allocated to the British Mk 13 bomb fitted with a Paveway kit. This weapon was originally used with the RAF's Buccaneer Mk.2 low-level strike aircraft, and later with the Panavia Tornado.

Country of origin: USA
Weight: 1000lb (453kg)
Diameter: 1ft 6in (457mm)
Length: 14ft 2in (4.32m)
Warhead: high explosive/fragmentation
Wingspan: 1ft 5in (0.49m)
Range: 4950ft (1500m) low altitude release
Guidance System: laser seeker

GBU-15

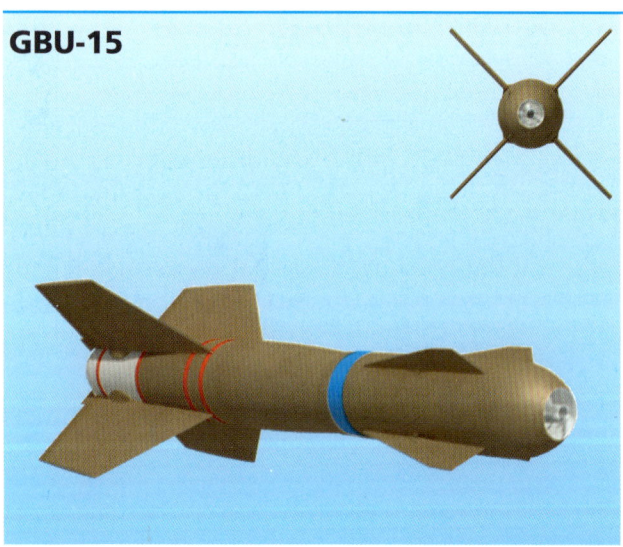

Description: The GBU-15 is an unpowered glide bomb designed to destroy high-value targets, and is carried by the F-15E Strike Eagle. It also has a long-range anti-ship capability with the B-52 Statofortress. In a direct attack, the pilot selects a target before launch, locks the weapon guidance system on to it and then launches.

Country of origin: USA
Weight: 2000lb (4400kg)
Diameter: 18in (457mm)
Length: 12ft 10in (3.9m)
Warhead: high explosive
Wingspan: 4ft 11in (1.5m)
Range: 5 to 15nm (9 to 28km)
Guidance System: TV/imaging infrared

GBU-16

Description: The GBU-16 Paveway II is one of the American Paveway series of laser-guided bombs and is based on the Mk 83 general-purpose bomb, but with a laser seeker and wings for guidance. The weapon is produced by Lockheed Martin and Raytheon, and is claimed to be accurate to within 3.6ft.

Country of origin: USA
Weight: 1000lb (454kg)
Diameter: 14.7in (360mm)
Length: 12ft (3.7m)
Warhead: high explosive
Wingspan: 4ft 11in (1.5m)
Range: more than 8nm (14.8km)
Guidance System: laser seeker

DIRECTORY

GBU-22

Description: The Mk 82 500lb (227kg) GBU-22 Paveway III was developed as an upgraded successor to the earlier weapons in the Paveway series, but it was not adopted by the US forces as its warhead was deemed to be too small to produce the desired effect against the types of target that were envisaged. However, it had some export success.

Country of origin: USA
Weight: 500lb (227kg)
Diameter: 10.8in (270mm)
Length: 11.5ft (3.5m)
Warhead: 500lb (227kg) blast/fragmentation
Wingspan: 1 ft 5in (0.49m)
Range: 1.86 miles (3km)
Guidance System: laser seeker

GBU-24

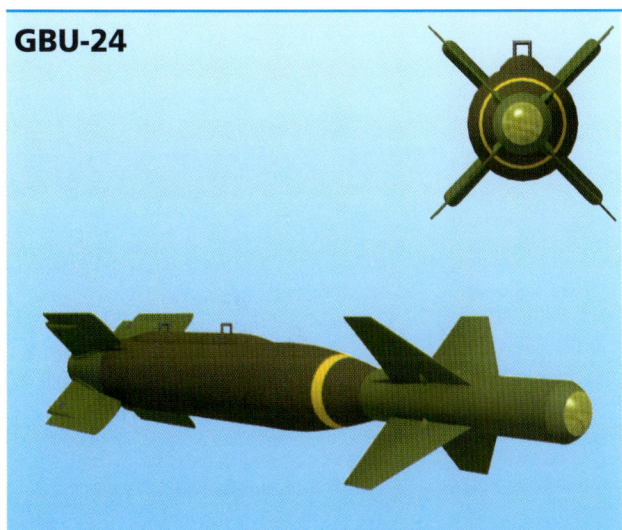

Description: The GBU-24 Paveway III has a greater gliding range than earlier members of the Paveway family. It is also more expensive because of its advanced guidance kit, and is better suited to deployment against well-defended, high-value targets. The GBU-24 is so precise that it can fly down ventilation shafts to destroy hardened targets.

Country of origin: USA
Weight: 2000lb (906kg)
Diameter: 14.6in (370mm)
Length: 14ft 2in (4.32m)
Warhead: high explosive penetrator
Wingspan: 5ft 5in (1.65m)
Range: over 10nm (18.4km)
Guidance System: laser seeker

GBU-27

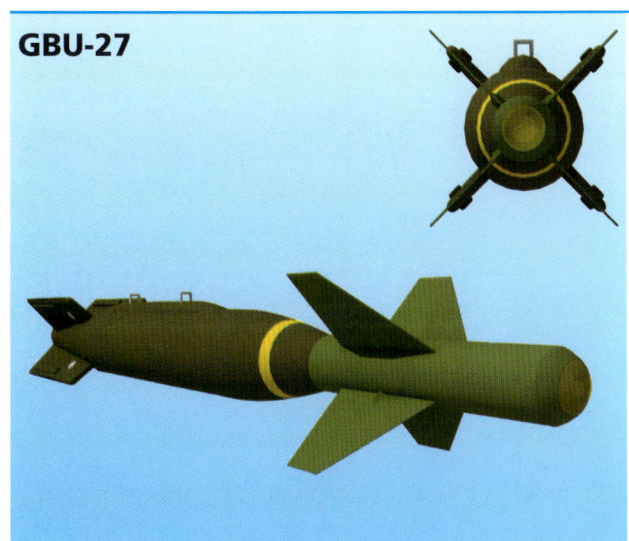

Description: The GBU-27 Paveway III is basically a GBU-24 guided bomb that was re-designed for use with the Lockheed F-117A Nighthawk 'stealth' aircraft. It is a 'bunker buster' and was deployed during Operation Desert Storm in 1991, and on one occasion an attack resulted in the deaths of 400 Iraqi civilians when an air raid shelter was destroyed in error.

Country of origin: USA
Weight: 2000lb (906kg)
Diameter: 2ft 4in (711mm)
Length: 13ft 10in (4.2m)
Warhead: high explosive, penetrator
Wingspan: 5ft 5in (1.65m)
Range: over 10nm (18.4km)
Guidance System: laser seeker

MODERN AIR-LAUNCHED WEAPONS

GBU-31 (MK84 JDAM)

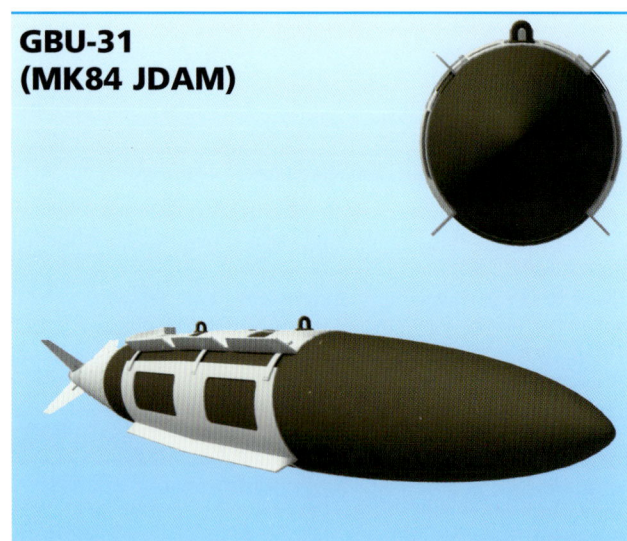

Description: The GBU-31 is a Mk 84 bomb fitted with the Joint Direct Attack Munition (JDAM) guidance kit. JDSM bombs are guided to their target by an integrated inertial guidance system coupled with Global Positioning System (GPS) receiver for enhanced accuracy, giving them a range of around 15nm (28km).

Country of origin: USA
Weight: 2039lb (925kg)
Diameter: 18in (458mm)
Length: 10.75ft (3.28m)
Warhead: high explosive
Wingspan: n/a
Range: up to 15nm (28km)
Guidance System: INS/GPS

GBU-32 (MK 83 JDAM)

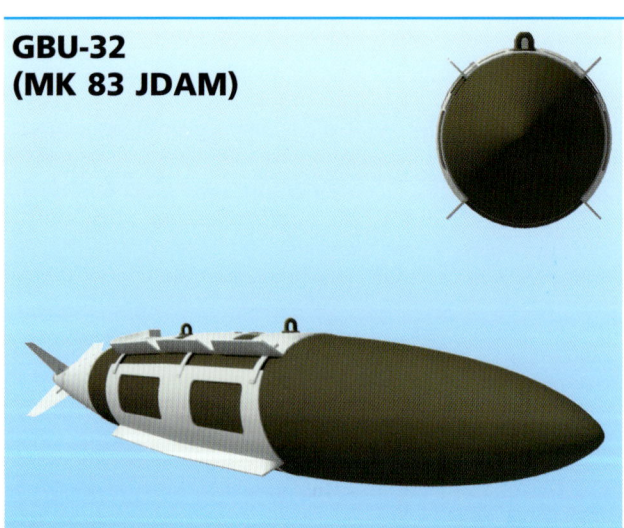

Description: The GBU-32 is a 1000lb (453kg) bomb fitted with a JDAM (Joint Direct Attack Munition) guidance kit that turns it into an all-weather 'smart' weapon, being guided to its target by an integrated inertial guidance system coupled with a Global Positioning System (GPS) receiver for enhanced accuracy.

Country of origin: USA
Weight: 1000lb (0.453kg)
Diameter: 15in (590mm)
Length: 9.9-12.7ft (3.0-3.9m)
Warhead: high explosive fragmentation
Wingspan: 19.6-25in (500-630mm)
Range: up to 15nm (28km)
Guidance System: INS/GPS

GBU-38 J (MK 82 JDAM)

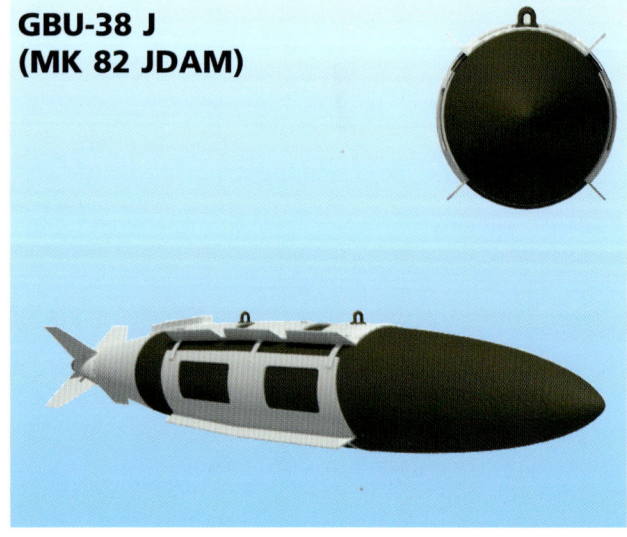

Description: The GBU-38 is a 500lb (227kg) Joint Direct Attack Munition (JDAM) weapon manufactured by Boeing and using the Mk 82 bomb case. It was first used in combat in Iraq in 2004, two Alabama Air National Guard F-16s destroying a two-storey building where a terrorist meeting was reportedly taking place.

Country of origin: USA
Weight: 500lb (227kg)
Diameter: 10.75in (273mm)
Length: 7.28ft (2.22m)
Warhead: high explosive
Wingspan: n/a
Range: up to 15nm (28km)
Guidance System: INS/GPS

DIRECTORY

GBU-39 SMALL DIAMETER BOMB

Description: The GBU-39 Small-Diameter Bomb (SDB) was developed with the intention of providing US strike aircraft with the capability to carry a pack of four small bombs instead of one large 2000lb (906kg) weapon. It has been developed in two versions, one with an INS/GPS system to attack stationary targets, and the other with a thermal seeker to attack moving objects like tanks.

Country of origin: USA
Weight: 285lb (129kg)
Diameter: 7.5in (190mm)
Length: 6ft (1.8m)
Warhead: dense inert metal explosive
Wingspan: n/a
Range: more than 60nm (110km) stand-off
Guidance System: GPS/INS

JP233 MUNITIONS DISPENSER

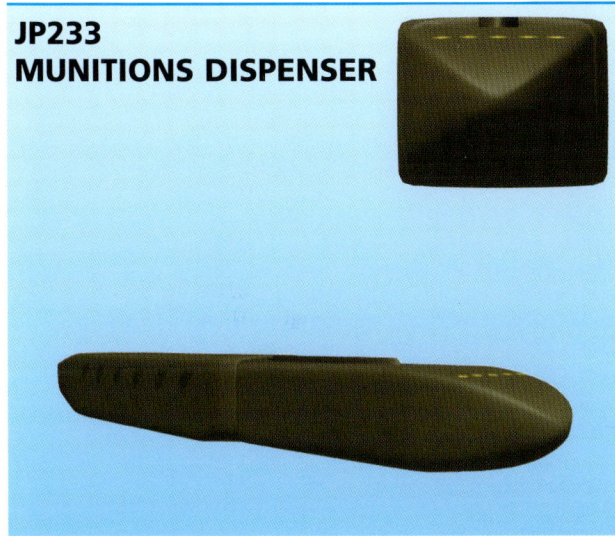

Description: The JP233 Munitions Dispenser was developed as a means of destroying Warsaw Pact runways and, by scattering sub-munitions, preventing their repair. The pod was built in two sections, the rearmost containing SG.357 anti-runway penetrators and the forward part HB.867 area denial mines. The system was used operationally by RAF and Saudi Arabian Tornado strike aircraft in the 1991 Gulf War.

Country of origin: UK
Weight: 80lb (28.5kg) (munitions weight)
Diameter: n/a
Length: n/a
Warhead: n/a
Wingspan: n/a
Range: n/a
Guidance System: none

KAB500KR

Description: The KSAB-500KR is an electro-optical fire-and-forget TV-guided bomb that was deployed with the Soviet Air Force in the 1980s and remains in widespread use today. Similar to the American GBU-15, it has a hardened, armour-piercing warhead capable of penetrating up to 4ft 11in (1.5m) of reinforced concrete

Country of origin: Russia
Weight: 1234lb (560kg)
Diameter: not known
Length: 10ft (3.05m)
Warhead: high explosive, armour-piercing
Wingspan: not known
Range: up to 10.6 miles (17km)
Guidance System: TV seeker

MODERN AIR-LAUNCHED WEAPONS

KAB500L

Description: The KAB-500L is a laser-guided bomb developed by the former Soviet Air Force, and is a standard FAB-500 general purpose bomb fitted with a guidance system. The weapon remains in use by the Russian Air Force and is also used by the Indian Air Force. The Chinese People's Air Force has developed a copy.

Country of origin: Russia
Weight: 1155lb (525kg)
Diameter: 15.7in (400mm)
Length: 10ft (3.05m)
Warhead: 837lb (380kg) high explosive
Wingspan: 2.5ft (0.75m)
Range: up to 6.2 miles (10km)
Guidance System: laser seeker

KAB1500KR

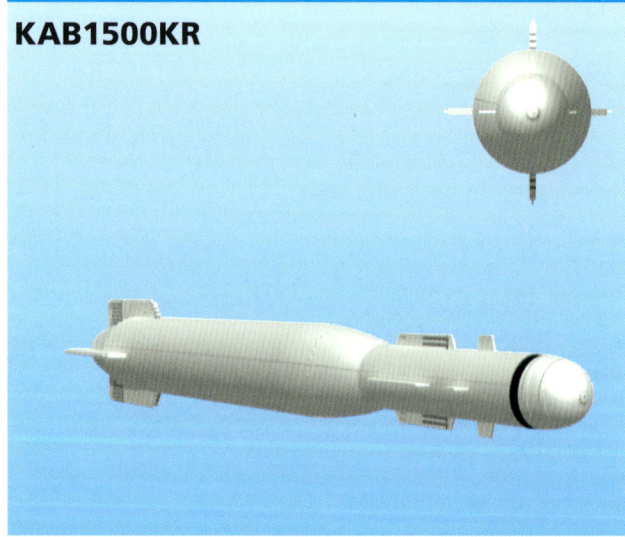

Description: The KSAB-1500KR is a much larger version of the KAB-500KR and can be fitted with high explosive, deep penetrating or thermobaric (fuel-air explosive) warheads. Its TV guidance system is pre-programmed and locks onto the target while still on the launch aircraft. The system can only be used in clear weather.

Country of origin: Russia
Weight: 3335lb (1525kg)
Diameter: 22.79in (580mm)
Length: 15ft (4.63m)
Warhead: high explosive, penetrator
Wingspan: 4.26ft (1.3m)
Range: up to 10.6 miles 17km
Guidance System: TV seeker

M117

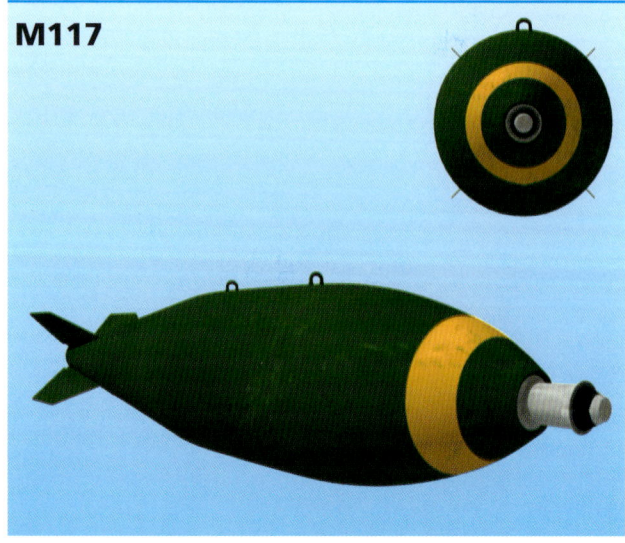

Description: The M117 is an air-dropped general-purpose 'iron bomb' widely used by the US armed forces, and has been in service since the time of the Korean War in the early 1950s. During the Gulf War of 1991, USAF B-52 bombers dropped some 44,600 M117s on Iraqi positions in Kuwait.

Country of origin: USA
Weight: 750lb (340kg)
Diameter: 16in (408mm)
Length: 7ft (2.16m)
Warhead: high explosive
Finspan: 20in (520mm)
Range: n/a
Guidance System: none

DIRECTORY

MK82

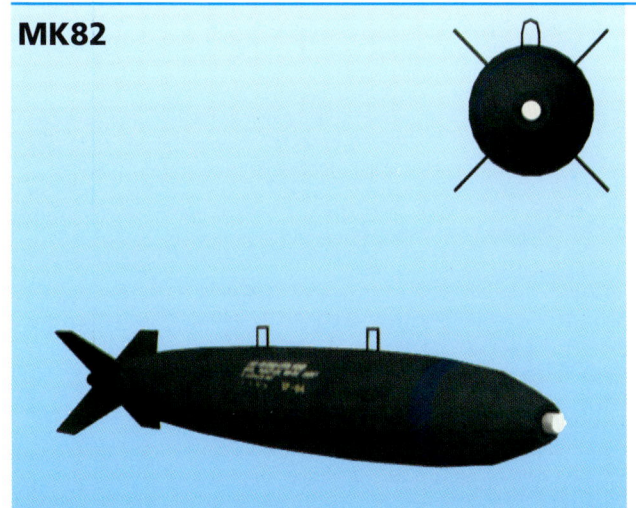

Description: The Mk 82 is what is known as a 'dumb bomb', a low-drag general purpose bomb. It is the most common weapon of its kind in the US arsenal and is the smallest bomb currently in service. It comes with a variety of fin kits, fuzes and retarders for use against different types of target.

Country of origin: USA
Weight: 500lb (227kg)
Diameter: 10.75in (273mm)
Length: 7.28ft (2.2m)
Warhead: high explosive
Wingspan: n/a
Range: n/a
Guidance System: none

RBK-250

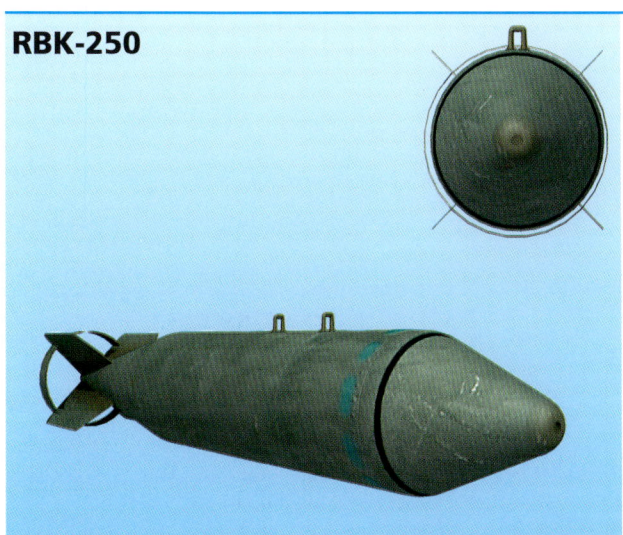

Description: The RBK-250 is a cluster bomb used by the Russian Air Force and various customer air forces; Russia is a major producer and exporter of cluster munitions. According to some reports, this weapon was deployed by the Russians during its operations in Georgia, an allegation vehemently denied by the Russian Government.

Country of origin: Russia
Weight: 551lb (250kg)
Diameter: not known
Length: not known
Warhead: cluster munitions
Wingspan: n/a
Range: n/a
Guidance System: none

MISSION PODS

AAR-50 NAVFLIR

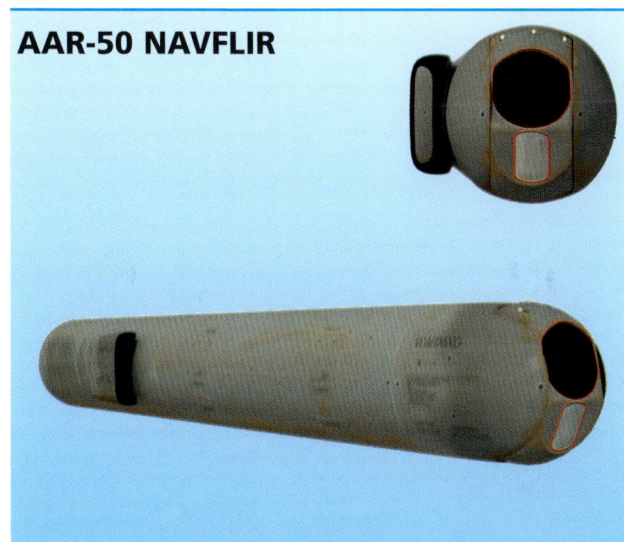

Description: The Hughes AAR-50 NAVFLIR (Navigation Forward-Looking InfraRed) was designed to provide strike aircraft with a low-altitude navigational capability at night and in adverse weather conditions. The pod-mounted system is carried by the US Navy's F/A-18C Hornet and Super Hornet aircraft, and uses advanced digital processing to provide the pilot with a high-quality TV-like image projected on the head-up display.

Country of origin: USA
Weight: 214lb (97kg)
Diameter: 9.8in (250mm)
Length: 6.5ft (1.98m)
Warhead: n/a
Wingspan: n/a
Range: n/a
Guidance System: n/a

MODERN AIR-LAUNCHED WEAPONS

ALQ 131 ECM POD

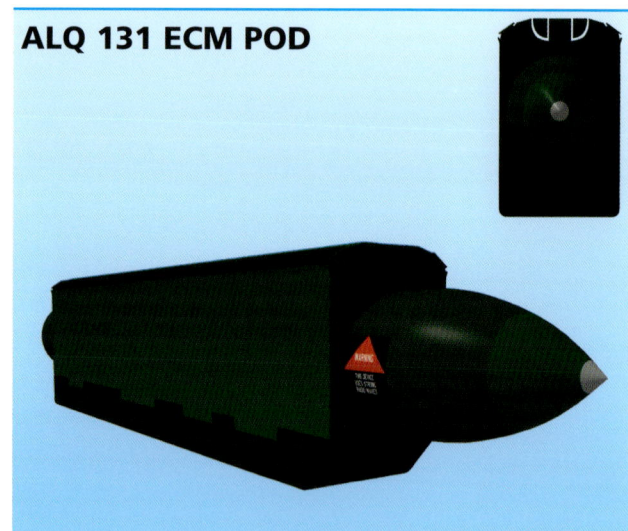

Description: The ALQ-131 is a self-defence jammer pod carried by most tactical aircraft in US service. It can be carried on any underwing ordnance station. The pod has been extensively used since 1976, and up to the end of 2009 it had supported well over 15,000 combat sorties by US aircraft worldwide.

Country of origin: USA
Weight: 674lb (306kg)
Diameter: 12in (300mm)
Length: 10ft (3.05m)
Warhead: n/a
Wingspan: n/a
Range: n/a
Guidance System: n/a

AN/AAQ-13 LANTIRN NAVIGATION POD

Description: The AN/AAQ-13 navigation element of the LANTIRN system provides high-speed precision attack capability at night and in adverse weather. It contains a terrain-following radar and a fixed infrared sensor, providing visual cues and input to the aircraft's flight control system. The infrared image of the terrain ahead is displayed on the pilot's Head-Up Display (HUD)

Country of origin: USA
Weight: 451lb (204.6kg)
Diameter: 12in (305mm)
Length: 6.5ft (1.99m)
Warhead: n/a
Wingspan: n/a
Range: n/a
Sensors: infrared, TFR

AN/AAQ-14 LANTIRN TARGETING POD

Description: LANTIRN (Low Altitude Navigation and Targeting Infrared for Night) is a system developed for use by the USAF's F-15E Strike Eagle and F-16 Fighting Falcon tactical fighter-bombers. It increases their effectiveness by enabling them to fly at low level at night and in all weathers to attack ground targets with a variety of precision-guided weapons. The system contains two pods: specification refers to the targeting pod

Country of origin: USA
Weight: 530lb (240.7kg)
Diameter: 15in (380mm)
Length: 8.2ft (2.51m)
Warhead: n/a
Wingspan: n/a
Range: n/a
Sensors: infrared/laser designating and ranging

DIRECTORY

APK-93 DATALINK POD

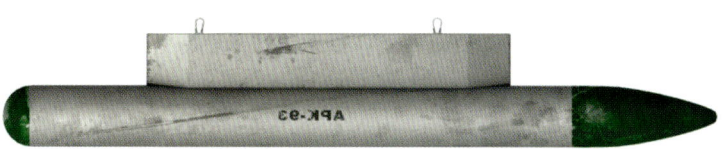

Description: The APK-93 is a Russian datalink pod and is carried primarily by the Sukhoi Su-30 Flanker tactical fighter and the MiG-27K. The data link allows imagery to be exploited almost instantly, enabling the pilot to assess situations and make rapid tactical decisions. The system is also used in the Kh-59 cruise missile.

Country of origin: Russia
Weight: not known
Diameter: not known
Length: not known
Warhead: n/a
Wingspan: n/a
Range: n/a
Guidance System: n/a

DAMOCLES POD

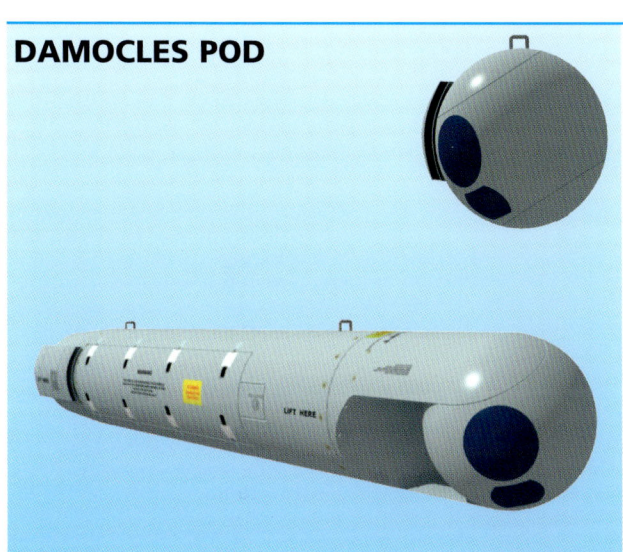
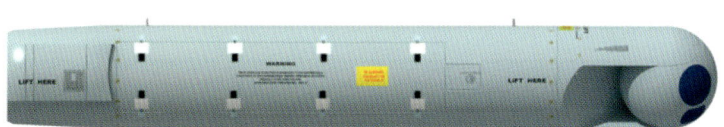

Description: Produced by the Thales Group, Damocles is a third-generation infrared targeting system. The infrared camera has two zoom levels for acquisition and tracking of the target. In good weather, the system can track large aerial targets at up to 20 nm. It is used on Mirage 2000, Super Etendard, Rafale and Su-30KM aircraft.

Country of origin: France
Weight: 660lb (300kg)
Diameter: 12in (300mm)
Length: 10ft (3.05m)
Warhead: n/a
Wingspan: n/a
Range: n/a
Guidance System: n/a

LITENING TARGETING POD

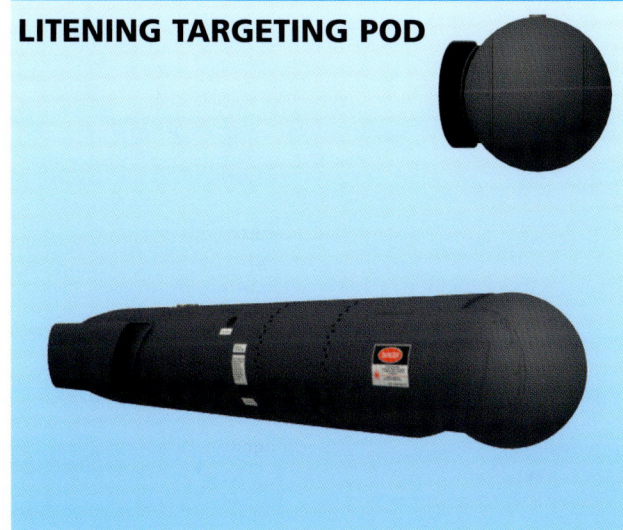

Description: Litening is a widely used target pod integrated and mounted externally on the aircraft. The target is displayed to the crew via a high-resolution, forward-looking infrared (FLIR) sensor. It has a wide field of view search capability. The pod is equipped with a laser designator for precise delivery of laser-guided munitions.

Country of origin: USA
Weight: 440lb (200kg)
Diameter: 16in (406mm)
Length: 7.25ft (2.20m)
Warhead: n/a
Wingspan: n/a
Range: n/a
Guidance System: n/a

MODERN AIR-LAUNCHED WEAPONS

PAVE PENNY TARGETING POD

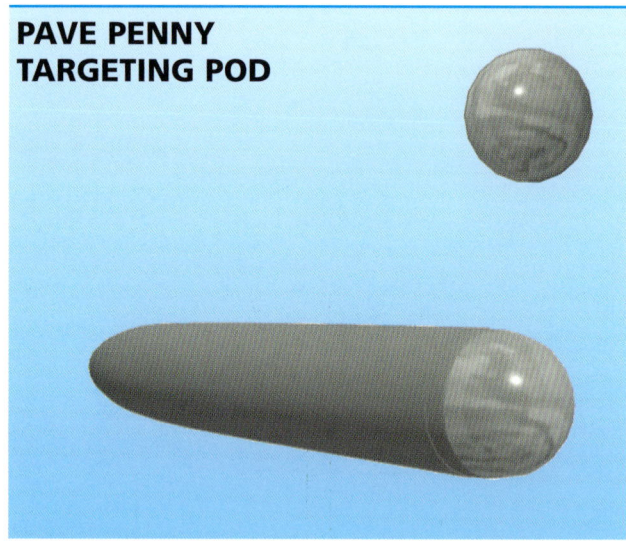

Description: The Lockheed Martin AN/AAS-35 Pave Penny is a laser spot tracker carried by US strike aircraft to enable the pilot to track a laser spot on the ground. The aircraft does not itself produce the laser beam, but the seeker searches for reflected laser light from other laser designators and the appropriate target information is displayed in the cockpit.

Country of origin: USA
Weight: 32lb (14.5kg)
Diameter: not known
Length: 31in (780mm)
Warhead: n/a
Wingspan: n/a
Range: 20 miles 32km)
Guidance System: n/a

SNIPER ATP POD

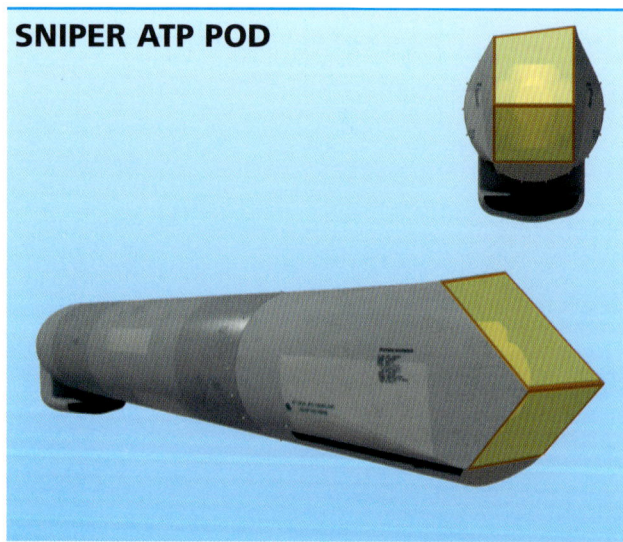

Description: The Lockheed Martin Sniper Advanced Targeting Pod, which is used on a variety of US, British and Canadian aircraft, was designed to produce much less drag than the systems it replaced. It incorporates a multi-spectral sensor capability with a high-resolution third-generation FLIR and CCD-TV. The dual-role laser offers an 'eye safe' mode for urban operations.

Country of origin: USA
Weight: 440lb (199kg)
Diameter: 11.9in (300mm)
Length: 7.8ft (2.39m)
Warhead: n/a
Wingspan: n/a
Range: n/a
Guidance System: n/a

SORBTSIYA ECM POD

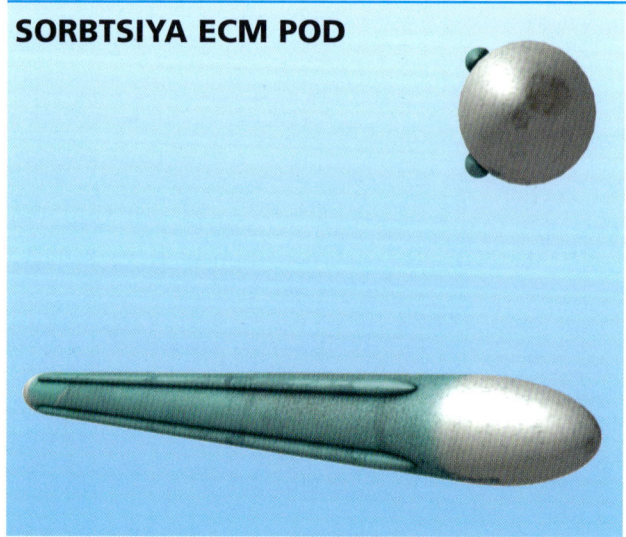

Description: Sorbtsiya is a Russian ECM jamming pod used by aircraft such as the Sukhoi Su-33, which carries one on each wingtip station. It is also used by the Su-30MKK fighters supplied to the Chinese People's Air Force, and by the Su-27 Flanker. The pod is reported to be very effective, and has been the subject of substantial export orders.

Country of origin: Russia
Weight: not known
Diameter: not known
Length: not known
Warhead: n/a
Wingspan: n/a
Range: n/a
Guidance System: n/a

INDEX

Entries in *italics* indicate photographs or illustrations.

A-10 Thunderbolt II 16, 20–7, *20–7*, 102, 174
AA-6 Acrid (R-40) *165*, *169*, *171*, 190, *190*
AA-8 Aphid-B (R-60M) *173*, *176*, *178*, 190, *190*
AA-9 Amos (R-33E) *165*, 169, 190, *190*
AA-10 Alamo-A (R27R) *149*, *157*, 191, *191*
AA-11 Archer (R73E) *149*, *151*, *153*, *155*, *157*, *161*, *163*, *165*, 191, *191*
AA-12 Adder (R-77) *165*, 191, *191*
AA-13 Arrow (R-37) 192
AAR-50 NAVFLIR (Navigation Forward Looking Infrared) mission pod 219, *219*
AASM (Armement Air-Sol Modulaire) 137, 197, *197*
Advanced Tactical Fighter Programme, U.S. 62
Afghanistan 6–7, 26, 41, *41*, 43, 50, 73, 87, 98, 115, 123, 139, 176–7, 182
AGM-65 Maverick 18, *21*, *24*, 25, 26, 38, *45*, 47–8, *49*, 54, *57*, *59*, 89, *109*, 113, *114*, *133*, *144*, 198, *198*, 208
AGM-69 SRAM (Short-Range Attack Missile) 82
AGM-78 Standard ARM (Anti-Radiation Missile) 198, *198*, 199
AGM-84 Harpoon 18, 38, 47, 54, 71, *83*, 113, 115, 129, *130*, 209, *209*
AGM-84H SLAM-ER (Short-Range Attack Missile-Expanded Response) 209, *209*
AGM-86C ALCM (Air-Launched Cruise Missile) 69, 198, *198*
AGM-88 HARM (Homing Anti-Radiation Missile) 15, 47, 49, 55, *83*, 119, 121, 199, *199*
AGM-114 Hellfire 199, *119*
AGM-119 Penguin 47, *139*, 210
AGM-129 ACM (Advanced Cruise Missile) 97
AGM-130 40–1, *42*, 199, *199*
AGM-154 JSOW (Joint Standoff Weapon) 37, 39, 42, 50, *51*, 54, 77, *88*, 90, 95, 96, *96*, *101*, 200, *200*
AGM-158 JASSM (Joint Air-to-Surface Standoff Missile) 85, *106*, 200, *200*
AIM-7 Sparrow 29, 30, 31, *35*, 47, *53*, 54, 192, *192*, 194
AIM-9 Sidewinder *15*, 20, *21*, 22, *24*, 25, 27, 29, 30, *31*, *32*, 33, *33*, *35*, 37, 38, 40, *44*, *45*, 47, 46, *49*, *50*, *51*, *53*, 55, *57*, *59*, 60, *61*, 64, 65, 67, 77, *77*, *81*, *83*, 100, *101*, *102*, *104*, 105, *106*, 106, *109*, *113*, *114*, 122, 137, *140*, *141*, 147
AIM-9J Sidewinder 192, *192*
AIM-9L Sidewinder 193, *193*
AIM-9M Sidewinder 193, *193*
AIM-9P Sidewinder 193, *193*
AIM-9X Sidewinder 194, *194*
AIM-54 Phoenix 17, 33, 53
AIM-120 AMRAAM (Advanced Medium-Range Air-to-Air Missile) 30, *31*, *32*, 33, *33*, 34, 37, 38, 39, *40*, *42*, *45*, 47, *47*, 49, 50, *51*, 54, 55, *55*, *61*, 64, 65, 66, 77, 100, *104*, 105, *106*, *109*, 115, *128*, *133*, 137, *137*, *139*, *141*, 147, 191, 194, *194*
AIM-132 ASRAAM (Advanced Short-Range Air-to-Air Missile) 54, *104*, 105, 115, *117*, *120*, 122, *122*, *125*, *128*, *130*, *133*, 137, *137*, *139*, *141*, 194, *194*, 195
air campaign 14–15
Air Launched Cruise Missile (ALCM) 18, 69, 89–90, 198, *198*
Air National Guard, US 50
air superiority 11, 31, *33*, 55, *125*, *128*, *133*, 141
Airborne Early Warning (AEW) 14, 15, 66, 135
airfields/runways, strikes against enemy 14, 15, 116, *117*, 118, 123
air-launched weapons:
 aircraft by aircraft 20–187
 directory 188–222
 history of 7–19
 air-to-air combat, birth of 8
 air-to-air missiles 16–17, *45*, *61*, *64*, 66, 77, *104*, 109, *149*, *161*, *165*, 190–7, *190–7 see also under individual missile name*
 air-to-ground weapons *21*, 36, *45*, *57*, *61*, *101*, *104*, 197–209, *197–209 see also under individual weapon name*
ALARM (Air Launched Anti-Radiation Missile) *120*, *128*, *139*, 200, *200*
Allied Force, Operation *119*
ALQ-131 ECM (electronic countermeasures) pod *21*, *22*, *24*, 25, *27*, *42*, *49*, 220, *220*
Al-Qaeda 50
AN/AAQ-13 LANTIRN (Low Altitude Navigation and Targeting for Night) pod 37, *39*, *40*, *42*, *47*, *49*, 55, 220, *220*
AN/AAQ-14 LANTIRN (Low Altitude Navigation and Targeting for Night) pod *42*, *47*, *49*, *57*, 59, 220, *220*
anti-radiation missiles (ARMs) 14, *15*, 47, 56
anti-ship missiles 14, 18, *35*, *49*, *52*, *53*, 71, *83*, *114*, *120*, *137*, *139*, *141*, *130*, *137*, *139*, *181*, *185*, 209–11, *209–11*
APK-93 datalink pod 221, *221*
area denial 87, 90
armour, attacks upon 9, 13, 22, *24*, 26, *57*, 77, 78, 82, *101*, 117
armour-piercing incendiary (API) rounds 23
AS-30L 201, *201*
ASM-135 anti-satellite (ASAT) missile 16, 17
ASMP standoff missile 137
atomic bombs, first use of *11*
AV-8B Harrier II 108–15, *118–15*
Avro Vulcan 12

B-1B Lancer *48*, 82, 84–91, *84–91*, 92, 182
B-2 Spirit 62, 91, 92–9, *92–9*, 200
B-29 Superfortress *11*, 70
B-50 Superfortress 70
B-52 Stratofortress *13*, 68–75, *68–75*, 79, 84, 86, 87, 91, 92, 197, 209, 214, 218
B-70 Valkyrie 88
Balkans conflict 26, 34, 40, 50, 58, 73, 90, 98, *119*, 123, 161, 201
balloons 7–8, 10
Bataan, USS 115
Betab 211, *211*
beyond visual range (BVR) 34, 46–7, 105, 124, 129, 131, 160, 162, 194, 196
Blackburn Buccaneer 123
BLG1000 211, *211*
BLU-109 48
'Bockscar' 11
bombs 17, 211–19, *211–19 see also under individual bomb name*
Brahmos 201, *201*
bridge-busting (infrastructure strike) 14, 43
Brimstone *101*, *117*, *120*, 129, *130*, 201, *201*
bunkers/caves/tunnels, strikes against (bunker-busting) 14, 17, 41, *42*, *48*, *48*, 143, *143*, *145*, 160

cameras 19
cannon, automatic 10, 16
 GAU-8 Avenger 20, 22, 23, 25
 GAU-12 103, 113
 Mauser *124*
 M61A1 rotary 30, 46, 65
 'Vulcan' 16, *28*, 38, 44, *52*, *60*, 65, *68*, 77
 see also under individual aircraft name
'carpet bombing' 14, 17, 71
CBU-87 (cluster bomb) *21*, 39, *39*, *40*, *51*, 98, 212, *212*
CBU-89 (cluster bomb) 90
CBU-98B (cluster bomb) *24*
CBU-103 (cluster bomb) 88, *88*, *102*
CBU-107 (cluster bomb) 38
chaff 58
chemical weapons 17, 18
'choke points' 43, 72

close air support (CAS) 13, 14, 20, *21*, 37, 40, *41*, 73, *109*, 111, *130*, 178
cluster bombs 17, 18, 20, *21*, 38, 39, *39*, *40*, 50, *51*, 56, 87, *98*, 187, 212, *212*
Cold War 26, 34, 82, 88, 92, 93, 123, 182, 184, 186
combat air patrol (CAP) 135
communication sites, strikes against 14
conformal fuel tanks 6–7, *19*, 30–1, 36
countermeasures 10, 14, 19, 25, 46, 56, 58, 63
 see also under individual countermeasure name
cruise missiles 18, 48, 69, 89–90, *122*, *152*, *183*, 185

Damocles pod 132, 221, *221*
Darter 194, *194*
'decapitation strike' 39, 175
decoys 14, 15–16, 17, 19, *58*, *118*, *167*
Desert Fox, Operation 50
Desert Shield, Operation *83*, 110
Diego Garcia 98
directory of modern air-launched weapons 188–222
dogfight 11–12, 17, 33–4, 131, 132, 156, 166
drogue parachutes 13
dumb (unguided) weapons 10, 17, 18, 20, *21*, 25, 26, 38, *45*, 50, 54, 56, 74, 90, 122, 218
Dwight D. Eisenhower, USS 54

EA-18G Growler 52
EF2000 Typhoon 124–31, *124–31*
electronic countermeasures (ECM) 10, 14, 19, 25, 46, 56, 63, 196, 222
electronically scanned array (ESA) system 236
Enduring Freedom, Operation 50
'Enola Gay' *11*
escorts, fighter 10, 12
Exocet *137*, 210, *210*
extended-range strikes 27, *57*

F/A-18 Hornet/Super Hornet 52–9, *52–9*, *83*, 102, *110*, 194, 219
F-4 Phantom 81
F-14 Tomcat 53, 54
F-15A-D Eagle 28–35, *28–35*, 62, *63*, 82, 129, 158, 162, 194, 199, 214, 219
F-15E Strike Eagle 6–7, *16*, 17, *19*, 36–43, *36–43*
F-16 Fighting Falcon *15*, 26, 44–51, *44–51*, 58, 102, 129, 132, 158, 162, 219
F-22 Raptor 60–7, *60–7*, 103, 129
F-35A/B/C/ Lightning II 26, 43, 50, 59, 102, 100–7, *100–7*, 115, 123, 129, 139
F-104 Starfighter 119
F-111 Aardvark 38, 76–83, *76–83*
FAB-69 *181*
FAB-250 212, *212*
FAB-500 *173*, *178*, 212, *212*
FAB-1500 213, *21*, *1293*
Falklands Conflict, 1982 *12*, 115, 193, 210
FAST (Fuel and Sensor, Tactical) 30–1
'ferry' missions 14, *31*
Fighter Control Officers (FCOs) 11
fire-and-forget 19, 31, 33, *145*, 196, 200
flares 58, *118*, *167*
Fleurus, battle of, 1794 7
fly-by-wire (FBW) control system 46, 127, *140*, 144, 150
'flying-wing' shape 92
Folding Fin Aircraft Rocket (FFAR) 205
Forward Air Control (FAC) 22, 25, 26
Forward-Looking Infra-Red (FLIR) system 25, 39, 58, *68*, 116, 121, 144, 221, 222
friendly fire 13, 110, 161
fuel tanks 6–7, 15, 19, *19*, 30–1, 36
 see also under individual aircraft name

GATOR mines *24*, 90
GAU-8 Avenger cannon 20, 22, 23, 25
GAU-12 cannon 103, 113
GBU-10 (Guided Bomb Unit) 213, *213*
GBU-12 (Guided Bomb Unit) *24*, *27*, 37, 39, 47,

223

INDEX

77, 120, 133, 145, 213, *213*
GBU-13 (Guided Bomb Unit) 214, *214*
GBU-15 (Guided Bomb Unit) *42, 81,* 199, 214, *214,* 217
GBU-16 (Guided Bomb Unit) *113, 114,* 214, *214*
GBU-22 (Guided Bomb Unit) 215, *215*
GBU-24 (Guided Bomb Unit) 43, 48, *49, 57, 59, 117, 125, 128, 129,* 215, *215*
GBU-27 (Guided Bomb Unit) 215, *215*
GBU-31 (Mk 84 JDAM) (Guided Bomb Unit) *18, 27, 45, 57, 71,* 98, *101, 104,* 216, *216*
GBU-32 (Mk 83 JDAM) (Guided Bomb Unit) *61, 51, 61, 114,* 216, *216*
GBU-38 (Mk 82 JDAM) (Guided Bomb Unit) *21, 45, 85, 90, 94, 109,* 216, *216,* 219, *219*
GBU-39 small diameter bomb (Guided Bomb Unit) *40, 61, 73,* 97, 103, *106,* 217, *217*
GLONASS (Global Navigation Satellite System) 186
GPS guided weapons *18, 19,* 26, 38, 48, 50, 65, *70,* 71, 73, 74, 87, 90, 96, 97, 105, 115, 121, 123, 129, 137, 143, 186
Gripen 140–7, *140–7*
ground-attack missions 8–10, 11, 13, *21* see also under individual aircraft name
guided missiles 10, 13, 14, *18, 19,* 26, 38, 48, 50, 56 see also under individual missile name
Gulf War, 1991 13, 26, 34, 39–40, 50, 58, 73, 77, 78, 81, 82, *83,* 115, 123, 161–2, 177, 201, 215, 218

hands-on-throttle-and-stick (HOTAS) 65, *135*
hard-target strike ('bunker-busting') 14, 17, *24,* 41, *42,* 48, *48, 143, 145*
High Explosive Incendiary (HEI) 23
High-Off-Boresight (HOBS) 106
HUD (Heads-Up Display) 106, 219
IFF (Identification Friend or Foe) 161
incendiary bombs 17
Indian Air Force *150, 153,* 155
infrared heat signature 17, 19, 25, 33, 39, 58, 63, 68, 116, 144
infrastructure strike 27, 43, 47, 85, 88, 175
interdiction 13–14, *24,* 40, 41, *51, 128*
Iraq 13, 26, 28, 34, 39–40, 50, 53, 58, 73, 77, 78, 81, 82, *83,* 90, 98, 115, 123, 161–2, 177, 201, 215, 218
IRIS-T (Infra Red Imaging System Tail/Thrust Vector-Controlled) *125, 128, 130, 141, 145,* 147, *194, 194*
iron bombs *26, 45, 50, 58, 155, 163, 173, 181*
Israeli Air Force 34, 50
Iwo Jima, USS 112

J-21 Jastreb 50
J-22 Orao 50
jammers 19, 58 see also under individual jammer name
Joint Air-to-Surface Standoff Missile (JASSM) *86,* 90, 105, 200, *200*
Joint Direct Attack Munitions (JDAM) *18, 18,* 38, *70,* 73, 74, *74,* 87, 90, *94,* 97, 98, 105
Joint Standoff Weapon (JSOW) 38, *39,* 50, 51, 95, *96, 96,* 97, 105, 200, *200*
Joint Strike Fighter (JSF) project 100, 102
JP233 munitions dispenser 217, *217*

KAB500KR *151, 155, 163, 178,* 217, *217*
KAB500L 218, *218*
KAB1500KR 218, *218*
Kargil War 162
Kh-15 (AS-6) Kickback *181,* 202, *202*
Kh-22 (AS-4) Kitchen 182
Kh-25L (AS-10) Karen 202, *202*
Kh-29L (AS-14) Kedge *149, 163, 171, 173,* 202, *202*
Kh-29T (AS-14) Kedge 203, *203*
Kh-31A (AS-17) Krypton *149, 153, 157, 169,* 203, *203*
Kh-31P (AS-17) Krypton 203, *203*
Kh-55 (AS-15) Kent *183,* 184, *185,* 204, *204*
Kh-59 (AS-13) Kingbolt *153,* 204, *204*
Kh-59M (AS-18) Kazoo 204, *204*
Kh-101 *183,* 205, *205*

Kormoran *120,* 210, *210*
Kosovo 98

LANTIRN (Low Altitude Navigation and Targeting for Night) pod 13, 18–19, 26, *37,* 38, *39,* 40, *42,* 43, *47, 49, 57,* 58, *59,* 82, 107, *136,* 220, *220*
LAU-68 rocket launcher *22, 109, 114,* 205, *205*
LAU-131 rocket launcher *21, 22,* 205, *205*
leaflets, dropping 14, 17
Libya 58, 81, *81*
LITENING targeting pod 75, *109, 113, 114,* 115, *117, 120,* 122, *128,* 129, 221, *221*
long-range missiles 13, 17 see also under individual missile name
low-altitude attacks 25, *49*
low-observable technology see stealth
low-probability-of intercept (LPI) 66

machine-guns 8, 16
Massive Ordnance Penetrator (MOP) 48, 97
Matra R550 Magic 194, *194*
Mauser cannon *124*
Meteor 141, 137, 196, *196*
Mica 137, 147, 195, 196, *196*
MiG-21 50, 147, 177, 203, 221
MiG-23 50, 162
MiG-29 150, 156–63, *156–63,* 191
MiG-31 164–71, *164–71,* 190, 192
MiG-35 156–63, *156–63*
mines, air-launched 18, *24,* 26, 38, 50, 88
Missileer, Douglas 77
missiles see under individual missile name
mission pods 219–22, *219–22* see also under individual pod name
Mistral 197, *197*
M117 bomb 218, *218*
M61A1 rotary cannon 30, 46, 65
Multi-Role Combat Aircraft (MRCA) 119

napalm tanks 17
NATO 26, 110, 144, 150, 151, 158, 161, 162, 164, 172, 174, 176, 181, 182
Northrop 98
nuclear weapons 10, *11,* 14, 17, 18, 38, 50, 58, 68, 71, 86, 88, 93, 156, 160, 184, 186

offensive counter-air operations *39,* 118
operational losses 10
Osirak reactor attack 50

Pave Penny pod *21, 22, 24, 27,* 222, *222*
Paveway bombs 38, 43, 48, *58, 76,* 105
Penguin anti-ship missile 210, *210*
precision strike 13, *27, 59, 81, 85, 107, 113, 114, 117, 136,* 160
Psychological Operations (PsyOps) 14, 26, 50
Python missile 197, *197*

radar 10, 11, 17, 28, 36, 46, 56, 63, 66, 127, 167 see also under individual radar system and aircraft name
RAF (Royal Air Force) 8–9, *118, 123,* 129, 194, 201, 214
Rafale 126, 132–9, *132–9*
RBK-250 cluster bomb *173,* 219, *219*
RBS-15F anti-ship missiles *141,* 147, 211, *211*
rear-area interdiction 90, 175
reconnaissance 11, 15, 19–20, 58
refuelling, in-flight 14, 43, 134
retarded bombs *13,* 17, 154 see also under individual bomb name
rockets 17–18 see also under individual rocket name
Royal Navy 102, 193

S-8 *151, 161, 176, 178,* 206, *206*
S-13T 207, *207*
S-24B 207, *207*
S-25LD 208, *208*
S-80M 206, *206*
S-88M 206, *206*
S-130F 207, *207*
Sagem AASM (Armement Air-Sol Modulaire) 137
SCUD missile *24,* 26, 73

'scout' aircraft 8
SEAD (Suppression of Enemy Air Defences) 14, 15, 17, 28, 37, 47, *49, 54, 55,* 56, 58, 79, *83,* 95, 96, 115, *120,* 121, *128,* 129, 137, *139, 149, 157,* 164, 170
search and rescue missions 25
searchlights 10
sea-skimming 18, 143, *143*
second member of crew 11, 40, 169
'self-escort' capability 38
shipping, attacks against 14, 18, *35, 49, 52, 53,* 71, *83, 114, 120, 137, 139, 141, 130, 137, 139, 181, 185,* 209–11, *209–11*
Short Takeoff and Vertical Landing (STOVL) 102, 103
SLAM-ER (Standoff Land Attack Missile, Extended Range) 54, *57*
Sniper ATP pod *24, 37, 39, 40, 42,* 222, *222*
Sorbtsiya ECM pod *151, 153, 155,* 222, *222*
South Ossetia War 177
Soviet Union 26, 28, 50, 86, 150, 176–7, 191
Soviet-Afghan War 50, 176–7
special forces missions 25, 40
'standoff' strikes 18, *31,* 38, *39,* 50, *51, 55, 85, 95, 95,* 96, *96,* 97, 105, 200, *200*
stealth 10, 14, 38, 60, 62, 63, 64, 92–9, *92–9,* 100, 127, 137
Stinger missile 176
Storm Shadow 105, *122,* 123, *125,* 129, 208, *208*
Strategic Air Command (SAC), U.S. 82, 90
Su-25 172–9, *172–9,* 191, 202, 207, 208
Su-27/30/35 & Chinese variants 148–55, *148–55,* 203, 221, 222
submunitions 17, 18
surface-to-air missiles (SAMs) 14, 86 see also under individual missile name
swing-role mission profile 124, 131, 135
'swing wing' *83,* 84–91, *84–91,* 123

Tactical Information Data Link System (TIDLS) 146
'Tank Plinking' 13, *77,* 78, 82
tankbusting/tank hunting 9, 13, 22, *24,* 26, *57, 77,* 78, 82
Taurus KEPD350 *145,* 147, 208, *208*
Tornado 116–23, *116–23*
Tu-22M Backfire 180–2, *180–2,* 202
Tu-95 Bear 186, 205
Tu-160 'Blackjack' 182–8, *182–6*
Turkey 50

United Nations 40, 50
USAF 28, 30, 35, 60, 93, 95, 102, 194, 197, 200, 212
 44th Fighter Squadron, 18th Fighter Wing *33*
 81st Training Wing 22
 aircraft see under individual aircraft name
 operations see under individual operation name
 weapons see under individual weapon name
U.S. Marine Corps 102, 110, *110, 111,* 112, *113,* 115
U.S. Navy *18,* 53, 77, 102, 103, 194, 200

V/STOL (Vertical/Short Takeoff and Landing) 108, 115
variable geometry ('swing wing') aircraft 84–91, *84–91*
Vectoring in Forward Flight (VIFF) 110
Vietnam War 16, 20, 26, 28, 70, 73, 79
'Vulcan' cannon 16, *28,* 38, 44, *52,* 60, 65, *68,* 77

weapons guidance systems 13, 18–19, 26, 38, 40, 43, 58, 82, 107 see also under individual guidance system name
Weapons Systems Officer (WSO) 39, 169, 201
wind-corrected munition dispenser (WCMD) 87, 88
World War I 8, *10*
World War II 8–10, *8–9,* 22, 69, 154

Yakovlev 102, 103

ZAB-500 napalm tank *176,* 209, *209*